FALSE FLAG

FALSE FLAG

Why Queer Politics Mean the End of America

Joy Pullmann

Since 1947
REGNERY
An Imprint of Skyhorse Publishing, Inc.

Regnery books may be purchased in bulk at special discounts for sales
promotion, corporate gifts, fund-raising, or educational purposes.
Special editions can also be created to specifications. For details, contact
the Special Sales Department, Regnery, 307 West 36th Street, 11th
Floor, New York, NY 10018 or info@skyhorsepublishing.com.

Regnery® is an imprint of Skyhorse Publishing, Inc.®, a Delaware
corporation.

Visit our website at www.regnery.com.
Please follow our publisher Tony Lyons on Instagram
@tonylyonsisuncertain.

10 9 8 7 6 5 4 3 2 1

Library of Congress Cataloging-in-Publication Data is available on file.

Cover design by John Caruso
Cover photograph: D.C. 6.10.23 by Anna Rose Layden—REUTERS

Print ISBN: 978-1-68451-587-5
eBook ISBN: 978-1-5107-8248-8

Printed in the United States of America

To my beloved husband, Nathaniel, and in gratitude to the faculty and students at Hillsdale College, truly my alma mater.

Contents

Introduction

> *"'The culture war' is not some fringe issue that icky social conservatives fixate on. It's real, it's systemic, it's foundational, and it's coming for you."*
> —Randy Barnett, constitutional law professor[1]

The 2010s and 2020s did not randomly explode with rainbow porn. They were presaged by decades of Social Marxism eroding natural human relations.

Since the Enlightenment, it has been increasingly popular in the West to believe that humankind is marching inevitably towards progress. What if, instead, Western societies are—rapidly—descending towards barbarism and chaos?

The warnings blare at us daily, but many people are too spiritually and intellectually deformed to recognize them. Others have blinded themselves by living inside a geographical, professional, or media-induced virtual reality. Still others grew up in a different time, or live in books, and cannot bring themselves to see what's right in front of their faces.

Throughout history, the common man has been a serf. But at least since the Reformation, the common man has learned to read and write, and, from the time of the American Revolution, to know and defend his basic natural rights. This elevated baseline, abnormal in human history, is descending. With it is declining the common man's ability and right to rule himself—once a pinnacle of civilizational clarity and achievement. The nation's ruling class is hastening this erosion by their lack of morals and hatred for American citizens' equal natural rights.

Western society is being erased by the purposeful destabilization of the institution that creates society: the natural family. Even the leading communist country, China, is ruled by people who understand that sexual chaos ultimately destroys every society. The leaders of the United States and other Western nations, however, appear to be too consumed with self-pleasuring to rule according to this basic reality. Their decadence, and their demands that we all ignore its devastating consequences, pose an existential threat to American happiness.

People who do not grow up in the homes of their two married, biological parents make, on average, worse citizens than people who do. Children afflicted by their parents' and communities' lack of sexual self-discipline have more trouble regulating their emotions, refraining from violence, following logical arguments, providing for themselves, achieving their potential, and respecting others' rights.[2]

They are also far more likely to demand public resources than to contribute them,[3] and to accelerate sexual chaos. Look into the background of a transgender person. You'll almost always find a parental divorce or another serious childhood trauma, such as sexual assault or porn exposure.

As this sexual cyclone sucks in Americans, our ability to sustain the way of life our Constitution requires is collapsing. Virginia's Bill of Rights encapsulates the universal belief of the American Founders

"That no free government, or the blessings of liberty, can be preserved to any people but by a firm adherence to justice, moderation, temperance, frugality, and virtue and by frequent recurrence to fundamental principles."[4]

As Thomas G. West, a prominent scholar of the Founding, explains, "security of rights requires—at least to some extent—public virtue. . . . [Language similar to that in Virginia's Bill of Rights] is found everywhere in the constitutions, laws, and other official documents of the states and in the federal Northwest Ordinance. The conviction that security of natural rights is impossible without public morality led to government support of cultivation of mind and character through religion, education, and other means."[5]

The American Founders believed no people could enjoy freedom without high standards of virtuous private behavior, and that key among those necessary virtues was directing sexual desires into families. The less Americans seek and display the virtues required to sustain families, the less capable they make themselves and the next generation of self-government. The fewer men become fathers, women become mothers, and both discharge those duties faithfully, the more people will demand that government attempt to replace fathers and mothers—a job government fails at, tragically and horrifically, every time.

Children without fathers are typically public charges.[6] Even giving single mothers more than the median national income in welfare[7] fails to help their children enjoy happier lives and more prosocial habits compared to children whose biological fathers and mothers marry for life. As a result, family chaos threatens Americans' natural right to the fruits of their own labors, for it takes from productive and healthy families to give to dysfunctional families—all without making them whole, because money can never buy love.

Children without mothers are less emotionally regulated, more anxious, and more emotionally dysfunctional.[8] Children who enter daycare as babies go on to commit more crimes, have worse social skills, and worse health.[9] All these attributes make them more likely not only to be public charges but also to support more authoritarian government that promises to keep them "safe"—like a substitute mommy.

Men and women without children are less likely to exhibit frugality and self-reliance, virtues central to self-rule. They are more likely to live for the moment than plan for the future, including their retirement. That makes them also more likely to be public charges, at the very least with respect to their foreseeable old-age needs.

Across the globe, families are increasingly disintegrating and failing to form. Unprecedented low birth rates threaten economic and political collapse across the world. Just half of children in the United States are raised in the environment most likely to make them capable of self-government: a home where their own two biological parents are in their first marriage.[10] The United States has the world's highest rate of children living in single-parent households, 23 percent,[11] partly due to our large subsidies for non-marital childbearing.

Stable families are a core societal precondition for limited government and self-rule. By destroying families, the identity politics state uses welfare to undermine the natural family's private provision of human needs. When half of America's citizens grow up in sexually chaotic homes, and all of us marinate in a sexually chaotic culture, only a minority of citizens will have the capacity for self-government. Thus a widespread lack of sexual virtue is an existential threat to both economic and social freedoms.

The "Pride" movement is a descendent of the Sexual Revolution—historically, logically, philosophically, and physically. Just as leading feminists projected their own family chaos onto politics[12]—"the personal is political," in the slogan of the day—today their transgender progeny project onto politics their own even worse family chaos. It's a vicious cycle.

Sexual chaos is a precondition for totalitarian government. People who cannot regulate their thoughts, emotions, and sexual behavior or provide for their own needs vote for government to replace these core functions of family. Feminism and now queer theory erase the natural and healthy interdependence between the sexes and substitute total war—not just vicious competition between men and women based on sex, but also internal war between each person and his or her very biology.

Destroying the family and ending its direction of sexual energies into creation and productivity erases people's capacity for self-government. People develop their ability to exercise self-restraint in childhood, at home. Controlling one's powerful sexual urges and directing them into establishing a mini-kingdom at home prepare people to manage their affairs without the demand for totalitarian government intervention in every aspect of life.

Family therefore threatens unlimited government, totalitarianism, the all-encompassing state, the Pink Police State, the managerial regime, or whatever else one wants to call government that usurps private functions and refuses to accept any boundaries. This means sexual identity politics throw individuals into relationship chaos, enabling government to seize ever-increasing power. Unlimited government—totalitarianism—is the end state of the Sexual Revolution. Its long march is why our country is in no condition for self-rule and won't be for generations.

The Pride flag stands for the Cultural Marxism seeking to destroy America. According to its own philosophers, Pride isn't about private bedroom behavior. It's about regime change. As the homosexual pedophile Michel Foucault put it, this mutation of Marxism seeks to "subvert the hierarchy," or destroy all natural authorities, including the authority of truth, of reality itself.[13] This is a call to permanent revolution against human norms, and the Pride flag marks the territory these revolutionaries believe they hold.

To control minute interactions between Americans, intersectional politics require massive bureaucracies that unite the judicial, legislative, and executive powers—directly subverting the US Constitution. This is, in fact, the very kind of tyranny the American Founding was designed to prevent.

Three million federal bureaucrats increasingly openly defy the law in pursuit of identity politics. They believe their insurrection is justified because special privileges for non-American and "queer" people constitute human rights; therefore, *any* action taken to protect these groups—up to and including violence—is righteous. As we will see in chapter 7, identity politics is these people's new religion.

Lawless bureaucrats and human resources professionals insert the federal government as a Big Brother into all economic interactions. Thus identity politics unites pagan religious impulses with government structures for enforcement and validation.

This intertwined religious and political system—a theocracy—is displacing basic rights precious to all Americans: the right to due process, the tyranny-limiting checks and balances of the Constitution and its division of state from federal power, the rights of free speech and freedom of religion, and the right to form autonomous natural families without government permission.

The US military and embassies all over the world have been flying the Pride flag alongside the American flag since 2011. To woke honchos like many US flag officers and corporate titans, unnatural sexual privileges exemplify America. In truth, they exemplify the illegitimate regime occupying our country.

So the Pride flag replacing the American flag on cars and front porches across the country is not just iconic. It's a symbol testifying to an underlying reality. The Pride flag celebrates regime change in the United States—and across the West. It is a symbol of unfettered license.

In the name of love, it stokes hatred: self-hatred, hatred of one's country, hatred of reality, and hatred of one's neighbors.

What else can we call an ideology that enables stripping the skin of a prepubescent child from wrist to elbow to construct a fake phallus, demanding taxpayer funding and endorsement of such Naziesque procedures?[14] What else can we call an ideology that allows one spouse to banish the other from seeing his or her own children every day even though that spouse has committed no crime, only married under inescapable no-fault divorce laws?[15] What else can we call an ideology that makes Americans hide their religions in a closet lest they lose the family business, close friends, a job, a career in law, finance, or medicine?[16]

Sexual Marxism is not love, it's hatred. It's hatred of fatherhood and motherhood, children, and all natural human connections. Without family, people go insane. They are only fit for mental institutions. It's no coincidence that's what our nation's streets increasingly resemble.

Depriving anyone of his natural family is cruel and evil, and it erases his capacity to rise to self-government. Yet that's what the Sexual Revolution does, and the Pride flag heralds it. The sexual chaos that this in-progress American Cultural Revolution is fomenting is a major precondition for totalitarianism. Yes, that *can* happen here, and it's already occupying Wall Street, Main Street, Congress, Hollywood, and all of your screens.

CHAPTER 1

"Pride" Is Really Just Sexual Marxism

"When law and morality contradict each other, the citizen has the cruel alternative of either losing his moral sense or losing his respect for the law."
—*Frédéric Bastiat*, The Law

Walk through any American neighborhood. The odds that a house with a Black Lives Matter sign also flies a Pride flag are high. It's a curious phenomenon given that African Americans are less likely than Americans of other racial backgrounds to support homosexual behavior.[1] More black Americans than non-black Americans—68 to 60 percent—also say a person's sex is given at birth and cannot be changed.[2]

Homosexuals, another part of this alleged cultural Marxist coalition, openly express antipathy towards relationships with black homosexuals.[3] Black homosexuals report much higher rates of discrimination inside the "LGBT community" than one would expect given all the PR proclaiming leftist identity groups are one big happy rainbow family.[4]

Otherwise hostile intersectional groups like these unite in their hatred of the Constitution and the social norms required to uphold it. That explains why they stand together even though they hate each other: because they hate something else more. The hatred the Pride flag represents isn't limited to the Constitution, nor to competing (and cooperating) groups represented by different stripes in the intersectionality rainbow. There is hatred, including self-hatred, at the very heart of this movement—hatred expressed brutally in the homosexual act itself, which can do irreversible physical harm to the participants,[5] and in the Joseph Mengele–level mutilations performed in the name of "queer rights."[6] LGBT policies mutilate human bodies as well as the US Constitution—and the peaceful way of life it exists to protect, through securing our natural rights.

The rainbow flag is the chief symbol of LGBT activism. It stands for the identity politics—also called intersectionalism and Cultural Marxism—that aims to destroy America. Let's hear from the creators of that symbol—the queer theorists and practitioners themselves.

A Symbol of Revolution

According to its own proponents, Pride isn't just about private bedroom behavior. It's about regime change.[7] Like any regime change, it requires violence. These realities are hallmarks of the Pride flag's story.

In 1964, a *Life* magazine article described San Francisco as "the gay capital of America."[8] Former Army medic Gilbert Baker designed the first pride flag for San Francisco Gay Freedom Day in 1978 at the request of city Supervisor Harvey Milk, a homosexual who sexually abused far younger teen boys.[9] Milk "requested Baker to design something that could stand as a symbol of pride for the LGBTQ community."[10] He came up with a rainbow flag.

A US National Park Service article includes a picture of Baker wearing a sequined dress and flying the flag in a San Francisco Pride march. The unsigned article directly connects the Pride flag to a "revolution" against American law and the imposition of a new form of "nationhood": "Baker became inspired by flags and the connections they had to identity, nationhood and revolution."[11]

After Milk was murdered in November 1978, the article reported, Baker wanted to cover the next year's Pride parade in rainbow flags "to show the world we would survive." So he had four hundred rainbow flags made for the 1979 Pride march in San Francisco. After that, residents of local homosexual neighborhoods kept them up.

In 1981, Baker joined the anti-Christian drag protest group The Sisters of Perpetual Indulgence. His stage name was Sister Chanel 2001.[12] The group is notorious for obscene behavior expressing bigotry and animus against Christians and heterosexuals, such as dressing up as Jesus Christ and engaging in sex acts the Bible calls evil.

At the 1990 International Lesbian and Gay Freedom Day Parade, Baker protested as "Pink Jesus." He marched covered in pink paint, wearing pink high heels, and with an American flag loincloth tacked to a crucifix with a sign that read, "Martyrs for Art." Next to him marched a topless woman and a man in drag.

Baker likened his displays to threats of violence: "The real connection to the public happens with the confrontation at the boundaries of fear. Art is like a gun that way."[13]

For a 1994 New York Pride parade celebrating the twenty-fifth anniversary of the Stonewall Riots, Baker helped construct a mile-long Pride flag. In defiance of permits requiring marchers to use less-trafficked streets, he and other homosexuals cut up the flag and took it outside the permitted march location to Saint Patrick's Cathedral in a display of anti-Christian animus.[14]

"This display of civil disobedience was a true celebration of the 25th anniversary of the Stonewall Riots. The event made national news and brought the pride flag into the mainstream," the National Park Service reported. In 2016, President Obama invited Baker to the White House, where Baker gave Obama a Pride flag he had hand-dyed. That flag is now in Obama's presidential library.

This brief history of the Pride flag illuminates recurring themes: hatred of order, authority, religion, sexual restraint, and norms of respect for others, especially children. The pride flag's creator understood himself as a sexual revolutionary, and he dedicated his life to revolting against the norms and laws that protected American peace and unity.

Splintering Identities

In 1999, Navy veteran and "transgender woman" Monica Helms created the light blue, white, and pink transgender flag.[15] Around that time, queer people increasingly began remixing Pride flags to represent the splintering of sexual identities.

The updated Pride flags included colors representing racial identities—always excluding people with light skin tones—and an ever-expanding list of sexual proclivities, such as intersex, non-binary, bisexual, pansexual, and queer. These new flags are an open endorsement of the connection between Pride and the rest of the identity politics groups. Despite monotonous chants of "diversity," all of the queer symbols exclude heterosexual people and those who accept their natural sex.

Initially, some homosexuals opposed recognizing racial minorities and transgender people in movement symbols and policies, arguing that gender dysphoria and race are different categories from sexual behavior. But they were quickly shut up with accusations that white homosexuals were less oppressed than transsexuals and African-Americans and therefore had no right to argue with them.[16]

In 2018 the nonbinary American Daniel Quasar designed the "Progress Pride flag." This increasingly popular symbol overlays the six-color rainbow flag with a triangle of black and brown—for skin colors—around the transgender triangle of light blue, pink, and white.[17] Boston began flying it in 2020,[18] and New York in 2022. The Biden White House flew this flag for pride celebrations in 2023. London Mayor Sadiq Khan switched city pride flags to the "Progress" version in 2020.[19]

This flag connects sexual identity politics with racial identity politics. It is a clear affirmation of the anti-Constitution doctrine of intersectionalism, the philosophy that would grant racial and sexual victim groups special government privileges on the basis of their identity.[20] The Constitution, in contrast, recognizes no protected classes and applies its restraints on government on behalf of all citizens equally.

Quasar demands to be addressed with "xe" and "xem" pronouns. The designer's website indicates that he dabbles in neopagan spiritualities. He claims, "I am a queer non-binary celestial object having a human experience" who "live[s] with anxiety and various other mental health issues."[21] He also designed a "cosmicgender" flag in 2021.[22]

New York state officials celebrated their decision to use the Progress flag in 2022 as representing the state's commitment to "equity," "inclusion," "diversity," and "progress."[23] When public officials installed a Progress Pride flag on New York City's Roosevelt Island in 2023, they connected it with President Franklin Delano Roosevelt's swap of the US Constitution for a competing political system: "The Progress Pride

Flag, which is on the Grand Stairs within the Four Freedoms State Park, was installed to be a symbol of solidarity with the LGBTQ+ community and a reminder of the collective progress needed to achieve the Four Freedoms outlined by President Franklin D. Roosevelt in 1941—the Freedom of Speech and Expression, Freedom of Worship, Freedom from Want, and Freedom from Fear."[24]

Competing with that fabric flag for the "state's largest" Pride flag were massive steps at the park, painted with a rainbow in June 2023. Here, too, leftists openly connected the pride symbolism with regime change in America. "Part of the park's mission in celebrating the four freedoms is to educate and inspire current and future generations to define those freedoms for themselves," FDR's great-granddaughter Julia Ireland told NBC News. "The pride flag will serve as a symbol of support and a reminder of the necessity of the human rights that my family worked towards."[25]

If every individual makes his or her own definition of freedom, the word is meaningless. Erasing the meanings of words allows totalitarians to abuse people by doing whatever they want and calling it "freedom," like Communist regimes do.

United in Hatred of American Norms

The Pride flag has become a potent symbol of identity politics. That permutation of Marxism would erase the US Constitution's protections of human rights and equality for all citizens. That's why identity-politics marches, riots, and protests feature the Pride flag even when those events aren't technically about sexual preferences.

On January 21, 2017, Communist organizers held a Women's March to protest the inauguration of Donald Trump. Key among their fears was his pledge—later fulfilled—to nominate Supreme Court justices who would uphold the Constitution by overturning *Roe v. Wade*.

On the same day as that first Women's March in Washington D.C., the *Washington Post* claimed, some four million joined marches across the country under the same branding.[26] These openly promoted a rebellion against the Constitution by promoting the lie that it secures a right to murder unborn children. The protests teemed with Pride flags, media reports showed.[27]

Fittingly, one of the official Women's March's eight "unity principles" was LGBTQIA policies.[28] The march organizers explained, "We firmly declare that LGBTQIA Rights are Human Rights and that it is our obligation to uplift, expand and protect the rights of our gay, lesbian, bi, queer, trans or gender non-conforming brothers, sisters and siblings. We must have the power to control our bodies and be free from gender norms, expectations and stereotypes."[29]

BLM materials went even farther, calling for destroying the nuclear family. BLM's "guiding principles" included not only pro-queer policies but also "the disruption of Western nuclear family dynamics and the return to the 'collective village' that takes care of each other."[30] BLM-sponsored materials for kids as young as kindergarten tell tykes "everybody gets to choose their [sic] gender."

A BLM "starter kit" for schools offered this script to introduce early elementary students to transgenderism: "Everybody has the right to choose their own gender by listening to their own heart and mind. Everyone gets to choose if they are a girl or a boy or both or neither or something else, and no one else gets to choose for them."[31]

Christopher Rufo, the premier journalist investigating Critical Race Theory, has reported myriad examples of leftists connecting sexual and racial identity politics in K–12 curricula. In the Buffalo, New York, public schools, for example, the "curriculum is explicitly opposed to Western epistemology, values, and institutions," Rufo reported. "Schools are instructed to promote the fourteen 'Black Lives Matter principles,' which teach students to disrupt 'Western nuclear family dynamics,' dismantle 'structural racism and white supremacy,' challenge 'cisgender privilege,' break 'the tight grip of heteronormative thinking,' and abolish 'sexism, misogyny, and male-centeredness.'"[32]

BLM and the Women's March, as well as the White House, have all expressed their commitment to intersectionalism, which they use to justify promoting sexual and racial politics in tandem. "Women's March is an intersectional movement," the organization said in a statement in 2018.[33] BLM cofounder Alicia Garza, who is queer, flatly stated, "It's not possible to abolish capitalism without a struggle against national oppression and gender oppression."[34]

United against a Common Enemy

Pundits on the right continually point out the contradictions inherent in intersectionality, including that homosexuals reject the female sex organs—mostly vulvas and ovaries—that participants in the Women's March hoisted aloft on signs and wore on hats. Critics also point out that researchers now believe sexuality is fluid and it's obviously a behavior, while race is not performative, but innate.

The Women's March foundered in 2019 on another of these contradictions: the enmity between George Floyd rioters, Palestinian activists, and Jews. From the earliest days of the Women's March, groups higher in the intersectional hierarchy treated white feminist marchers with open contempt because of their skin color and support for inborn sex distinctions.[35]

What unites all these identity groups is their wholesale rejection of natural rights and the American way of life based upon them. That rejection is at the core of identity politics, and particularly of Queer Theory, which denies that a stable human nature exists.

This is why the George Floyd protests of 2020 and beyond, which emerged directly after the Women's March self-destructed, also often featured Pride flags and other rainbow gear. It's why several BLM protests focused on the deaths of the transgender people in police custody,[36] and BLM protesters projected a rainbow onto a statue they wanted the city of Richmond, Virginia to tear down.[37]

A Kinetic Revolution

Before there was Black Lives Matter, there were the Stonewall riots. Stonewall is a keystone of American queer history. In those riots, queer activists physically fought the authorities for three days. Today that sort of thing is called an insurrection—at least when the people who do it can be coded as on the political right.

Violence and lawbreaking are repeat themes for queer activists, some of whom believe that laws to restrict sexual exhibitionism are illegitimate.[38] The activist group Queer Nation, for example, was founded in 1990 to revive violence against the state in service of queer politics.

Queer Nation claims it is a descendent of Stonewall and was founded by participants in the queer "resistance" organization ACT UP.[39]

ACT UP is infamous for acts of "civil disobedience" that included disrupting a Roman Catholic Mass for AIDS victims in Philadelphia, throwing condoms at Mass-goers and the presiding archbishop.[40] The organization eventually included more than forty chapters. Its initial New York City organizers agreed to perform demonstrations that aimed to "mystify," "enchant," and "terrify." (Again, using "terror" for politics is called "domestic terrorism" when people on the right are accused of it.) The New York City ACT UP's chapter invaded restaurants and bars to provoke clashes with patrons and police with "sex positive" public actions including hundreds of people making out.

"That was one of the things that [white Queer Nation activists] wanted to do: a lot of civil disobedience," one of the group's organizers told reporters in a 2019 retrospective.[41]

In July 1990, according to the organization, "Queer Nation rallie[d] outside the homes of two bashers to alert the neighborhood that 'your neighbors are bigots.'"[42] In, 1991, like myriad leftist organizations, this one petered out because of infighting and public disapproval

Identity Marxists' use of violence is often not spontaneous. It is planned. As in the cases of ACT UP and BLM, violence is part of their program.

Angela Davis is a highly influential critical theorist who married sexual and race politics in service of Communism. She studied with Marcuse, who said Davis, like the Weather Underground, "had taken the critical theorists to their logical conclusion: violent resistance against the state."[43] As Rufo notes in his 2023 book, *America's Cultural Revolution*, "Davis was one of the first to argue that the fight against oppression must include the fight against racism, patriarchy, and capitalism. 'The Socialist movement must never forget that while the economic struggle is indispensable, it is by no means the sole terrain of significant anti-capitalist activity,' she wrote during her incarceration. The movement must obliterate the entire superstructure that holds the system in place, particularly the architecture of racism and the 'family-based structure of oppression.' . . . By dissolving the social bonds that sustain the mode of production, she believed, the revolutionary could begin to undermine the entire capitalist society."[44]

Now a professor at the University of California at Santa Cruz, Davis came out as a lesbian in 1997. In the 2020s, this Communist Party member was a highly visible BLM supporter who urged that the riot-laden movement must encompass sexual politics. BLM cofounders Patrisse Cullors and Alicia Garza are also queer.[45]

Love Doesn't Mutilate People

Queer activists march under the banner of love, but regularly use violence to accomplish their goals. Beyond the street violence, there is the violence of transgender "medicine."

Queer politics not only wars against sexual restraint and basic decency in the streets, it also makes war on human bodies inside hospitals and doctors' offices. Just as feminism's war on our sexed bodies creates a demand for brutalizing children with surgical abortions and abortifacients, so queer politics' war on our bodies demands brutalizing children with "gender transitions."

This isn't love, but its opposite. There is no other word than "hatred"—except, perhaps, "evil"—to describe what transgender policies do to humans. Anyone who looks at the truth and doesn't agree is beyond the reach of reason and empathy.

A 2022 interview with one of Oregon Health Science University's (OSHU's) top transgender surgeons provides all the evidence anyone should need that queer ideology makes war on humans. In it, Dr. Blair Peters admits that "experts" like him have no idea of the life-long effects for their patients of amputating their penises or breasts and constructing false penises from forearm skin.[46] Indeed, as research admitted in multiple federal court cases shows, "No high-quality evidence supports using puberty blockers and cross-sex hormones to treat children with gender dysphoria, and multiple studies suggest that such interventions are potentially dangerous."[47]

As the *New York Times* admitted in August 2023, "Pediatric gender medicine is a nascent specialty, and few studies have tracked how patients fare in the long term, making it difficult for doctors to judge who is likely to benefit." The article noted that US gender clinics are so overwhelmed with demand they regularly prescribe high-dose hormones to kids with very little screening.

Reuters found that the number of transgender American children ages six to seventeen tripled from 2017 to 2022.[48] It's surely increased since then. The United States has gone from one gender clinic that opened in 2007 to more than one hundred today, the *New York Times* reported.[49] What happens in those can only be described with words like "Nazis" and "hell."

To achieve a vaginoplasty—the transformation of a penis into something approximating a vagina: "surgeons first cut off the head of the penis and remove the testicles," documented Rufo, from hospital handbooks. "Then they turn the penile-scrotal skin inside out and, together with abdomen cavity tissue, fashion it into a crude, artificial vagina."[50] Thanks to the help of newly acquired robots, the OSHU hospital staff can do two of these procedures per day.

As Rufo reported, "This procedure is plagued with complications. OHSU warns of wound separation, tissue necrosis, graft failure, urine spraying, hematoma, blood clots, vaginal stenosis, rectal injury, fistula, and fecal accidents. Patients must stay in the hospital for a minimum of five days following the procedure, receiving treatment for surgical wounds and having fluid drained through plastic tubes. Once they are home, patients must continue on transgender hormone treatments and manually dilate their surgically created 'neo-vagina' in perpetuity; otherwise, the tissue will heal, and the cavity will close."[51]

What is the likelihood people subjected to such procedures become lifelong dependents on their fellow Americans? Obviously extremely high. People wrapped up in debilitating gender confusion and converted into expensive lifelong medical patients are not top-shelf candidates for self-governing citizens who respect others' natural rights to their lives and property.

Moral Monsters Spawn Surgical Monsters

Blair Peters, a "queer surgeon" who insists people use the pronouns "he" and "they" for him, describes performing genital surgeries not just to convert penises into the appearance of vaginas, and vice versa, but also to accommodate bizarre identities and Frankenstein genitals. "There's some people that come in and they embrace a nonbinary gender identity and they envision more of a nonbinary type of appearance to their genitalia . . ." he said. "There's a lot more of like a spectrum of procedures now that are available, and a lot of them kind of falling, maybe between the two [sexes] or outside of the two. So I think it's becoming more of a field where it's less about reinforcing this binary view of genitalia and anatomy and more so embracing the person's own unique concept of themselves. And me, as a surgeon, my whole goal is helping you self-actualize how you see yourself internally."

He describes sometimes taking breast sizes down but not eliminating the breasts entirely, so that women can let their smaller breasts show on days they want to be seen as women and "bind" them on days they want to look more masculine. Sometimes women keep their vaginas and add a penis, with or without a fake scrotum. Sometimes men keep their penises and add breasts. Some patients, Peters says, want neither sex's genitals, but a "nullification" of genitals, or something else of their own design: "People with nonbinary identities make up a large portion of the TGD [transgender and gender diverse] community."[52]

These are not just the statements of one rogue doctor. They represent the cutting-edge consensus of his field. An Unherd contributor quoted presenters at the 2022 World Professional Association for Transgender Health (WPATH) conference as saying, of transgender surgeries on children's bodies, "We're building the plane while we're flying it," and, "What [these patients] want may not be physically possible."[53]

Another surgeon, who mutilates genitals in San Francisco and Austin, Texas, has publicly proclaimed that he practices genital "nullification," "non-binary," and "eunuch" procedures. Like Peters, plastic surgeon Curtis Crane will sew a fake penis onto a woman while preserving her vagina, add a fake vagina while retaining a man's penis, or create an entirely "smooth" genital area.

Crane's medical team performs some one thousand genital mutilations per year and "boasted of a one- to two-year waitlist and claimed to have one of the highest volumes of transgender surgeries in the United States." He claims his surgeries enact the leftist ideology that sex is "nonbinary" and redress historical "inequities."[54] In a 2023 medical journal article, Peters and coauthors claimed that hospitals and surgeons that won't provide "nonbinary" surgical options are instruments of white supremacy.[55]

Nobody who "nullifies" his genitals is likely to be physically capable of starting his own family. That erases one of the key institutions of private-sector support for people throughout life—another way of making these bodily modified people lifelong public dependents. This ideology is moving at breakneck speed into the lives of children, destabilizing their understanding of reality, and decreasing the likelihood they form stable families—and making more customers for gender clinics.

The chief psychologist at a children's hospital's gender clinic in 2018 supported children expressing "identities" that include human-animal hybrids and surgically altering kids' bodies to fit those identities. Alongside "gender-fluid" and "gender non-binary" children, University of California School of Medicine professor Diane Ehrensaft listed "gender hybrids" on a slide talk.

Gender hybrids, Ehrensaft said, include gender "minotaurs" and "Priuses." The former is a mythical beast that is half man and half bull, and the latter Ehrensaft described as "half boy and half girl." She noted that many of these children love mermaids. "We are in the midst of a gender revolution and the children are leading it. And it's a wonderful thing to see," Ehrensaft said at the San Francisco Public Library in 2018. She explained that transgenderism is the logical outcome of feminism's erasure of distinctions between the sexes, which is now moving into erasing distinctions between species.[56]

From Kink to Genital Surgery and Back Again

The erasure of distinctions between species spreads kink to children who may very naturally and innocently enjoy playing at being dinosaurs or mermaids. It should go without saying that subjecting children to sexual chaos retards their ability to govern themselves and therefore form the next functioning generation of a self-governing society. Rather than encouraging sexual self-restraint and serving one's family and neighbors, sexual chaos erodes self-restraint and encourages decadence and dissipation. One of the most startling manifestations of this trend is "furries."

"Furries" began partly as a homosexual fetish. One sex partner acts like a dog and the other like his owner. "Dogs" dress the part, which sometimes involves elaborate costuming.

The kink concept spread from queer circles into kindergartens when the LGBT floodgates opened after the Supreme Court's 2015 *Obergefell v. Hodges* decision erasing sex distinctions in marriage. The trend also collided with cosplay fandoms of videogames and cartoons, and "furries" soon meant dressing not just like dogs but every character under the sun.

Some furries do it for the innocent fun. Others combine the role playing with sexual fetishes and mental illnesses. Kids as young as eight and six are drawn in by the colorful animal characters, finding them online on TikTok and other social media—which makes furry-dom a prime place for groomers and predators. In 2017, a pedophile ring full of furries was busted in Pennsylvania.[57]

A furry convention spokesman told *Rolling Stone* they confine adult programming "such as kink safety panels" to evenings, with a "strict" policy against pulling out condoms for orgies at the public events until "after dark."[58] Sex toy companies make replicas of animal genitals and other furry products that kids can easily find online when searching for furry content.[59]

People often get into furry behavior through pornography. A homosexual who published a documentary on furries told the *New York Post*, "Furry porn is really beautiful."[60] A 2013 survey found that 96 percent of male furries and 78 percent of female furries watched furry pornography, on average, forty-one and ten times per month, respectively.[61]

There's also a significant overlap between queer identity and adopting a furry persona. Furries were almost three times more likely to identify as non-heterosexual than non-furries, according to a 2012 meta-analysis of research.[62]

There's nothing wrong with dressing up in costumes or having sex. But there's a lot wrong when people can't—or won't—direct their energies into higher forms of art, commerce, and expression, or tell the difference between fantasy and reality. Adults dressing up as stuffed animals and looking at cartoon porn indicates a refusal to assume the responsibilities of adulthood. And that is a threat to the constitutional way of life needed to sustain republican freedoms in America. Given that at least some gender surgeons will apparently do anything a customer wants, it's also likely the furries trend will result in some surgical body modifications to make people look more like animals. In fact, that's already happening too.

The Transgender Dragon

The cross-species body modification that queer ideology legitimizes goes far beyond people donning cat suits. People are increasingly asking surgeons to split their tongues to look like a snake's,[63] or to tattoo their eyeballs black so that they look like animals or demons. Before eyeball tattoos, people try out a cat's- or snake's-eye looks with non-medical contact lenses.[64]

The most famous example is "Lizardman," a former PhD student who had his entire body tattooed with lizard scales, his tongue forked, his teeth sharpened, and silicone implants placed under his skin to give it large, lizard-like bumps.[65]

A self-proclaimed "transgender dragon" goes by the name Tiamat Eva Baphomet Medusa. (Baphomet is a demon's name.) Medusa had his ears and nose amputated. He's had horn bumps implanted under his forehead skin, his body tattooed with scales, and the whites of his eye tattooed green. His tongue is also forked. Medusa has also surgically castrated himself and implanted breasts. A *Vice* reporter who interviewed Medusa called him "beautiful." (He's wrong.)

It won't surprise you to learn that this wildly deformed man is deeply hurting.

As a child, he told *Vice*, he was abandoned in the desert. Medusa grew up with a stepfather he says was abusive and a chaotic nuclear family. When young, Medusa was raped by two men. He later contracted HIV. The diagnosis set him on the path towards trans-species body modification.

"Frightened that HIV would take her [sic] life, she decided to shed the skin she was born into, to leave behind humanity itself," writes *Vice* reporter Diana Tourjee. Tourjee, a transgender man with fake breasts, identifies with Medusa: "I am unable to cleanly separate the kind of body modification that altered my sex, and the taboo procedures Tiamat endured to become her vision of herself."[66]

Body modifications like these project people's inner chaos onto their bodies. Transgender and transhuman people are telling us they're in a lot of pain. Medusa, for example, told Tourjee he smokes marijuana most mornings. He said he'll also be on psych meds for life. He calls his strange appearance "a defense mechanism" against further trauma like his homosexual rape.

In a pattern tragically common with badly abused people, hurting individuals often try to resolve their abuse with abuse. No compassionate person would let them. No compassionate person would say that splitting one's tongue, toking up on opposite-sex hormones, wearing a fur suit and barking in the streets, or cutting off one's genitals is a compassionate solution for agony.

Telling people the lie that identity can be detached from biology is psychological abuse. It hurts the vulnerable most. The reality is that queer ideology feeds mental illness, human rights abuses, cultural decadence, and social breakdown. It's not loving, it's hateful and destructive.

What Homosexuals Call Marriage Isn't

Homosexuality has been a minority practice in just about every civilization for all of human history. Postmodernist homosexuality, however, is different. Rather than keeping homosexual acts out of the public eye, and acknowledging they cannot constitute a marriage because they do not produce children, neo-Marxist sexual politics demands public recognition of non-procreative sexual practices.

That was not the case in, say, ancient Greece, where homosexual acts were common but also widely lampooned by major poets including Ovid and Aristophanes. In ancient times, homosexuality was a laughed-at lewd fetish mostly indulged in on war campaigns away from wives and families, and an instrument of domination over the weak; not a "marriage."

The ancients who engaged in homosexuality understood that marriage is about children, and therefore requires a man and a woman. They believed marriages were only heterosexual even if some elite men violated—usually younger, including prepubescent—males.

Today, the vast majority of homosexuals do not pursue lifelong monogamous relationships, nor do most want to.[67] As homosexual writer Andrew Sullivan wrote in his 1989 case for letting gays call their relationships marriage, "Much of the gay leadership clings to notions of gay life as essentially outsider, anti-bourgeois, radical. Marriage, for them, is co-optation into straight society." Sullivan hoped that granting homosexuals marriage licenses would reduce their promiscuity.[68]

In 2010, NPR interviewed a transgender man who had written a book arguing that marriage is "a failing institution" and that licensing queer marriage means "only giving that right to people who are willing to conform to this narrow notion of a long-term monogamous partnership sanctioned by the state."[69] This perspective matches that of myriad influential queer theorists, from the Frankfurt School communist Wilhelm Reich to key feminists (many of whom were lesbians) to Camille Paglia to the thirteen queer authors of 2011's "Against Equality: Queer Critiques of Gay Marriage."[70]

To queers, marriage often doesn't mean lifelong monogamy. Even when they are in a relationship, many queers have sex with people besides their usual partner. When they do couple, homosexuals break up at far higher rates than opposite-sex couples, sometimes as much as double the rate.[71]

None of this is what people understand by the term "marriage." Homosexuals who obtain a marriage certificate and maintain monogamy are a tiny minority of a tiny minority[72]—yet this wildly unrepresentative situation has been presented to Americans as the aspirational queer lifestyle. Outside the mainstream, however, queer media openly recognize the jealousies produced by constant cruising and cheating, as well as the high anxiety produced by an obsessive focus on appearance.[73]

Destroy the West by Dissolving Marriage

Also out of the public eye, a number of queer theorists have stated that their object is not marriage, but to destroy sexual norms and, therefore, Western society. "[T]he queer theorists argue, there is no 'human nature' that cannot be transcended or obliterated through the application of culture and science," notes Rufo.[74] Before their pursuit for centralized political power after Stonewall, social critic Camille Paglia notes, homosexuals "were absolutely scathing. Going against every possible social convention."[75]

"I still cannot understand the longing of so many otherwise free-thinking gays for the imprimatur of traditional marriage, which seems to mimic and valorize heterosexual formulas and precedents," the lesbian and self-described transgender Paglia said in 2018, echoing a position common among pre-*Obergefell* queer theorists and homosexual writers.[76]

Early feminists' openly stated goal of destroying marriage laid the foundation for the same among their intellectual descendants in queer and gender studies. The 1977 National Women's Conference, for example, openly pushed for homosexual preferences.[77] Key feminist Shulamith Firestone, an acolyte of the communist[78] Wilhelm Reich, argued, "Just as the end goal of socialist revolution was not only the elimination of the economic class *privilege* but of the economic class *distinction* itself, so the end goal of feminist revolution must be . . . not just the elimination of male *privilege* but of the sex *distinction* itself" (italics original).[79]

Reich argued that destroying monogamy and the natural family would lead to communist revolution. A member of the infamous communist Frankfurt School, Reich coined the term "sexual revolution." In his book *The Sexual Revolution*, Reich argued for sexualizing children and punishing people who disagreed with encouraging every family member's participation in "free love."[80] Refusing to affirm every sexual act another might engage in, Reich claimed, was "oppression" and "abuse" that the state should punish.[81]

The same theorists who supported queer sexuality led the charge for weakening marriage for everyone through no-fault divorce laws. As the common thread between identity groups is hatred for Western civilization, the common goal is destroying republican government's foundations in the father-led nuclear family: "Feminists like Herma Hill Kay, who shaped the Uniform Marriage and Divorce Act, supported no-fault divorce as a way to destroy the patriarchal family and liberate women," notes Hillsdale College political science professor Kevin Slack.[82]

Kate Millett's 1960s feminist catechism declared that feminists' goal was to "make cultural revolution" by "destroying the American family," which they would accomplish by "destroying monogamy." They'd do all that, these leading second-wave feminists chanted at their meetings, "By promoting promiscuity, eroticism, prostitution, abortion, and homosexuality."[83]

Like many leading feminists including Simone de Beavoir, Angela Davis, Gertrude Stein, and Virginia Woolf, Millett was a lesbian. She was also known for sexual aggression, including repeated attempts to rape her sister.[84]

Ending Sexual Restraint Destroys Societies

Before queer forerunners switched to pursuing the legal benefits and centrality of marriage licensing, they were strongly aginst it.[85] That suggests their sudden reversal towards pursuing in name what they had openly sought to destroy was a new tactic to achieve the same goal. Certainly, the destruction of the natural family is increasing apace as a direct result of the adoption of queer policies. That means destroying a key bulwark of limited self-government.

With the advent of the 1960s Sexual Revolution, Rufo writes, quoting queer academics, "Suddenly, drag was not a private performance but a statement of public rebellion. The queens began using costume and performance to mock the fashion, manners, and mores of Middle America."[86] Queer activists directly target "heteronormativity"—that is, the reality that only a man and woman make babies and that married parents are the best-positioned to raise them well.

Fighting heteronormativity means making war on social health, because child-producing marriages direct sexual energies into creativity, sacrifice, and production. This basic sociological reality has been established for centuries.[87]

As Thomas West points out, the American Founders acknowledged the obvious and universal truth that "marriage has a civilizing effect not only on children but also on adults. [Declaration of Independence signer John] Witherspoon writes that the single life 'narrows the mind and closes the heart.' Other early magazine articles reinforce this view. A 1791 essay states that 'while other passions concentrate man on himself, love makes him live in another, substitutes selfishness.'"[88]

An Oxford and Cambridge anthropologist's 1934 review of five thousand years of history "found that the greater a culture's sexual restraint, the greater that culture's accomplishments. Monogamous cultures could build and grow, produce art, music, architecture, and science, expand economies, and create space for people to flourish. But [J. D.] Unwin found that as soon as a culture abandoned monogamy, particularly premarital chastity, it collapsed within three generations." Limiting and productively directing sexual energy fuels cultural strength.[89]

Conversely, unlimited sexual license destroys cultures. A sexually unrestrained culture traps citizens within their sexual desires. Whether with furries or with the multiplication of gender identities, people over-focus on pleasuring themselves and lose their drive for better pursuits.

Erasing Marriage Was an Op

So at this point it's quite clear homosexual "marriage" was an op. As Nathaniel Blake writes, "the LGBTQ movement was built on a lie, and it is now breaking the promises it made to secure support from ordinary Americans."[90]

That lie is that queer people were "born this way." The last ten years' explosion in queer identification, coupled with social science research's failure to find a gay gene,[91] as well as its findings that sexuality is fluid,[92] indicate that cannot be true. If people are "born queer," the explosion in young people identifying as transgender simply wouldn't be happening.

And it's clear that identification is encouraged by social conditioning. As journalist Abigail Shrier writes in *Irreversible Damage*, "Those who teach gender ideology do not make adolescents transgender. They simply fill kids' heads with gender options and ideology. Then, when the adolescents do experience a crisis, the heroic solution readily bobs to mind." The multiple-hundred-fold increase in children seeking transgender mutilation[93] coinciding with the saturation of culture in queer imagery and ideology indicates that people aren't born queer—a piece of evidence that erases any claim to legal privileges for immutable characteristics.

The survival of Western culture depends on strong natural families and government structures that protect rather than destroy those families. In homes and institutions like schools, whose authority descends from homes, culture is passed on to children authoritatively in the form of normative moral judgments, loyalties, and distinctions. When one learns both at home and in school to restrain one's passions, it frees the soul to participate in self-government through rational thought and dialogue: logic, argumentation, and debate. This rational self-government culminates in Western culture and its highest expression, the American form of constitutionally limited government.

Sexual politics makes war against Western culture by attacking its origins in the father-headed household.[94] Identity politics is an assault against the families who discipline their sexual relations within lifelong monogamous relationships. Its explicit goal is to overthrow Western civilization by overthrowing marriage and the families marriage naturally creates. Committed Cultural Marxists in the recent past, like the 1970s domestic terror group Weather Underground, followed New Left philosopher Herbert Marcuse's "theory, outlined in his book *Eros and Civilization*, that sexual and political liberation are intertwined. They broke up monogamous relationships and asked members to submit their sexuality to the collective in order to surpass bourgeoise norms and 'commit suicide as a class.'"[95]

Sexual politics seeks to enact the Communist Manifesto's demand for the "abolition of the family" as a means to abolish property and "bourgeoisie" social norms.[96] Marxist critical theory's demand for "inverting the hierarchies,"[97] as applied by sexual identitarians, practically works out to destroying marriage, the relationships between parents and children, and all strong male leadership.[98] This is what sexual revolutionaries mean by their ubiquitous call for "smashing the patriarchy."

Sexual politics' true goal is not simply to grant government privileges to a tiny percentage of Americans who claimed discrimination—but who could have found workarounds such as powers of attorney to facilitate hospital visits between homosexual couples, or pro bono lawyers to write their wills and defend them in court. The goal was to destroy organic families as a mediating social institution that naturally limits government. The queer activist Masha Gessen made this explicit at a writer's festival in 2012.

"It's a no-brainer that the institution of marriage should not exist," Gessen said, voicing the stance of Karl Marx, Friedrich Engels, and the Cultural Marxist Frankfurt School to loud applause. ". . . Fighting for gay marriage generally involves lying about what we're going to do with marriage when we get there. Because we lie that the institution of marriage is not going to change. And that is a lie. The institution of marriage is going to change—and it should change and, again, I don't think it should exist."[99]

Queer theorists and practitioners aren't kidding that they want a Marxist cultural revolution. They have openly proclaimed that everywhere from street protests to "academic" journals for a hundred years. This revolution is already well underway in far-left states such as California, Illinois, Minnesota, and New York. LGBT laws that are replacing the normative American way of life and its original form of government are at the spearhead of this violent regime change.

CHAPTER 2

Identity Politics Is a Bureaucratic Insurrection

"A more brazen abuse of our authority to interpret statutes is hard to recall."
—Justice Samuel Alito, dissenting from the decision of the
Supreme Court in *Bostock v. Clayton County*

Since 2012, Jack Phillips has been harassed in courts for living his Christian faith. Despite winning a US Supreme Court case in 2018, he continues to be persecuted. Phillips was first hauled in front of an extra-judicial tribunal known as the "Colorado Civil Rights Commission" for refusing to create a cake to celebrate homosexuality. Contrary to media lies that he denies service to queer people, Phillips offered to sell a homosexual couple anything in his shop, and even to create any cake they liked except for a custom cake explicitly endorsing sex acts that Christianity calls sin.[1]

Rather than wholeheartedly affirming his First Amendment rights and the clear unconstitutionality of identity politics commissions and laws, the Supreme Court ducked. It ruled that the commission had shown "a clear and impermissible hostility" against Phillips's religious beliefs. There was plenty of evidence of that: emails between commission members showed them comparing Phillips's First Amendment–protected expression of his religious faith with defenses of the Holocaust and slavery.

Inspired by Phillips's case, another Colorado man asked three other local cake shops to create cakes expressing disapproval of homosexual acts. They all refused. When that man filed discrimination complaints about these refusals of service, the Colorado Civil Rights Commission ruled against him.[2]

On the same day in 2017 that the US Supreme Court announced it would take Phillips's case, a transgender lawyer named Autumn Scardina called the shop to demand that Phillips bake a cake celebrating transgender mutilation. During the trial in that case, Scardina said his goal was to "correct" the "errors" of Jack Phillips's "thinking." Scardina also said if his suit were dismissed, he'd call Phillips's Masterpiece Cakeshop *the very next day* and demand another offensive cake to prompt another lawsuit.

Scardina alleges that the Colorado Anti-Discrimination Act gives him the right to force Phillips to produce creative work to Scardina's taste—which, if you think about it, is essentially an act of enslavement, forcing Phillips to do work to Scardina's specifications against Phillips's will and conscience. Rather than punishing Scardina's attempt to weaponize state institutions on behalf of his bigotry, a Colorado trial court agreed with him.[3] So did the Colorado Court of Appeals, in 2023.[4] Phillips has appealed to the Colorado Supreme Court. Eighteen state attorneys general filed a brief against him, arguing Christianity is illegally bigoted.[5] These cases have kept Phillips in court for more than a decade now.

The famous baker's modest shop sits in a Denver-area strip mall. Phillips told me he has lived near there all his life. He doesn't plan to leave Colorado, because Americans' constitutional rights should be protected even in Democrat-run states: "Every American should be free to live according to their conscience. That is protected by the First Amendment."[6]

As Phillips's saga illustrates, identity politics depends on and works through the bureaucracy. Together, activists and bureaucrats foment regime change. Public officials have openly unmoored themselves from any pretense of fidelity to the law and the Constitution. That's so last century. We're in the midst of a multi-stage coup against our constitutional way of life.

Phillips's famous case is high-profile proof that queer activists' political program would negate the Bill of Rights, Declaration of Independence, Constitution, and the historic American way of life that embodies these documents. Voluminous evidence of their program can be uncovered by simply examining the laws and regulations these activists support.

Guilty until Proven Innocent

Note that Jack Phillips's ordeal began not in a constitutionally created court, with all the protections that the Constitution guarantees in actual court proceedings. The "Colorado Civil Rights Commission" is part of the executive branch of the state government, not the Colorado judiciary. It's part of what's called "the administrative state." Using the administrative state to coerce Americans to live the way LGBT activists demand violates all of Americans' constitutionally secured rights, as well as other natural rights that the Constitution leaves for states and individuals to protect.

For one thing, when an executive agency opens an investigation or proceeding against Americans, courts defer to the government, not the accused citizen, under the doctrine of a 1984 Supreme Court case known as *Chevron*.[7] This reverses the common law standard of "innocent until proven guilty." It marks the end of due process rights, which are constitutionally secured in multiple amendments.[8] In administrative courts, Americans are assumed guilty until proven innocent.[9] That's also a theme of LGBT ideology, which marks heterosexuals as born with evil "cis privilege," making them illegitimate participants in public life.[10]

Government agencies act as the judge, jury, and prosecution in cases tried in administrative law courts, violating the Constitution's separation of powers. Further, in administrative law cases, often the accused cannot compel testimony in his favor, get legal representation, confront those testifying against him, or be protected from the "excessive fines" forbidden by the Eighth Amendment.[11]

Only wealthy Americans can afford to pay legal fees for a decade. The legal fees for standing up to government agencies will bankrupt the average citizen.

Like most Americans, Phillips is not wealthy. In 2022, friends fundraised to buy his family a newer secondhand van, partly so he could help take care of his daughter, who is a single mother, and his grandchildren. The van he had owned before the fundraiser was twenty-two years old with more than two hundred thousand miles on it.[12] If buying a new van was a stretch, funding a decade-long battle up to the Supreme Court is inconceivable.

Having to fight the same charges in court for more than a decade, even after you have been cleared by the Supreme Court, is a "cruel and unusual" punishment by any reasonable person's standard. It also violates the Fifth Amendment's prohibition against double jeopardy, prosecuting a person more than once for "the same offence."

Breaking the Constitution is like breaking the Ten Commandments: when you violate one part of it, invariably you will violate others. That's exactly what the administrative state and the cultural Marxists that have seized control of it are doing.

Destroying America with Lies about Equality

The effect of identity policies is not "equality," as we're constantly told. It's slavery, injustice, and enmity between Americans. These policies are an attempt to force Christians—indeed, all serious religious believers and even all dissenters from woke policies in America—into homosexuals' fabled closet. As Wyoming pastor Jonathan Lange observed of Phillips's case, "If the First Amendment's right to 'free speech' is only valid when it is an 'exercise of religion,' constitutional protections are denied to the non-religious. That should trouble everyone."[13]

Identity policies erase equality by stripping fundamental natural rights from all Americans, and substituting for them the unequal favoritism of government officials. The new identity politics regime has also established non-constitutional entities as a shadow government more powerful than the judicial, legislative, and executive branches established in state and national constitutions.

As Illinois Gov. J. B. Pritzker told a room of queer activists as he was signing a law to queer K–12 curricula and fund transgender surgeries with tax dollars, "Those of you in this room know better than anyone that marriage equality was never the endgame."[14] The endgame is erasing American constitutional government and the way of life it reflects and protects. Below, to back up that statement, is a sampling of recent totalitarian proposals pushed by queer activists.

A 2024 bill would establish Maine as an "LGBT sanctuary state" by protecting any doctor who illegally mutilated transgender children in another state, banning Maine from extraditing them for prosecution.[15] The bill also would allow Mainers to sue *other states'* officials for obeying their state laws protecting children from transgender mutilations.

If passed, it would "catastrophically destabilize our constitutional order,"[16] said Tennessee Attorney General Jonathan Skrmetti. Sixteen state attorneys general sent a letter to Maine's legislature warning them the legislation could "trigger a rapid tit-for-tat escalation that tears apart our Republic."[17]

A 2022 New York law requires social media companies to police their users for "hate speech"—meaning, of course, speech queer people don't like. The law sets up a system whereby citizens report complaints to bureaucrats, who investigate and issue daily fines of $1,000 per alleged violation. It also allows the state attorney general's office to make companies produce documents for state "investigations" outside the safeguards in the regular court system against such totalitarian fishing expeditions.[18]

The law essentially extends college DEI snitch lines called "bias reporting systems" to everyone in New York state—indeed, to anyone who uses the services of companies that operate in New York state, such as any social media. "Forcing private companies to set speech codes is a way to circumvent the First Amendment," lawyers told the *Epoch Times*.[19] The law is tied up in court.

A 2023 "hate speech" bill the Democrat-run Michigan House passed would make it a crime "to cause someone to 'feel terrorized, frightened, or threatened.'"[20] So how someone chooses to feel could make another American guilty of a crime. The bill also gives "sexual orientation" and "gender identity" protected-class status, effectively giving legal advantages to those who identify as queer. Policies like these, pushed allegedly on behalf of queer Americans, erase all Americans' constitutional rights to free peaceful speech.

"One merely needs to look at the scores of cases brought against schools, churches, businesses, and individuals around our country," law professor William Wagner told The College Fix. "Proponents use these laws to silence and financially cripple those who dare to adhere to a different viewpoint and oppose their agenda."[21]

Months later, the Democrat-run Michigan Supreme Court began forcing every judge and attorney in the state to use transgender pronouns or refrain from using pronouns altogether.[22] In October 2023, the US Department of Health and Human Services began also requiring their more than eighty thousand employees[23] to use false pronouns.[24] The HHS claims its policy applies not just to employees but also "visitors," "which means anyone who steps foot into an HHS facility or program now [allegedly] has to comply," noted Roger Severino, the former director of HHS's Office of Civil Rights.[25]

The policy forces all seekers of justice in Michigan and all HHS employees to assume the false leftist position on transgender pronouns. It also essentially handicaps people who acknowledge that pronouns correspond to sex by forcing them into awkward speech to avoid pronouns, and putting them in danger of slip ups that may endanger them professionally.

In 2017, California required health-care workers to use false pronouns or face up to a year in jail. In 2021, a federal court ruled the law unconstitutional, with the judges telling California lawmakers that they supported forcing false pronoun use, but not via threats of jail time. [26]

This is compelled speech, and not merely for state employees, but also for private citizens such as nurses and doctors, and lawyers and their clients in court. It's obviously against the First Amendment's guarantee that individuals control their speech, not the government. These provisions claim to show "empathy" and "respect" for gender-confused people, while exhibiting zero empathy or respect for the people who know sex is immutable. Such regulations condemn those who acknowledge immutable sex with the implication that their accurate understanding of reality is unkind, false, even cruel.

True freedom includes the freedom to not only be wrong but to contradict those in power. Nobody has freedom if his freedom is limited to things that don't matter, like what color socks to wear or what TV show to watch.

It's totalitarian to force people to assert things they believe are false. It's also an abuse of power. Such policies publicly humiliate those who disagree with leftists by compelling them to lie or to submit to the subjugation rituals of awkward speech in order to be employed in the legal system or seek justice through state courts.

Bostock: The Next *Roe v. Wade*

The 2020 Supreme Court decision *Bostock v. Clayton County* is perhaps the pre-eminent example of the lawlessness of queer ideology, which fulfills feminism by erasing distinctions between the sexes. Like Jack Phillips's case, it also illustrates how the unconstitutional bureaucracy subverts constitutional government for queer privileges.

President Trump–appointed Supreme Court Justice Neil Gorsuch wrote the 6–3 majority opinion, joined by Republican-appointed Chief Justice John Roberts and the court's four Constitution-haters. *Bostock* parallels the 1973 Supreme Court decision *Roe v. Wade* in multiple ways. Both court majorities were appointed by Republicans.[27] Both decisions were obviously unconstitutional. Both enacted dramatic judicial overreach, and their evil consequences continue.

Like *Roe*, *Bostock* was also a Supreme Court stamp of approval on a lawless Democrat president's move, and a pretext for more lawlessness from another. In 2014, Obama Attorney General Eric Holder announced the US Department of Justice was shoehorning the concept of "gender identity" into the word "sex" in the 1964 Civil Rights Act prohibiting "sex discrimination."[28]

Transsexual Chase Strangio is an American Civil Liberties Union lawyer for one of the cases decided in *Bostock*.[29] An in-depth report by an Alabama judicial panel in 2024 found that other lawyers for the

ACLU and similar activist organizations pursuing transgender litigation— including the Southern Poverty Law Center, National Center for
Lesbian Rights, and Lambda Legal—engaged in legal "misconduct" by
attempting to get their cases assigned to friendly judges to set precedents
favorable to their cause.[30] Contrary to Gorsuch's claim that the decision
would only affect Title VII, the ACLU's Strangio saw it as the foundation for expanding LGBT policies in every aspect of federal power.[31]
He turned out to be completely right.

"The arguments that we made completely resonated with Gorsuch,
which is who we were targeting," Strangio said. "And he basically
adopted our briefs in full to create this opinion that I think will serve
not just the LGBTQ community, but serve the expansion of justice in
civil rights litigation generally in really incredible ways."

Banning Employers from Acknowledging Sex Differences

Gorsuch and LGBT activists argued that the federal law prohibiting
discrimination on the basis of sex encompasses not only women, but
also queer people. Gorsuch reasoned that the law requires punishing
any employer who doesn't treat the sexes as interchangeable: "An
employer who fires an individual for being homosexual or transgender
fires that person for traits or actions it would not have questioned in
members of a different sex," Gorsuch wrote in *Bostock*. "Sex plays
a necessary and undisguisable role in the decision, exactly what Title
VII forbids."[32]

If this is the way the law must be understood, it is an immoral
and unconstitutional law that abrogates Americans' natural rights.
Gorsuch's reasoning would require erasing all sexual differences everywhere that federal laws banning employers from acknowledging differences between the sexes apply. That's obviously stupid, because men
and women are, in fact, different. We cannot be transposed. It makes

sense to treat men and women differently in some circumstances, and Americans have commonsensically done so since the Founding.

This decision is also evil because judges legislating from the bench are tyrants. They deny us the right to govern ourselves by changing the meaning of the laws we have given our consent to. It also violates the Constitution's separation of powers, which protects Americans' natural right to self-rule by prohibiting non-elected judges from changing the laws. Only the elected legislature is supposed to do that. The role of the judge is to apply the legislature's laws to real-life situations, not to repeal their meanings.

"A society governed by the rule of law must have laws that are known and understandable to the citizenry," Justice Brett Kavanaugh noted in his dissent. "And judicial adherence to ordinary meaning facilitates the democratic accountability of America's elected representatives for the laws they enact." In a ruling posing as "strict textualism," Gorsuch even apparently claimed the Civil Rights Act legitimately changes in meaning over time(!): "Title VII's prohibition of sex discrimination in employment . . . has repeatedly produced unexpected applications."

Violates Law, Language, History, and the Constitution

The *Bostock* dissent penned by Justice Samuel Alito and joined by Justice Clarence Thomas notes that American laws, legal proceedings, and culture have always distinguished between sex and sexual orientation. *Bostock*, in contrast, expanded "sex discrimination" to include "sexual orientation and gender identity discrimination."

Bostock contradicted not just thirty out of thirty Court of Appeals decisions, but also the federal agency charged with enforcing identity politics protections laws, the Equal Employment Opportunity Commission (EEOC). Even that wildly leftist agency had never previously claimed that Title VII created special protections for sexual orientation and gender identity by using the word "sex," the justices noted.

"[T]he Court's conclusion . . . necessarily means that the EEOC failed to see the obvious for the first 48 years after Title VII became law," the dissent notes. "Day in and day out, the Commission enforced Title VII but did not grasp what discrimination 'because of . . . sex' unambiguously means."

The dissenting justices pointed to multiple historical proofs contradicting *Bostock's* claim that the 1964 law had always required businesses to allow employees to cross-dress at work, use inaccurate pronouns, put men in women's bathrooms, and all the other sexual orientation and gender identity (SOGI) privileges. These include the fact that at the time of the law's passing, and for three decades afterward, the US military discharged homosexuals. The word "transgender" didn't exist until years after the law passed, and the term "gender identity" seems to have first appeared in an academic article the same year Title VII was passed.

The transgender activists who won the *Bostock* case denied historical, legal, and linguistic realities. Outrageously, Gorsuch and Roberts went along with their lies, adopting their magical thinking that insisted these federal identity politics laws *always* included privileges for LGBT people.

"Those who claim to be victims of Biden's affirmation of these legal protections are really angry about legal rules that were drafted by Congress decades ago and affirmed by the Supreme Court in June," Strangio fabulized, discussing Biden's first-day-in-office executive order applying *Bostock* to all federal agencies.[33]

If these legal protections "were drafted by Congress decades ago," then why did it take a Supreme Court decision and dramatic executive action fifty years later to put them into effect? Because nobody thought any federal laws encompassed sexual preferences until *Bostock*.

Indeed, LGBT activists spent decades between the 1964 Civil Rights Act and 2020, when *Bostock* was decided, demanding their identity group get its own carve-out in federal "antidiscrimination law." That means not even LGBT activists believed the Civil Rights Act protected homosexual, transsexual, or any other queer identity. This betrays the fact that *Bostock* was an egregious exercise in legislating from the Supreme Court bench, just like *Roe v. Wade.* It depended entirely on butchering the United States' supreme law, the Constitution.

The Supreme Court Doesn't Know How Sex Works

As a key part of his purportedly textualist argument, Gorsuch uses the following illustration (and another like it): "[T]ake an employer who fires a transgender person who was identified as a male at birth but who now identifies as a female. If the employer retains an otherwise identical employee who was identified as female at birth, the employer intentionally penalizes a person identified as male at birth for traits or actions that it tolerates in an employee identified as female at birth. Again, the individual employee's sex plays an unmistakable and impermissible role in the discharge decision."

Wrong. A man who dresses up as a woman is not analogous to a woman dressing up as a woman. He's analogous to *a woman dressing up as a man.* An employer firing an employee for cross-dressing is firing people not for their sex, but for their *behavior.* Gorsuch's scenario doesn't just change the participants' sex but also their *behavior,* as Justices Alito and Kavanaugh noted in their dissents.

Gorsuch's analogies don't work for homosexuality, either. Substituting a man for a woman in a sexual encounter does not result in the same bedroom behavior. In fact, technically, a man cannot engage in sex with another man, because their relations can never cause procreation, the scientific meaning of the word "sex." For mammals—and all other creatures who reproduce sexually—the act isn't sex if offspring cannot result.

Apologies that the Supreme Court's detachment from basic biology forces me to make this crude observation, but two-man relations do not involve the same orifices as man-woman relations. Neither do two-woman relations. You simply cannot substitute a naked man for a naked woman in the sex act and call it the same. It isn't, because men's and women's bodies are *different*. Men simply don't have the orifice for sex that women do. Two protrusions or two cavities don't fit together the same way one protrusion and one cavity do.

Thus Gorsuch's analogies and wordsmithing are simply false, and obviously so. *Obergefell v. Hodges,* the 2013 Supreme Court decision erasing marriage, was wrong on this count as well.

Apparently our Supreme Court has no idea how sex works. Not only that, they insist on writing their false and ignorant account of sexual encounters into jurisprudence and federal law.

Basic biology aside, who are Supreme Court justices to tell Americans that "An individual's homosexuality or transgender status is not relevant to employment decisions?"[34] Those things are absolutely relevant to some employment decisions, such as whether a man should supervise people he is sexually attracted to while they're undressing—as a homosexual sports coach of boys would be. It's relevant to whether a lesbian will be helping a woman fit a bra, or examining her naked in a doctor's office. It's relevant to who teaches kindergarteners—should it be a man wearing a dress with fake, bouncing breasts?[35]

Gorsuch's reasoning implies that there are no rational or legally permissible distinctions between the sexes. This would eliminate single-sex dormitories, sports teams, clubs, and lingerie shops, people's ability to choose the sex of their OB-GYNs, and more. Congress denied it was doing any of this when it passed the sex-related amendments to the Civil Rights Act in 1964.

Even if sexual behavior and crossdressing *were* completely irrelevant to all employment decisions—and they're not—it's none of the government's damned business who Americans freely associate with or why. This is exactly how federal "discrimination" law nullifies Americans' fundamental natural rights.

Another Pretext to Trans Everything

More than one hundred federal laws ban Americans from making distinctions based on sex, Justic Alito noted. He predicted "far-reaching consequences" such as ending single-sex sports, forcing religious Americans to violate their beliefs to participate in the marketplace, forcing men and women to house together in domestic violence centers and college dorms, and forcing people who pay insurance premiums—which, thanks to Obamacare, is all Americans—to fund transgender medical mutilations.

Besides all that, of course, "the position that the Court now adopts will threaten freedom of religion, freedom of speech, and personal privacy and safety," wrote Alito. Gorsuch had claimed that "we do not purport to address bathrooms, locker rooms, or anything else of the kind," maintaining that the decision was only applicable to employment law. Neither queer activists nor the Biden White House paid any attention to that distinction, and Gorsuch and Roberts were fools to expect they would. Or perhaps they did expect what Biden did with their decision, and welcomed it.

"Every state considering anti-trans bills barring trans people from sports must now consider that they will face a US government that is not facilitating anti-trans discrimination but actually enforcing Title IX's protections to stop it," Strangio wrote of LGBT activists' plans to employ *Bostock*. "Every employer, every landlord, every health care provider that is considering firing or evicting or denying health care to a transgender person must now think about the fact that all three branches of the federal government have made clear that anti-LGBTQ discrimination is illegal."[36]

The administration declared that it would apply the Supreme Court's reasoning to federal programs for education, housing, immigration, food subsidies, and every other federal agency. The existence of a large federal bureaucracy gives leftists more fronts on which to wage their culture war on the American way of life. They wield the unconstitutional power of the bureaucracy[37] vigorously. "Under *Bostock's* reasoning, laws that prohibit sex discrimination . . . prohibit discrimination on the basis of gender identity or sexual orientation, so long as the laws do not contain sufficient indications to the contrary," said Biden's Inauguration Day executive order.[38]

In 2021, the EEOC changed its regulations regarding employers' recognition of sex distinctions. Their new "guidance" said employers of fifteen or more Americans must now allow employees to cross-dress at work, use opposite-sex bathrooms and showers, and force colleagues to use the wrong pronouns for them. The regulations also said businesses must force customers to interact with transgender people despite their personal preferences.[39]

On March 2, 2022, the US Department of Health and Human Services issued regulations telling Americans that federal disability protections now included *Bostock's* gender identity and sexual orientation privileges. This meant that federally funded health-care entities—which is almost all of them—must provide gender mutilation, cross sex hormones, and all the rest of "gender-affirming care." If they didn't, not only might their federal funds be yanked, they could be liable for penalties under the Americans with Disabilities Act.[40] These and other parallel regulations across the federal government were immediately challenged in court, and the cases are ongoing.[41] Alito was right: "The entire Federal Judiciary will be mired for years in disputes about the reach of the Court's reasoning."

An Anti-Constitution Wishlist

Identity politics relies heavily on non-constitutional agencies, and on ostensibly private "popular front" organizations. These pretend to agitate from outside the government but are essentially indistinguishable from government in policy, personnel, and funding, just as in Communist China.[42] In 2020, the sex-politics agitators Human Rights Campaign released a "Blueprint" outlining eighty-five demands for the executive branch.[43] After Joe Biden was inaugurated, his administration started following these activists' orders.

That would be shocking—if this were a private group instead of a popular front mask for the far-left permanent bureaucracy. Multiple HRC board members and employees held Biden and Obama administration posts.[44] Its current president previously campaigned for Obama,[45] and multiple staffers have campaigned for Hillary Clinton.[46]

Key items on HRC's wishlist included:

- Appointing openly LGBTQ figureheads into prominent positions, "including "the first-ever openly LGBTQ cabinet secretary"[47]
- Axing federal contracts with religious charities such as homeless shelters, detox programs, preschools, and food banks
- Yanking accreditation—and thus eligibility for federal student funding—from religious colleges unless they disavowed sexual morals
- Essentially establishing the United States as a "sanctuary country" for all foreigners who claim to be LGBT
- Funding LGBT agitation abroad
- Hiring federal workers based on race, sex, and sexual preferences.

The Biden administration immediately implemented many of these demands, starting the day Biden assumed office. The HRC "Blueprint" had asked the president to apply "*Bostock v. Clayton County* across all agencies enforcing civil rights statutes and provisions."[48] On Inauguration Day, Biden signed an executive order obeying that demand to extend *Bostock* into every conceivable part of the federal government.[49]

The HRC wants to apply queer ideology to every aspect of American life, using the bureaucracy as the tip of their spear. The "Blueprint" is essentially a road map for using the unconstitutional parts of the federal government—the vast majority of its bureaucracy—to erase even more of the Constitution. Essentially every item on the Bill of Rights is targeted, plus key portions of the rest of the Constitution, such as its separation of powers.

Erasing the Bill of Rights

The First Amendment conflicts are obvious and perhaps central. The "Blueprint" demands, for example, that the federal government ban therapists from helping clients struggling with gender dysphoria and unwanted sexual attractions, even if their clients want that help. This is a ban on free speech and freedom of association.

The "Blueprint" attacks the First Amendment more insidiously in demanding the federal government "provide a publicly available list of colleges and universities that have received religious exemptions" from obeying federal regulations requiring them to treat men as women.[50]

The only way the Feds can provide a list is if colleges file for exemptions, which the law doesn't require, Alliance Defending Freedom lawyer Greg Baylor said in an interview. Since the 1980s at least, he said, religious education institutions have been presumed exempt from the law without needing to file any paperwork. The Human Rights

Campaign wants the Feds to require colleges to log their exemptions and for the government to publish that list "to out them as bad bigoted schools so they can shame them," Baylor said.[51] In other words, this activist group is demanding policies that will allow them to engage in anti-speech, anti-religion pressure campaigns against targets that the federal government has helped them identify.

Again, like Communist "popular front" "cultural groups" that are actually extensions of the government, HRC petitions for things that the people who run the government—some of whom used to be their colleagues and may be again in the future—want to do already. This gives the government a pretext for carrying out their mutual plans. The government, in turn, helps this "private" group run social pressure campaigns to punish any dissents from the party line.

Federal agencies began telling K–12 Christian schools to file these exemptions in 2022, not disclosing that the schools are automatically exempt and don't need to file any paperwork to get the exemption.[52]

Shoving Christians into Economic Ghettos

The blueprint also threatens equal access to every federal dollar for religiously affiliated people and organizations, requiring Americans to violate their consciences in order for the government to treat them equally in doling out their own taxpayer funds. This is a huge deal, because federal contracts and grants employ more people than the federal government does.[53] In 2022, federal grants equaled $700 billion,[54] nearly what taxpayers spend on the US military.[55]

That's not all. Federal spending now equals approximately one-quarter to one-third of everything Americans spend or create every year.[56] Half of that spending is transfer payments.[57] Wealth redistribution in the form of state and individual transfer payments was 76 percent of non-interest federal spending in 2023.[58] So federal contracts, grants, and transfer payments make up perhaps the majority of the US economy, and LGBT activists want to use all of them to make the *entire* US economy available only to people who take a loyalty oath to their ideology. Pretty communist.

Essentially, queer activists want to use the federal government's huge size and spending as hush money to erase Americans' First Amendment rights to say and believe the truth. Their vision is not limited to economic activity, either. The "Blueprint" applies queer ideology to every federal entity, including the US military. The goal is to use every lever of federal power to force Americans to do and say what LGBT activists want. That is un-American and totalitarian: it assumes the right to tell people that they may not act as if they believe anything other than what government sanctions.

Damage Vulnerable Americans' Bodies or Else

The HRC "Blueprint" demands that Americans—parents, teachers, therapists, nurses, doctors—be forced to assist in treatments and procedures that violate their deepest beliefs. It demands that everyone be forced to use male pronouns for women and female pronouns for men—in other words, to lie. This violates the First Amendment's guarantees of free speech and freedom of religion. Among other medical industry changes, the "Blueprint" demands that the federal government:

- force taxpayers to pay for expensive drugs that enable sex with HIV-positive people
- require all health-care providers—including those religiously affiliated—to provide mutilating transgender therapies and lie about the sex of transgender patients

- force taxpayers to pay for soldiers and federal prison inmates to receive mutilating transgender therapies
- and require the US military to accept and keep transgender and HIV-positive recruits. The previous, opposite policy had been "based on sound science tied to the need for HIV medications and the danger of cross-infection through shared blood."[59]

Even More Disappearing Constitutional Rights

The HRC "Blueprint" threatens the Second Amendment with demands for federal data collection to push gun control: "The lack of this data . . . impedes the development and implementation of evidence-based interventions to address gun violence affecting LGBTQ communities."

The Fourth Amendment secures "the right of the people to be secure in their persons, houses, papers, and effects, against unreasonable searches and seizures." The "Blueprint" pushes the federal government to help minors hide transgender medical treatments and payments from their parents, whether their parents' health insurance or Medicaid pays for the treatments.

Reaching around parents to collect data on and manipulate the medical treatments of their children, using their insurance and other health information to do so, seems a pretty obvious violation of this provision. It makes families insecure in their own house and health records, including from the government-abetted seizure of their children. So does the demand for the federal government to force women in prison, homeless shelters, and domestic violence shelters to share housing with mentally ill and often violent men.

The Fifth Amendment says, "No person shall . . . be deprived of life, liberty, or property, without due process of law; nor shall private property be taken for public use, without just compensation." The Supreme Court's *Bostock v. Clayton County* decision adding "gender identity" to the word "sex" in federal antidiscrimination law violates this provision, for it takes these constitutional rights of citizens without due process. The due process of law is for Congress to define what it means by "sex" and for courts to adhere to what Congress has written. It's a violation of Americans' due process rights for courts to legislate from the bench.

The Sixth through Eighth amendments to the Constitution provide citizens multiple due process rights against adversarial government action. These include allowing an accused person to confront those testifying against him, compel testimony in his favor, to have legal representation, and to be protected from "excessive fines" and "cruel and unusual punishments."

The Ninth Amendment says, "The enumeration in the Constitution, of certain rights, shall not be construed to deny or disparage others retained by the people." This means the Constitution does not name every natural right of American citizens that government must protect. We have more rights than the Constitution specifically names.

The Tenth Amendment, the last item in the Bill of Rights, says, "The powers not delegated to the United States by the Constitution, nor prohibited by it to the States, are reserved to the States respectively, or to the people." In other words, the powers the Constitution doesn't give the federal government still belong to the people and the states. The administrative state has taken many of these powers from the people and their states, such as zoning (the federal government is now redesigning neighborhoods for DEI)[60] and public relief for natural disasters and indigence.

Because of Fourteenth Amendment jurisprudence, all the Bill of Rights protections now apply to state governments, as well as the federal agencies. Queer politics threatens them all.

Teaching Kids about Homosexual Touching

Queer totalitarianism reserves to itself the right to control people's homes and family life. Nowhere is this more visible than the queer takeover of education, which reaches all the way to babies in daycare and toddlers watching PBS.[61]

California, Colorado, Illinois, New Jersey, Oregon, Rhode Island, Washington state, and Washington, D.C., require sex education to inform students about LGBT sexual practices. California, Colorado, Connecticut, Illinois, Nevada, New Jersey, and Oregon require LGBT instruction in all public schools, and permit it as early as preschool if teachers desire.[62] In 2020, the California Teachers Union decided to use its massive clout to push for policies allowing twelve-year-olds to get transgender hormones during the school day without their parents' knowledge.[63] Illinois required all public schools to teach queer history in social studies starting in July 2020 and buy only instructional materials that include such information.[64] Parents in California may not opt their children out of public school lessons on gender identity, and teachers don't have to notify parents of these lessons.[65] California uses federal funds to pay for transing its social studies curriculum. The state prioritizes the poorest school districts ("Title I") for trainings on how to add LGBT materials in every class.[66]

These governments are following 2012 curriculum recommendations from the queer activist group GLSEN, an acronym derived from its former name, the Gay, Lesbian, and Straight Education Network.[67] GLSEN marks "access to inclusive curriculum" as one of its "four core supports" that "improves school climates for LGBTQ+ youth." The other three are "comprehensive nondiscrimination and anti-bullying policies, supportive educators, and access to [LGBT clubs at school]." GLSEN offers an "Inclusive Teaching Guide" that shows teachers how "to weave intersectional LGBTQ+ inclusive content into all aspects of the curriculum."

School districts following GLSEN and other pro-queer outfits expose preschoolers to "polyamorous" and lesbian families. They also affirm gender dysphoria, telling three-year-olds, "Sometimes people use their bodies to help them know their gender, and some people know their gender in their heart." Special-needs students watch a video about a "gender-fluid" cross-dressing eleven-year-old.[68]

GLSEN bullies people into abusing children like this by explicitly tying in-school sexual exposure to "anti-racism": "in alignment with our mission and our research findings, GLSEN supports inclusive curricular standards that require affirming representation of the contributions and lived experiences of LGBTQ+ people, people who are Black, Indigenous, and people of color (BIPOC), people with disabilities, and all marginalized communities."[69] Despite bullying like this, 67 percent of Americans support parent freedom to opt out their children to inappropriate or morally objectional instruction like this, and 58 percent of Americans—a 12-point increase since 2021—oppose schools forcing students and teachers into using false pronouns.[70]

When visitors reach GLSEN's website, they find a large alert banner that says, "You can quickly leave this website by pressing the Escape key three times, or tapping three times quickly on mobile. To browse this site safely, be sure to regularly clear your browser history." At the top of every page on its site is a similar button. It's obviously to prevent parents from knowing if their children are reading the site.[71]

The Equality Act continually before Congress would require all schools to teach queer sex-ed and history,[72] like GLSEN wants. Like *Bostock*, the act would expand the word "sex" in federal civil rights laws to encompass "sexual orientation" and "gender identity." As legal analyst Inez Stepman writes, the act would force all health professionals to treat men as women, force violent men into women's shelters and prisons, allow males to erase women's sports, and force everyone to lie that some men are women and some women are men.[73] It could also force churches to perform homosexual ceremonies.[74] It is *Bostock* on steroids.

Christians Need Not Apply for Federal Funds

As part of its comprehensive program to push queer policies through the bureaucracy, in May 2022 the Biden administration banned from food welfare distribution any institution that does not allow boys into girls' bathrooms, use transgender pronouns, and allow staff to cross-dress at work.[75] That includes schools, child and adult daycares, emergency shelters, afterschool care programs, and disabled care centers, *including religious ones*. It also included any entity accepting food stamps, which is most grocery and convenience stores. This is using bureaucracy to commandeer the economy for extremist sex politics.

"As a result" of the new regulations, said the US Department of Agriculture (USDA), which administers federal food programs, "state and local agencies, program operators and sponsors that receive funds from FNS must investigate allegations of discrimination based on gender identity or sexual orientation. Those organizations must also update their non-discrimination policies and signage to include prohibitions against discrimination based on gender identity and sexual orientation."[76]

The USDA had changed the definition of the word "sex" in federal antidiscrimination law to include "gender identity." It claimed this redefinition was "consistent with the Supreme Court's decision in *Bostock*." [77] Myriad other federal agencies did the same, perhaps most infamously the US Department of Education in a Title IX rewrite finalized on April 19, 2024 despite 240,000 public comments, a "record number."[78] Just like *Bostock*, the Biden administration's Title IX rewrite inserted the concept of "gender identity" into the word "sex," shoehorning gender-distressed males into legal preferences designed to benefit women.

Just like *Bostock*, these regulations contradicted the law. Lawmakers in 1972 did not mean to provide federal encouragement for gender dysphoria. Title IX was intended to ensure equal opportunity for women in education. Everyone knows that, even if some people lie about it. Although Title IX gives religious institutions automatic exemptions, several were still harassed and forced to go to court under these new regulations.

A California Christian preschool where 40 percent of children are low-income, in a community where nearly one-third of residents are foreign-born, was denied federal food funds in December 2022 for refusing to put boys in girls' bathrooms.[79] Before being kicked out of the federal food program, it had received $3,500 to $4,000 per month to feed needy kids during the school year and in the summers. In January 2024, the government settled the case, likely to avoid a court precedent.[80]

Also in 2022, a Christian school in Florida was denied participation in the school lunch program on account of its religious beliefs. Nine days after pro bono attorneys filed a lawsuit on behalf of the school—and just a few days before the school year began—its funds were restored.[81]

The Biden administration made all these changes outside of legally required procedures, the Government Accountability Office said.[82] The administration pushed the policy on schools before following legally required rulemaking processes, which pushed the policies into place while they couldn't prompt lawsuits that might delay or end them. It's another example of the constant overlap between LGBT politics and lawlessness.

The Managerial State Makes War against Self-Government

Such policies subvert the foundation of the United States: Christianity. The American Founders believed limited government could not flourish without the people adhering to Christianity. That's because Christianity teaches people virtue, a necessary precondition for self-government.

Republican self-government is not possible without adherence to Christian precepts, which identity politics seeks to stamp out of American life in favor of a vicious pagan tribalism. Degrading the morality of the people destroys their capacity for self-government by enslaving them to their passions.

As Charles Hayward has written, "The managerial state cannot tolerate self-governance, because it implies people do not need the managerial regime to decide what is best. And a people lacking self-governance, what was always recognized as an enslaved people, is ideal fodder for the managerial state. Thus, the main focus of the managerial system for the past seventy years has been breaking down self-governance in society, emancipating the atomized self from any intermediation other than with agents and tentacles of the managerial state."[83]

Members of the three-million-strong federal bureaucracy now openly defy the Constitution over Pride issues. They believe their insurrection is justified because special privileges for queer people constitute human rights. Therefore, any reduction of these privileges is morally abominable, and any action taken to protect them morally righteous.

This is why we see incidents of, for example, Texas university officials holding video calls about how to circumvent state laws banning identity politics instruction,[84] and California law school deans publicly discussing how they violate the state constitution's prohibition of racial preferences.[85] After the Supreme Court ruled in 2023 that racism in admissions is unconstitutional, the Biden administration instructed colleges in how to violate the Constitution by admitting students based on race.[86] The White House might have engaged in the same insurrectionary behavior if *Bostock* had affirmed sex differences.

There is no arguing or compromising with these leftist jihadis engaged in a holy war. The only way to stop them from completing their mission to destroy our country is public mockery, firing them for insubordination, and stripping their financing and prestige. As Aristotle argued, the base are ruled only by pain and pleasure.

CHAPTER 3

A Hundred Years of Regime Change in America

"At the federal level, the Constitution and documents like
the Federalist Papers no longer explain how government
actually works. Indeed, they expose its illegitimacy."
—Kevin Slack, War on the American Republic[1]

Americans aren't stupid. Daily, we see examples of the government flexing its power to destroy citizens merely for saying the "wrong" word.

At the time of this writing, prominent examples include the US Department of Education opening a "civil rights" investigation into journalist Chris Rufo for allegedly using . . . an accurate pronoun.[2] They also include the Federal Trade Commission deciding to investigate Elon Musk after he bought Twitter[3] and the Justice Department going after one of Musk's companies for allegedly not hiring enough foreigners.[4]

Those are ridiculous lawfare exercises, and they will cost millions. Musk can afford the costs of the world's largest government going after him for political differences, but ordinary people cannot. That's likely a motivating factor in Musk promising that X (formerly Twitter) will fund people's legal defense in cases arising from their speech on his platform.

Smart people and companies without the millions to stand up to unhinged bureaucrats' fury—or the desire to waste millions on such an effort—keep their heads down and mouths shut to avoid being bank-rupted defending their Constitutional rights to free speech, freedom of association, and freedom of religion. This means Americans today effectively don't have Constitutional rights unless they are rich enough to afford lawyers. The vast majority of Americans aren't.

There are more than 185,000 pages in the Federal Register.[5] It's impossible for anyone to comply with laws that voluminous. That morass allows one petty bureaucratic dictator to make any American guilty until he can prove himself innocent at great expense. We are all de facto criminals whose crimes are just waiting to be found by a motivated government official. Bureaucrats have the power to unilat-erally charge, investigate, prosecute, and declare guilty anyone they decide to target, all before the matter is allowed to reach a court of law.[6]

Thus, government officials have power to coerce simply through "asking" for something. Imagine that a person with the power to ruin your life[7] because you made some non-PC remark that the person thinks could violate Title VII is asking for a favor. You wouldn't want him to get mad and start looking for all the crimes[8] you're surely guilty of, would you? What if he were to refer you to the US Department of Justice for prosecution of your speech crime?[9]

Mafia government like this results from Progressives having spent the past hundred years substituting tyrannical government for Constitutional government in the United States. The "diversity, equity, and inclusion" regime equals a civil war against the US Constitution and the way of life it reflects and protects.

The ideology Americans variously call wokeism, intersectionalism, identity politics, critical theory, and Cultural Marxism is anti-authority, and therefore pro-anarchy.[10] The size of the government deceives people about its lawlessness. Cultural Marxism engenders the kind of civil "rights" that supplant the Constitution instead of supplementing it. Marxist identity rights are truly a regime change in the United States.

To understand how this regime change is occurring, we need to look at how the American Founders understood natural rights. It will illuminate how intersectionalism replaces limited self-government with slavery. We'll focus on how sexual politics fuel such a regime change.

What Is a Natural Right?

The rights that the Constitution exists to protect are not merely desires. Rights are not needs like food and medical care, either. That's because, as Argentinian President Javier Milei pointed out in 2023, human needs and desires are potentially infinite, while resources are always limited.

In addition, if our needs were rights, we could essentially force other people into slavery. For medical care to be a right, the doctor's labor and skill must belong to others instead of to himself. For food to be a right, the farmer's labor, skill, and property must belong to others instead of himself. Call it whatever collectivist term you want—socialism, communism, tyranny—all are slavery.

We can disguise the slavery by playing Rube Goldberg games, but taking the results of one man's labor to provide another man anything beyond the equal security of his own natural rights is slavery. Slavery can be partial or full. Today, American taxpayers are partial slaves, working to provide for "entitled" populations *far* beyond the expenditures required to equally secure all citizens' natural rights. The vast majority of federal activity and funding now concerns transfer payments to groups that receive vastly more than they contribute.[11]

Expanding government beyond solely securing natural rights cannibalizes natural rights. Consider, for example, how the United States' unprecedented massive national debt, largely a result of entitlement and other non-Constitutional spending, endangers our national security.[12] US meddling in foreign wars diverts resources from direct threats such as securing our borders.

The Founders believed the chief duty of a just government was to protect citizens from violence. Our government has strayed far from that core mission, using identity politics and entitlement bribes to hide the fact that it has become a predator. That's an existential threat because a welfare state takes effort, funds, and security away from local police, from our national defense, and from a functioning justice system that is necessary to secure our real rights.

So if a need cannot create a right, where do rights come from? According to the American Founders, rights come from God. Yet recognizing natural rights doesn't require deep or sectarian theology. As Hillsdale College politics professor Thomas West's masterful work explains, "Independently of the Bible, the founders believed that human reason is also able to grasp that a first principle animates the world. This principle they called the God of nature—by which they meant God insofar as he is known by reason's inferences from the orderly structure of nature, including human nature. Believers and unbelievers alike could accept this understanding of God."[13]

Rights are what a rightly informed person, looking at nature, can see that God has given to all mankind. These include, as the Declaration of Independence says, life, liberty, and the pursuit of happiness. In numerous documents and speeches, the Founders added the right to property—to be secure in the fruits of one's own labor, protected from both government and highway robbery.

"All human beings by nature do possess life, liberty, the ability to pursue happiness, the ability to acquire property, and a mind that forms opinions by reason and conviction. These natural possessions, the 'property' we all own by nature, are the principal rights of man," West writes.[14]

Other natural rights that a just government must recognize flow logically from the "headwater" natural rights to life, liberty, property, and pursuing happiness. For example, the right to self-defense is a logical extension of the right to life. The right to speak one's mind and worship according to one's conscience are extensions of the rights to liberty and the pursuit of happiness. People cannot be happy when they are forced to live and speak lies.

What Does "Equality" Really Mean?

Key to understanding sexual politics is understanding what the American Founders, in contrast, meant by political equality. Today, our anti-Constitutional government interprets equality as sameness: the same outcomes for individuals regardless of their differences, which include sex. That is exactly what identity policies require.

The American Founders would have considered such a system of government tyrannical, because people are different. We cannot all achieve the same outcomes in anything, from hair color to earning power to artistic ability to fertility. In accord with the obvious fact that each person is born with different interests and capacities, the Founders believed equality means *equality of liberty.* We cannot all look, act, and achieve the same, but we all can have the same freedom to speak, naturally form families, use our minds and bodies to provide for ourselves, and worship.

"In the founders' understanding, equality as a political principle cannot conflict with liberty because *equality and liberty mean the same thing*," West writes (emphasis added). "Human beings are born equal in the sense that they are born 'equally free and independent.'"[15]

This applies to the sexes in obvious ways. Men and women are clearly physically different. Men cannot bring life into this world. Women are poor at physically defending themselves. The sexes are naturally unequal in many respects. This must affect how men and women use their liberties, but it did not, for the Founders, change the fact that men and women have the same natural right to political equality. We have the equal natural rights to freely use our capacities. Men and women both should rise to the capacity to fully govern themselves.

To our ears, that may sound like a call to equal suffrage. But in the Founders' day it was a call to equal virtue. The capacity for self-government, and therefore for political equality, is not bestowed by governments. It comes from character. In this aspect of humankind, men and women *are* the same: both sexes, like the people of all races, have souls. The soul is the part of ourselves that engages in vice and virtue. Men and women's souls are both equally capable of virtue, in ways that their bodies are *not* equally capable of childbearing, or self-defense.

Because our souls are embodied, the way men and women *express* the same virtue is often distinguished by sex. For example, pregnancy and childbirth require great courage of women. These are matters of life and death, necessary to the survival and flourishing of a woman's family and community. Men cannot display courage in childbirth, of course, but they obviously excel in other courageous feats such as defense of their homes and families.

The constitutions of the five earliest and most populous American states "affirm that 'no free government, or the blessings of liberty, can be preserved' except by adhering to certain virtues" that "continued to be taught and promoted by government well into the twentieth century," West notes. The lists of virtues from those five constitutions "all include justice, moderation, temperance, industry, and frugality, except that Virginia omits 'industry.'"[16]

The equality the Founders sought was not the totalitarian attempt to equalize every outcome—making the same numbers of women as men (or transgender as naturally gendered people) fight terrorists, hold cabinet posts, or become lawyers. Their understanding of equality meant allowing people the equal freedom to create their own lives and be responsible for their choices, which *naturally leads to unequal outcomes.* For the Founders, "'created equal' . . . means being free from the domination of others, being independent of their control or rule.' All are equal with respect to the right to rule themselves."[17] If we want freedom, inequality of outcomes is a diversity we all should celebrate.

"Equality of results," on the other hand, "can only be achieved by coercion—by taking away the equal liberty of some by violence in order to make others 'equal.'"[18] Identity politics openly embraces tyranny by demanding equality of results instead of equality of freedoms.

In fact, identity politics seeks not equality, but the inversion of natural hierarchies. It punishes people who use their freedoms to create order and excellence from their individual capacities, and instead celebrates degeneracy, dependency, and unbridled emotions. Its coercion intrudes deep into people's private lives to achieve these evil goals.

The Founders called such a situation both tyranny and anarchy. In Federalist 51, Bill of Rights progenitor James Madison points out, "In a society under the forms of which the stronger faction can readily unite and oppress the weaker, anarchy may truly be said to reign, as in a state of nature where the weaker individual is not secured against the violence of the stronger."

Is There a Natural Right to Marry?

Like the social compact—citizens' agreement to form a society that secures their rights—marriage works to secure citizens' rights. Pertinent to our topic, the natural right to marry descends from the right to pursue happiness.[19] As we have seen, marriage also contributes to developing the character citizens need for self-government. Thus "the founders held marriage to be not 'arguably' but indispensably necessary for the securing of natural rights," West notes.[20]

History demonstrates that blood ties tend to provide the most security and joy available in human life. They are the foundation of every culture and society. Societies emerge from family stability and expansion, as families grow into "clans" or "tribes," which sometimes turn into nations.[21]

Marriage also directs dangerous sexual energies into productive behavior, which benefits everyone in multiple ways. In the first place, it reduces jealousies and social controversies—what we might call "drama." People who don't cheat on each other or change sexual partners contribute to social peace.

Marriage also tends to improve the character of the spouses and the children their marriage begets. Due to an intimacy unlike any other, husbands and wives can learn how to love others more intimately than single people can. Children learn from their parents' direction how to be less selfish, lazy, and cruel, and more kind, thoughtful, and self-disciplined. Parents tend to give their children close personal attention because they naturally love their children in a way that strangers and neighbors naturally don't.

Marriage also reduces poverty. It legally joins two people who can work together to provide for the family they create. Poor people are more likely to violate others' natural rights, either by stealing or by obtaining others' property through welfare. And people who make children without first marrying are the most likely to be poor.

The Founders were less attentive to what people did naked behind closed doors than to the costs and penalties that their private sexual choices might impose on the public: children created without a secure legal attachment to the support, care, and protection of their biological mother and father. While laws in the Founders' era criminalized premarital sex and homosexual acts, West notes that "they were hardly ever enforced except when behavior became 'open and notorious.'"[22] The Founding generation's prime legal concern with sex was its potential either to damage or to secure others' rights.

"A 1781 Maryland law embodies the founding orientation. . . . ," West explains "In this law, the cost of welfare for single mothers is the sole concern, not the act of fornication itself. The immorality that is subject to legal penalties is not the indiscretion of the individual, but harming the rights of others by bearing a child without adequate means of support."[23]

The Founders' governments paid close attention to marriage and sex because they naturally generate children. Not only does "a lasting community need[] children who will become the next generation of citizens,"[24] "From the perspective of the social compact, the main purpose of the 'union of the parents' is the 'common care' of the children," West writes.[25] Because the best environment for the next generation of citizens to grow up in is a home headed by their married father and mother, the state has a strong interest in promoting robust marriage laws and penalizing breaches of the marital agreement such as abandonment and adultery.

Marriage cannot be a natural right for homosexuals because homosexual interactions *cannot* create a family. Homosexual relationships can never produce natural children, nor any of the family relationships that extend from procreative capacity (aunts, uncles, cousins, grandchildren, and so forth). This removes a key reason for government to acknowledge or preference homosexual encounters.

There is no government interest in a sexual relationship that has no capacity to produce children. It's purely a private matter. Since homosexual activities cannot possibly produce a child, there's no government interest in, nor a natural right to, those activities.

In contrast, the organic capacity to produce kids means that there are serious public consequences to any male-female sexual relationship. Even heterosexual couples using contraception can—and often do—make children together. Yet no homosexual interaction can ever generate children.

Sex is a scientific term for the procreative act. Homosexual relations are not—and never can be—procreative acts. Homosexuals can never physically unite in the way that a man and woman can, nor fulfill that physical unity in the form of a naturally resulting child. So homosexual relationships cannot be marriages because they do not actually include sex nor produce children; therefore, there is no natural right to those relationships that governments must affirm.

The public interest attached to marriage arises because lifelong marriages between one man and one woman are by far the most effective way of creating self-governing, competent, happy children as the next generation of citizens. No other form of sexual relationship improves on natural marriages, statistically speaking.[26]

In fact, the vast majority of criminals are created by sexual relationships in which the parents fail to commit to each other for life for the good of the children.[27] Lack of marriage between biological parents is also responsible for the vast majority of poverty, mental illness, suicide, and all other manner of deficits that seriously threaten citizens' natural rights.[28] Society and government have a strong interest in ensuring that as many children as possible are born into the homes of their married biological parents who stay committed for life.

Those who would argue that homosexuals' pursuit of happiness requires state licensing of their relationships need to argue that those relationships have a public benefit. They also need to grapple with the Founders' Aristotelian understanding of the word "happiness," which is different from what it means today. Aristotle famously defined happiness as "an activity of the soul in accordance with virtue." The Founders understood happiness this way as well. So to argue for erasing sex distinctions in marriage as a natural right requires a complete argument for sodomy and mutual masturbation as activities of the soul in accord with virtue. Answering that argument would require another book, or several, but suffice it to say that it's not self-evident, and the Founders would never have accepted such an argument.

Absent a credible case for the positive virtue of homosexual sex acts, the fact that homosexual encounters cannot produce children should suffice to demonstrate that the state has no legitimate natural rights–based interest in such private behavior. Indeed, the fact that a high percentage of the population is now satisfying their sexual desires through encounters that cannot produce children creates an existential crisis for a nation, which will soon have no children to continue its existence. This is the direction of all Western, and Westernized, nations already.

"Civil Rights" vs. Natural Rights

Many people don't even know there's any difference between the "civil rights" that are destroying our Constitutional way of life and the true civil rights that are guaranteed in the Bill of Rights and that preserve and protect that way of life. All privileges and protections that the government grants *should* be consistent with the the way of life the Constitution both enables and depends on. Real civil rights and our natural rights are meant to go hand in hand. Today, however, "civil rights" and our true rights are usually in conflict.

Until the waning of the Founding era, civil rights were often seen as synonymous with natural rights. "One of the principal sponsors of the 1866 Civil Rights Act described civil rights as 'the absolute rights of individuals, such as the right to personal security, the right of personal liberty, and the right to acquire and enjoy property.'"[29] Those are also the three core natural rights.

West notes the Founders believed there were two main kinds of civil rights: those for "the basic protection of person and property" of all people in the United States, citizens and noncitizens; and the civil rights accorded only to citizens. Some civil rights are appropriate for government to guarantee to all people within US borders, while other civil rights are appropriate only for citizens. Founding-era bills of rights specify many in both categories.

Among the civil rights afforded to American citizens but not to foreigners is the right to vote. The civil rights accorded to everyone inside the United States include, "the right to equal protection, i.e., equal enforcement, of criminal and civil laws that protect person and property. . . ." according to West. "Most importantly, this requires procedural judicial rights when government seeks to deprive someone of life, liberty, or property, such as the right to confront witnesses, to hire legal counsel, to a jury trial in criminal and sometimes also in civil cases, and to immunity from cruel and unusual punishment."[30] These are procedural rights that secure natural rights.

Governments promise to secure citizens' natural rights in exchange for their allegiance, the sacrifice of some of their natural rights (such as, in the case of paying taxes, one's natural right to one's property), and social contributions. True civil rights are mainly the working out of how governments fulfill their obligations to secure citizens' natural rights.

For example, the Second Amendment guarantees Americans' natural right to potentially lethal self-defense. Self-defense is a natural right pursuant to every individual's natural right to life. Civil rights respecting the Second Amendment might include, for example, laws setting the age of legal adulthood, at which point one is considered fully vested with and responsible for exercising the Constitutional right to self-defense.

In the Founding era, twenty-one was the typical age at which male citizens were required to join a posse if requested, sit on a jury, own a gun, and drill with the local militia. Now eighteen is the usual age for legal adulthood (except for drinking alcohol). The precise age most people are responsible enough to bear the duties of the social compact is not prescribed in natural law. So governments set the specific age, as a civil right that is a means to securing citizens' natural rights.

All Rights Include Duties

According to the Founders, rights and duties *always* go together. That's another way you can know whether something is a natural right: if it includes a duty. The current version of the Virginia Bill of Rights makes this connection clear. It's a beautiful encapsulation of many core Constitutional principles, so here's a slightly longer excerpt than necessary to make that point: "That no free government, nor the blessings of liberty, can be preserved to any people, but by a firm adherence to justice, moderation, temperance, frugality, and virtue; by frequent recurrence to fundamental principles; and by the recognition by all citizens that they have duties as well as rights, and that such rights cannot be enjoyed save in a society where law is respected and due process is observed."

If one has the right to life, he also has the duty to preserve his own life. People fulfill this duty by working to pay for their own food, homes, basic medical bills, and health insurance for extreme medical bills.

People also fulfill the duty to preserve their lives by banding together for individual and community self-defense, such as training for responsible self-defense in the home and defense of their neighbors in shopping malls and schools. Parents fulfill their duty to preserve the lives of the children they brought into this world by working to provide for their children's needs—and marrying before making children, because that allows a husband and wife to divide the labor needed to sustain a household, the most effective way to provide for an entire family.

Conversely, there can be no right without a corresponding duty. If people allege a right to medical care but will accept no duty to pay for the medical care they receive, medical care cannot be a right. (This is one reason nobody has a right to "trans-affirming medical care.")

That is not a right, it is an entitlement. And entitlements are immoral, because they force Peter to work to pay for Paul's goods. That's how false rights cannibalize real ones: here, the false right to medical care cannibalizing the true right to the fruits of one's labor.

The Founders did believe in a moral duty to prevent fellow humans from starvation, so long as it did not cause those providing it to starve. Those on the public dole were required to work to support themselves as much as possible—a requirement that some 80 percent of Americans still support—and they provided only the bare minimum to stay alive: food and shelter. This was meant to encourage people to better themselves and to reduce indigents' infringement on their neighbors' rights to the fruits of their labor.

When Natural Rights Conflict

As the Declaration of Independence notes, the purpose of government is "to secure these rights." Its purpose is not to *give* rights or privileges. In fact, it cannot do so. People have those rights outside of government, from God himself (or, for those who don't believe in God, from the objective natural order). The government's purpose is to *recognize and protect* people's pre-existing natural rights. That's why governments' chief duty is to repel violence—one cannot enjoy any natural right if one is dead.

As West explains, "A right that is natural belongs to every human being because they are human. . . . A legal right is granted by government and can be taken away by government. What is naturally right comes from human nature and 'can never be erased,' no matter what laws a government may pass. It is inalienable."[31]

The Founders knew that natural rights sometimes conflict. In such cases, prudence was required to decide which right to prioritize. A basic example is the conflict between the right to property—the fruits of one's own labor—and government carrying out its duty to protect individuals' right to life. To provide national and local self-defense in the form of an army, navy, and local police, government needs revenue. That's why it imposes taxes.

But taxation violates property rights. It takes from some to give to others: it takes from farmers, accountants, and grocers to give to soldiers and policemen. That's slavery, right? Not always.

The Founders believed the only way infringing on some part of citizens' natural rights could be justified is if the government infringes on one right *only as much as is required* to secure another right. They believed that people in a society give up some portion of their natural rights to achieve secure a broader portion of their natural rights.

You pay taxes so that police will show up if a robber breaks into your home. The Revolutionary Army often lacked provisions and compensation for the troops dying to establish an independent country because states didn't want to impose the taxes necessary to secure the national defense. That endangered the country, and thereby its people's natural rights. Therefore, it was just to impose taxes to secure the national defense then, and it still is.

It's a sop to this reality that today politicians pretend they want to spend money on legitimate purposes like "national security," "school safety," and "infrastructure" even though they often use the money for completely different purposes. In a crooked way, they are acknowledging that there are illegitimate and legitimate reasons to take taxpayers' earnings.

The Founders believed that when people enter a social compact, or agree to remain in a certain society, they give up a small portion of their natural rights in order to secure the greater part. That is why all taxes are not, as Frederic Bastiat claimed, "legalized plunder." Taxes are just *to the extent* they are imposed to secure natural rights. A good government taxes everyone *only* the amount necessary to protect their lives and property from murderers, vandals, and robbers.

Taxes are unjust, however, to the extent they are used for redistribution, because redistribution infringes on the natural right to enjoy the fruits of one's labor, as well as on the natural duty to provide for oneself. Redistributive taxes violate able-bodied individuals' duty to provide for themselves and their neighbors' right to be secure in the fruits of their own labor.

Human beings do not have a natural right to food, clothing, medical care, housing, and so forth, so government may not take the labor of some to provide these things for others. As Abraham Lincoln noted, redistribution schemes revive "the same old serpent that says, 'You work, and I eat; you toil and I will enjoy the fruits of it.'"

When Consent Endangers the Minority

A frequent natural rights conflict highly pertinent to sexual politics occurs when what the majority wants at the moment[32] would brutalize some people's (or all people's) equal natural rights. This is a conflict between the natural right to consent to one's government and other natural rights, such as to life, religious expression, or property.

A classic example the Founders frequently referenced was when a majority votes itself access to the pocketbooks of a minority. One version of this is "land reform," that is, stealing and redistributing properties from wealthy landowners to the propertyless poor. Another is when the elderly, who vote in higher proportion than the young, vote to obtain the fruits of younger people's labor instead of providing for themselves or relying upon their families.

Majorities tend to abuse minorities if everyone's rights are not equally protected by legal and cultural barricades the majority cannot breach. That is why we have a Constitution, and why many of its provisions are structured as they are. The government our Constitution created is designed to prevent majority bulldozing of rights—what the Founders called a "majority faction."[33]

"When consent endangers the very purpose of government, one of two things must be done if individual rights are to be secured," West notes. "One is to qualify the consent principle so that the will of some or all of the people is excluded from government, allowing government to protect rights. The other solution is to arrange the political institutions and form the character and minds of the people in such a way that they will have less opportunity, and less desire, to oppress others."[34]

In sexual politics, queer people are often cast as the minority, but essentially all the power backs their projected grievances. Backers of queer policies include US bar associations, the most-boosted media companies, Fortune 500 companies, Silicon Valley, Wall Street, most teacher training, higher education, teachers' unions, medical associations, the majority of representatives in Congress, all of Hollywood, the nation's ruling political party (Democrats) and all of its controlled opposition. The percentage of Americans pursuing non-heterosexual naked encounters may be in the single digits, but the entities cultivating this interest group to push anti-Constitutional politics are clearly an economic, legal, and cultural majority.

This dynamic of tyrannical majorities (and often tyrannical minorities) voting away citizens' equal natural rights encapsulates US politics for more than a century. The rainbow coalition is just the new face on this accelerating trend of replacing the Constitution with a competing form of government—a regime change.

The Stealth Coup against the Founders

So the American Founders built our supreme laws—our state and national constitutions, bills of rights, and the like—on the principle that government's chief function is to secure the citizens' natural rights, which come from nature and nature's God. This understanding and the system that rests on it have been under siege for a long time.

That argument has been made by highly competent scholars elsewhere. Here we'll summarize some of the key legal and cultural shifts that created a "living constitution" to compete with—and now supersede—the real one. Both constitutions reflect not just laws but an entire way of life, because all laws project and reflect an understanding of morality, and shape the people who live under them.

Woodrow Wilson marked the first prominent shift towards replacing the Constitution with its competitor, the administrative state. The theories of Wilson, a president of Princeton University, were the zeitgeist among the American intelligentsia of his time. They imported their anti-American vision of governance from Europe, especially from German universities and the managerial ruler Otto Von Bismarck, who established the world's first welfare state.

While most Americans maintained classic Protestant beliefs for several more generations, in the Progressive Era the ruling class was apostatizing from Christianity and the system of government it had generated. They applied hot new Darwinian thought to government.

This led to Progressives' rejection of the Founders' stable, objective natural order created by God, which expresses unchanging natural rights that predate the government and that every human bears equally.

Instead, Progressives professed an ever-shifting, unstable human nature that the smartest (Progressives, of course) could shape: "By controlling the environment, humans could guide the process of evolution instead of being chaotically tossed about by it," Hillsdale College politics professor Kevin Slack summarizes.[35]

Under Progressives like Wilson, government would no longer respect human nature and attempt to conform itself to an objective reality outside of human control. Instead, it would attempt to shape human nature. Government would deify itself.

Instead of believing that paradise would one day be realized for humans by the Supreme Creator after He enacted perfect justice, the ruling class of Wilson's day believed in seeking utopia on earth. The philosopher Eric Voegelin famously characterized this disposition of the early Progressives as "immanentizing the eschaton"—attempting to make heaven on earth.

"Democracy," said the early-twentieth-century Progressive intellectual leader and cofounder of *The New Republic* Herbert Croly, "must stand or fall on a platform of human perfectibility."[36]

Then as now, the Progressives rerouted religious energies into their political project, which helps explain why leftism often acts as a religion. Many poorly catechized American Christians who either don't know that the Bible explicitly rejects such efforts,[37] or don't actually believe in the Bible, were and still are taken in by the Left's attempts to substitute government for God in attempts to eradicate the world's evils.

"Under withering assault by biblical textual criticism, Darwinian evolution, and German idealism, educated Americans increasingly rejected the Christian and republican orthodoxy," writes Slack.[38]

Just like the religious leaders of the Progressive Era, who hollowed out the Bible with "higher criticism" while lying (to themselves as well as to others) about what they were doing, American political leaders hollowed out the Constitution while publicly professing to still support it and other Founding documents and symbols Americans cherished. They sucked out its body and blood and paraded around in its skin.

No Sin Equals No Need for Restraining Rulers

Wilson, who was elected with only 41 percent of the national vote on account of Theodore Roosevelt's third-party candidacy, delivered an infamous speech during his 1912 campaign for president. In it, writes scholar Charles Murray, Wilson "said to the electorate some of the same things he had been saying in his written work since the 1890s."[39] "All that progressives ask or desire is permission—in an era when 'development,' 'evolution,' is the scientific word—to interpret the Constitution according to the Darwinian principle," Wilson said.[40]

As Murray points out, Wilson was expressing the "consensus" among the day's American intellectuals. They believed the Constitution was outmoded, and therefore should be discarded. They believed in "experts" (themselves, of course) managing the populace, not self-government by citizens. So they set about "dissolving the people, and electing another,"[41] in a process that has taken approximately a hundred years.

Wilson believed "A new constitutional structure must replace the old separation of powers and checks and balances" of the Constitution, Slack writes. ". . . . A new 'living' constitution was needed to reinterpret the document for a changing social organism. The old Constitutional questions had been historically solved in favor of democracy and majority rule, but now, as society became more complex, the need arose for a 'science of administration' that could act with more efficacy and speed in response to changing purposes."[42]

These early Progressives first theorized and then enacted the competing regime of the administrative state. Sometimes called the regulatory state, or today the Deep State, the administrative state was *designed* to displace the Constitution's system of checks and balances, rule by consent of the governed, security of citizens' equal natural rights, and division of government into executive, legislative, and judicial. The bureaucracy is war against the Constitution.

"Wilson was the foremost American expositor of the theory of the 'living constitution. . . .'" explains Charles Kesler, a government professor at Claremont McKenna College. ". . . . Though the founders' Constitution and its three branches need not disappear, the government's lifeforce would flow increasingly through the new constitution overlying the formal one. . . . The whole point was to transfer the original Constitution's legitimacy to the new one."[43]

With a Congress also deeply influenced by Progressivism, Wilson took several key steps towards establishing the administrative state as a competing constitution. He set the stage for government control of money by instituting the Federal Reserve system. Wilson led Congress's creation of the Federal Trade Commission, another quasi-governmental agency tasked with the police powers of pre-emptive investigation into private affairs with no proof of lawbreaking—a clear violation of the Fourth Amendment—and non-judicial prosecution.

Wilson also continued fellow Progressive Teddy Roosevelt's rejection of the Founders' foreign policy, which had respected other nations' right to self-determination. Both believed in interfering with foreign nations' domestic affairs, something the Founders believed violated foreigners' natural rights. Most notably, in his second term Wilson violated his own campaign promises not to drag the United States into World War I, a messy conflict involving zero American interests. This also spawned the League of Nations, the precursor to the United Nations.

Although their inroads were still limited by the provisions of the Constitution and the people's understanding of their natural rights, Wilson's presidency and the takeover of America's intellectuals by European philosophy laid the groundwork for transformational anti-Constitution changes under Franklin Delano Roosevelt. In a strategy seized on by every leftist president since, Roosevelt used a national emergency to ram through structural changes that permanently installed the administrative state.

The Origin of Group Rights

Progressives' political Darwinism also spawned the concept of "group rights," later turned into "identity politics," to replace equal natural rights. Like his fellow intellectuals, Wilson argued that human rights evolved with history. They were not natural, stable, eternal, or God-given. Like humans' very bodies, their rights evolved over time.

For Progressives like Wilson, "Rights came from the group or groups to which one belonged, and from their stage of development," notes Kesler.[44] "The State [as Wilson capitalized it] emerged from a shared religious, cultural, ethnic, and linguistic identity, and necessarily expressed that identity."

Kesler quotes the managerial theorist Mary Parker Follett, from 1918: "If my true self is the group-self, then my only rights are those which membership in a group gives me. The old idea of natural rights postulated the particularist individual; we know now that no such person exists. The group and the individual come into existence simultaneously; with this group-man appear group-rights. Thus man can have no rights apart from society or independent of society or against society."[45]

To Progressives, rights are not inherent in every human being, but a function of group membership. They emerge like life did, from the mud.

They can be created, and discarded, in a process of elite-directed evolution. Government gives rights—and government can take them away.

These philosophical developments against human agency and moral responsibility and towards seeing people as masses to be molded by technocrats occurred between the early Progressive era and its successor, liberalism.[46] The influential philosopher John Dewey was first a Progressive and then a liberal—when Progressivism disintegrated with Americans' disillusionment after World War I. Dewey's "revolt against the liberalism of the founding goes back through [German philosopher G. W.] Hegel to Rousseau, who was the first to suggest that man has no definite nature but only the quality of malleability," West writes.[47]

Dewey drew two influential conclusions from this assumption. First, because man is the product of his society, "self-reliance and individuality are largely illusory," notes West. He quotes Dewey: "the state has the responsibility for creating institutions under which individuals can effectively realize the potentialities that are theirs."

In other words, people are not truly responsible for either their successes or failures. Society is. If the person is wrong, blame his environment. He must have randomly evolved in a maladaptive direction due to surrounding conditions. Therefore, if something is wrong, no individual can be held responsible. Society is to blame, and it, not he, must be changed.

"This means there must be something like a cradle-to-grave welfare state, financed by government supervision of production and distribution of wealth," West notes.

The second conclusion that Dewey drew from his assumption that human beings have no definite nature is that there are "no natural or divine standards defining the right way of life for man," West writes. Therefore, "To say with Dewey that man in himself is nothing is another way of saying that he is essentially a victim or essentially disabled. Here is the source of the New Liberal preoccupation with victimized groups."[48]

The political Left always pushes group rights and erodes individual rights because one of its foundational tenets is the malleability of human nature, not its constancy. In rejecting the American Founders' understanding that eternal truths exist that apply to all men—such as that murder, rape, and slavery are wrong in every culture, time, and place—and that despite many cultural differences, all humans share a nature, the Progressives unleashed their system of unnatural rights that eventually grew to overthrow the Constitution.

Never Let a Crisis Go to Waste

In a shifting and uncertain time, President Franklin Delano Roosevelt began a massive program of erasing Americans' natural rights by turning them into grants of government power. He began by adding false rights, confusing Americans about what rights mean. He furthered it by establishing what amounts to a fourth branch of government, the administrative state (or executive agencies). That fourth branch competes with the Constitutional branches of executive, legislative, and judicial, and unites all of their powers to achieve unlimited government force.

Roosevelt famously made this explicit in a 1941 address to Congress. In his "Four Freedoms" speech, he tacitly rejected the Founders' view that governments are obligated to protect their citizens' rights and respect the rights of other nations to do so for themselves. Instead, Roosevelt demanded worldwide adoption of "four essential human freedoms":

- "freedom of speech and expression—everywhere in the world"

- "freedom of every person to worship God in his own way—everywhere in the world"
- "freedom from want . . . everywhere in the world"
- "freedom from fear . . . anywhere in the world."[49]

There's a direct line from Roosevelt's conception of government to the Biden White House's October 2023 statement proclaiming "the United States' commitment to promoting and protecting the human rights of Intersex persons globally"[50] and offering deep condolences for a transgender student's suicide while barely acknowledging illegal immigrant murder of a Georgia college student in March 2024.[51] Roosevelt's utopian view entirely disregarded human nature and therefore worked to erase Americans' natural rights. Especially his unnatural economic rights grew to do so.

"Roosevelt was advocating a civil right to a comfortable existence that the founders would have rejected," West writes. ". . . . For Abigail Adams and the founders, Roosevelt's dictum—'necessitous men are not free men'—a recipe for enervation of mind and spirit, for dependency and the suffocation of real virtue. For her, only necessitous men can be free men. Only in 'contending with difficulties' do the soul's strengths come to be cultivated and perfected."[52]

To promise "freedom from fear"—let alone "anywhere in the world"—is a promise of totalitarianism. It promises government management of people's feelings. Yet government cannot control people's reactions. Nobody can but the individuals themselves. Regulating one's emotions is a key part of learned maturity.

Not even very dedicated mothers can protect their children from every negative emotion—and when one tries, psychologists call her a "devouring mother." Such mothers infantilize—and thus ultimately destroy—their children, keeping them from self-sufficiency and moral agency. So Roosevelt was truly arguing that the government must prevent citizens' emergence into adulthood.

We see demands for "freedom from fear" in sexual identitarians' demands that the government protect them from speech that hurts their feelings and force their fellow citizens to lie about the meaning of marriage. We see it in claims that men must have access to women undressing in locker rooms, or they might be so sad they will kill themselves. We see it in the insistence that we must allow doctors to mutilate adolescents for life, or the children are societally licensed to kill themselves in revenge for others' not obeying their very strong feelings.

A president openly sympathetic to Communism and advised by highly placed Communists,[53] Roosevelt created legal structures to eventually bring about totalitarian government. He upped the ante on Progressives' efforts to bust up Big Business by seeking to make government the fascist "senior partner" of the private economy.[54] Rather than increasing competition through trust-busting and anticompetitive actions, under Roosevelt the government began to manage the economy both directly and indirectly.

Following the playbook of tyrants, despots, and communists after him, Roosevelt used a national emergency to "fundamentally transform" American government. The Supreme Court initially resisted Roosevelt's barrage, but after being threatened with court-packing it flipped and began greenlighting Roosevelt's revolution in ways that are now impossible to reverse.

Almost Everything the Feds Do Is Unconstitutional

Charles Murray points out the Social Security Act as an instructive example. The Founders had emphatically stated that the "general welfare" clause of the Constitution does not simply allow Congress to spend on anything it wants.[55] It can only spend taxpayers' money on the actions the Constitution explicitly authorizes. That obviously does not include taxing some people to pay for others people's retirement.

Yet, a cowed Supreme Court allowed Social Security to go into effect, ruling against history and the text of the Constitution in a decision that meant, as Murray describes, "Congress could spend on pretty much whatever it wished that it deemed to be for the *general welfare*" (italics original).[56] That—and multiple other Roosevelt-era Supreme Court precedents like it—was the beginning of the end of Constitutional government in America.

Today, no court will revive the accurate pre-New Deal understanding of the Constitution. If the Supreme Court reversed its erasure of the meaning of the "general welfare" clause, it would negate almost everything the federal government does, as Murray notes. It would immediately end Medicare, Medicaid, food stamps, the Department of Education, and multitudes of government contracts. This would upend more than half the economy,[57] "signing the Supreme Court's death warrant" and "throw[ing] the country into chaos."

Given these practical reasons that FDR's unlimited expansion of government cannot be reversed, Murray says, "there are no Constitutional ways to restrain Congress from spending money on whatever it wishes to spend money on."[58] That has allowed the federal government to effectively erase the Constitution by coercing Americans to give up their Constitutional rights. Today, that is the majority of its functions, Constitutional scholar Philip Hamburger of Columbia Law School points out.

"The government increasingly controls Americans not merely along the Constitution's avenues of control—which run through acts of Congress and the courts—but also along an additional pathway, administrative power," Hamburger explains in his 2021 book, *Purchasing Submission*. "Indeed, administrative edicts and adjudications nowadays vastly outnumber congressional statutes and court decisions. Put another way, though the United States remains a republic, there has developed within a very different sort of government. The result is a state within a state—an administrative state within the Constitution's United States."[59]

The next presidential administration to significantly increase this competing system of government within the United States was Lyndon B. Johnson.

Lyndon Johnson's Insurrection

Johnson also seized on a national crisis to fundamentally transform America, in this case John F. Kennedy's assassination. Under Roosevelt, the federal government had begun hiring people based on race,[60] with explicit racial quotas. Because of this systemic racism, government was disproportionately staffed by black workers by the 1960s,[61] a reality that continues.[62]

Since Roosevelt, presidents had demanded race-conscious hiring in federal agencies and contractors. It was Johnson, in 1968, who added "sex" as a federally protected identity group to those executive orders,[63] paving the way for the Obama and Biden administrations to shoehorn in "gender identity" forty years later, with the help of the Supreme Court. Johnson's pivotal 1964 Civil Rights Act forced these identity politics practices on the private sector wholesale.[64]

The Civil Rights Act was part of Johnson's sweeping Great Society initiative, which also included creating Medicare and Medicaid, direct federal funding for education from pre-kindergarten through twelfth grade, federal interference with local housing, and a major food stamp expansion. The Civil Rights Act, along with the unlawful regulatory practices[65] the law helped spawn, became a cornerstone of the false rights regime that today displaces the Constitution. The Civil Rights Act also imported identity group politics into other domains, notably sex distinctions.

Between Roosevelt and Johnson, courts had recognized racial discrimination on the basis of "disparate treatment"—in other words, demonstrated unequal treatment on the basis of race.[66] Yet after the Civil Rights Act, courts increasingly began using a standard that federal agencies had pioneered under Roosevelt called "disparate impact." The Supreme Court sanctioned this approach in 1971, using the Equal Employment Opportunity Commission's "theory of systemic racism that expanded its domain from intentional individual discrimination to 'disparate impact.'"[67]

This means courts began punishing people and organizations not based on any proven racial discrimination but for *any* unequal outcomes between racial groups—notwithstanding mitigating facts such as if black workers had lower achievement or worked fewer hours. This explicitly violated federal civil rights laws,[68] including the Civil Rights Act, section 703(j) of which prohibits "preferential treatment to any individual or group . . . on account of an imbalance which may exist with respect to the total or percentage of persons of any race, color, religion, sex, or national origin employed . . . in any comparison with the total number or percentage in any community, state, section or other area or in the available workforce or community."

Yet, courts soon sanctioned regulatory agencies' demands that government and private businesses adopt the identity quotas that the law flatly banned. Judges and executive agencies almost immediately negated major provisions of a law that Congress had passed, effectively installing themselves as unelected representatives.

This is all business as usual today for our anti-Constitutional legal system, which leaves the citizenry no ability to consent to the rules that run our lives—a key natural right—because most judges are unelected and all bureaucrats are. The two collude with each other, entirely out of reach of the voters, to write laws in which citizens can have no real say.

"[T]he radicals outflanked public opinion by taking over the agencies that implemented the 1964 Civil Rights Act," Slack notes. "They overturned its mandate of equal opportunity to institute preferential treatment. . . . The most radical proposals entered into law without congressional debate and were even antithetical to the agencies' originating statutes."[69]

Insurrectionary from Its Inception

One of the worst offenders was the Equal Employment Opportunity Commission, an agency created by the Civil Rights Act. This agency laser-focuses on the "equity" agenda today, and at its inception it fueled sexual politics.

"Almost from the moment of its inception the EEOC began issuing regulations that violated both the language and the spirit" of its authorizing law, University of California at Berkeley political scientist Robert Detlefsen explains.[70] In 1978, Congress gave EEOC the exclusive power to regulate Title VII, which affects (formerly) private employment. The EEOC's legally unhinged sexual and racial rulemaking was quickly cloned inside just about every federal agency with its own "office for civil rights."[71]

This gave rise to doublespeak about these diversity laws: tell the public the law *bans* identity preferences while the interpreters of that law have since its inception used it to *force* identity preferences. It's technically true that the law bans preferences based on race, sex, and now sexual orientation; but in practice that has always been 100 percent false. That's because the administrative state has decided the law means the opposite of what it states. That's an insurrection—against the rule of law.

As Barry Goldwater pointed out in his 1964 presidential campaign, the Civil Rights Act, like the New Deal, is flatly unconstitutional. It voided the natural right to freedom of association guaranteed explicitly in the First Amendment and implicitly in the Tenth Amendment. Detlefsen pointed out that the Civil Rights Act also shifted civil rights laws from *prohibiting* behavior to *forcing* behavior.

Until the passage of the Civil Rights Act, racial preferences had been applied to government agencies and contractors. The Civil Rights Act expanded them to *all* organizations with fifteen or more employees, essentially commandeering Americans socially just as Roosevelt had commandeered them economically. In collusion with executive agencies, courts then expanded the law even further, beyond forcing *group-neutral* private association to forcing *systemic preferences* for non-majority groups.

The law ended freedom of association—it claimed the right to tell private companies whom to hire. The interpretation of the law, however, went a step beyond that Constitutional violation into another: forcing employers to hire people with specific government-privileged characteristics. This was the dominant interpretation of the law by 1971,[72] essentially as soon as the Act went into effect. This means the civil rights regime fueling today's culture war was already locked into place by the end of the 1960s.

These "fundamental changes . . . that would affect the lives of millions of people . . . proceeded according neither to some constitutional command nor to a broad public consensus," notes Detlefsen. "Rather, the changes merely reflected the preferences of officials in the executive branch."[73] A system of federal agencies large enough to compete with—and usurp the powers of—Congress is what Progressives wanted all along. There is no other way to describe it than a regime change. And it was largely complete by the end of the 1960s.

More than thirty years ago, Detlefsen amassed the evidence to demonstrate that government-enforced group rights emerged before President Johnson. It was already so entrenched in the 1980s that President Ronald Reagan failed to fulfill his promises to end already pervasive government discrimination against whites, men, and heterosexuals. In a 1993 paper, Detlefsen showed that by then big businesses had cultivated internal constituencies favorable to anti-white programs, including the workers hired because of racial and sexual preferences and the human resources offices that taught everyone government-enforced discrimination was a good idea.[74]

By 2023, every Fortune 100 corporation in the United States had pledged allegiance to "the ideology of diversity, equity, and inclusion,"[75] a mere enlargement of this century-long trend. After all, larger businesses had been incentivized or flatly required to use racial preferences since the 1930s. Detlefsen also noted that big businesses know forcing government paperwork and procedures on everyone protects them from leaner competitors. That means the identity rights regime also fights market competition, driving up prices and driving down consumer choice and innovation. As always, there is no real division between economic and social policy.

A Rival Constitution

"The changes of the 1960s, with civil rights at their core, were not just a major new element in the Constitution. They were a rival constitution, with which the original one was frequently incompatible—and the incompatibility would worsen as the civil rights regime was built out," notes Christopher Caldwell in his incisive 2020 book, *The Age of Entitlement.*

He says the legal innovations of the 1960s, themselves rooted in the 1930s, "had given progressives control over the most important levers of government, control that would endure for as long as the public was afraid of being called racist . . . all aggrieved minorities now sought to press their claims under this new model of progressive governance."

Cultural Marxists seized the "civil rights" templates for government discrimination on behalf of government-privileged identity groups. That has substituted a new form of government—by judicial and administrative decree—for consent of the governed in accord with equal natural rights.

Caldwell argues that the ever-growing civil rights apparatus amounts to extremely costly social engineering that has proven "to be the mightiest instrument of domestic enforcement the country had ever seen."[76] Its legal structures have created "an opening to arbitrary power."[77] It opens the door to totalitarianism: "Once bias is held to be part of the 'unconscious,' of human nature, there are no areas of human life in which the state's vigilance is not called for," he notes.[78]

Caldwell also argues that Congress and presidents spent the fifty years after Johnson's reign buying Americans' silence about the administrative state selling their Constitutional birthright to deliver government privileges for favored identity groups. In setting the foundation for unlimited government, the 1960s regime change required transforming the United States into essentially a soft totalitarian system, in which government buys peace among groups with borrowed money. That softness is hardening, more quickly every year.

With Social Security, Medicare, and deficit-funded tax cuts and defense spending, presidents from Johnson to Obama bribed Baby Boomers into accepting a massive welfare state for government-defined minorities—in other words, racial and sexual reparations. Voters would never have approved those directly. Deficit-funding both systems of government worked uneasily until the Obama era, when the monumental deficits it could not fail to create began to visibly mar what remained of the private economy.

At that point, it became apparent to more voters that the US government does not work the traditional way, the way children used to be taught in school. The three branches—executive, legislative, judicial—don't really run the government. That means voters don't really run the government. That explains why elections haven't seemed to change major national policies since Progressives installed executive agencies.

Barack Obama, Caldwell says, became the first president to openly govern on the basis of the identity regime instead of the Constitutional form of government it displaced.[79]

How Feminism Paved the Way for Transsexualism

After the 2015 *Obergefell v. Hodges* Supreme Court decision forcing states to erase the sexes from marriage, the Obama administration projected celebratory rainbow lights onto the White House. After the Court gave transsexuals the right to dress up as the opposite sex and demand pronoun police at work in its June 2020 *Bostock v. Clayton County* decision, Obama tweeted a picture of the 2015 rainbowed White House.[80]

These two court decisions were entirely detached from the Constitution in every way imaginable. Even pro-homosexual lawyers noted the *Obergefell* decision was largely "based on dubious and sometimes incoherent logic," and unmoored from the best legal arguments for a Constitutional right to same-sex marriage licenses.[81] It is preposterous to argue the framers of the Fourteenth Amendment or any other part of the Constitution intended to confer a legal right to "marry" on two people of the same sex. That was unthinkable at the time of the Constitution's ratification, and of the ratification of the Fourteenth Amendment.

Indeed, legal arguments for a "Constitutional right" to homosexual marriage licenses directly contradict the Founders' clear acknowledgements, in the laws they passed and the public addresses they made, that men and women are different and that the primary reason for any state interest in marriage is the children whom marriages may produce (and whom same-sex coupling cannot).

Both of these court decisions relied heavily on the false feminist idea, codified in the 1964 Civil Rights Act and fulfilled in transgenderism, that the two sexes are interchangeable. Feminism is simply women identifying as men—just not as transparently as transsexuals.

George Mason University law professor Ilya Somin observed that *Obergefell* used the same chief argument Supreme Court Justice Neil Gorsuch used in *Bostock*: "laws banning same-sex marriage discriminate on the basis of sex."[82] Of course, that argument goes back to the 1964 Civil Rights Act and the more than one hundred similar statutes now marbled throughout federal law. But it's ridiculous to say that acknowledging sex differences is "discrimination." Men and women are obviously physically different in many meaningful ways, and these differences often do matter for everyday life and public policy.

Only cruel fools, for example, would send pregnant women into combat. Only cruel fools would say employers must hire transsexual men to fit women for bras, perform massages, do crotch waxing, or even just greet customers wearing cross-dressing attire that makes the public square disorderly, sexually charged, and hostile to children.

Instead of the idiotic contemporary pretense that men and women are the same and that treating them as different when it matters is "discrimination," the American Founders recognized sex differences as important to many aspects of life. Their vision of equality was opposite the vision of equality promoted in "anti-discrimination" law, which undermines the Constitution and the Constitutional way of life.

"Many people today think women's liberty and well-being are better secured when the law allows for complete sexual freedom and treats men and women the same, and when women are encouraged to compete with men in the job market," West writes. "The Founders thought laws allowing sexual license, ignoring the real differences between the sexes, and not just allowing but pushing women into the job market threatened women's liberty and well-being."[83]

Today, the Founders' view is vindicated by the transgender men demanding access to women's private spaces; the mutilation of bodies (disproportionately women's) in transsexualism and abortion; the growth in unhappy single men and women; plunging birth rates that threaten our national solvency; the two-income trap; and the rape culture engendered by widespread unmarried sex. The refusal to acknowledge sex differences has caused all of these problems, and it is what unites the Cultural Marxist ideologies of feminism and transsexualism.

Men and women are not the same. We are equal in value, we have eternal souls equally beloved of God and endowed with the equal right to be ruled only by our consent. *That* is what the Founders meant by equality. It is not that all people are the same in their natural talents, physical features, or inheritance—an obviously absurd proposition. The natural right to equality is the equal right to liberty, meaning to not be ruled without one's explicit consent.[84]

The Cultural Marxist understanding of "equality" is destroying Americans' birthrights of government by consent and equality before the law, and with these we're losing our nation's happiness.

CHAPTER 4

Pride Devours Itself

"I now recognize that any revolution must be a permanent one, in the sense meant by Karl Marx and Friedrich Engels—that a perpetual revolutionary class must exist, remaining independent from the political machinery of its day and constantly pressing for a more radical future, even after great victory."

—Freddie deBoer[1]

Six months after he won a second presidential term, Barack Obama reversed his previous public position and said "same-sex couples should be able to get married."[2] That year, 2012, Obama's State Department began using US tax dollars to promote homosexuality abroad.

From 2012 to 2015, the Obama administration spent $41 million plus an unspecified "portion of $700 million" to promote queer politics internationally, the *New York Times* reported. Obama also spoke about the issue to "hostile audiences" abroad.

That effort caused more harm than benefit to queer foreigners, interviewees told the *Times*: "The US support is making matters worse. There's more resistance now." Africa's most populous nation, Nigeria, criminalized homosexuality and homosexual activism in 2014. Nigerian activists told the *Times* they didn't think those laws would have passed without the American government pushing LGBT policies.

"Before, these people were leading their lives quietly, and nobody was paying any attention to them," a Nigerian homosexual advocate told the Times. "Before, a lot of people didn't even have a clue there were something called gay people. But now they know and now they are outraged; now they hear that America is bringing all these foreign lifestyles."[3]

In 2017, the *Washington Post* also documented queer activism, creating a backlash.[4] Asian countries with large Muslim contingents, former Soviet Union nations including Russia, and African countries "all responded to increased pressure about LGBT policies during the Obama administration with punitive laws, policies to protect children from homosexual propaganda, and even police crackdowns on LGBT establishments and social circles," noted Stefano Gennarini, director of legal studies at the Center for Family and Human Rights, in 2018.[5]

American, European, and UN pressure on traditional societies often worsened conditions for LGBT people, he wrote. In 2023, the *Washington Post* again reported on this dynamic across the Middle East and Asia. "Lebanon, Jordan and Turkey have always stood out in the region on LGBTQ issues. All have queer scenes, all have hosted Pride parades or similar events," the *Post* noted. Yet all three were experiencing a shift in both street-level and government-level opinion, towards limiting the expression of queer sexual preferences.[6] The more people see queer sexuality in the public square, the less the majority supports it.

"The campaigns that promote homosexuality want to destroy the family," said a Jordanian scholar, according to the *Post*, calling on her government to reduce the visibility of queer sexuality in their society. The Turkish government arrested more than three hundred people at a 2022 Pride parade and banned the event entirely in 2023.

Undeterred, from 2020 to 2023 the Biden administration sent $4.1 billion around the world to push queer politics. The more than 1,100 grants funded DEI programs in Serbia, queer political activist groups in Armenia, and a study on the effects of transgender hormones on Thai women, reported the *Epoch Times*.[7]

Americans Don't Like 24/7 Pride Either

Backlash against queer saturation also became a phenomenon in the United States. A November 2023 poll showed an eleven-point drop in support for same-sex relationship licensing among American teens and twenty-somethings from 2021 to 2023,[8] from 80 to 69 percent. Leftists had expected a continued climb towards the near-unanimous support that, for example, interracial relationships enjoy in the United States.

Also in 2023, Gallup found a seven-point drop in the percentage of Americans willing to label homosexual relationships morally acceptable, from 70 to 63 percent. Republicans' moral approval of homosexual relations fell 15 points in the poll, from 56 percent to 41. Democrat moral approbation of homosexual relations fell from 85 to 79 percent.[9] The poll also found a seven-point increase in Americans opposing transgender athletes on opposite-sex sports teams. The support for putting athletes only on teams that match their sex was 69 percent—a blockbuster number in polling.[10] Even a majority of Democrat respondents supported requiring athletes to play on teams that match their natural sex.

The same poll also found an increase—from 51 to 55 percent—in Americans saying that "changing one's gender" is "morally wrong."

A PPRI poll out in June 23 found similar trendlines. It showed the belief there "are only two gender identities" increasing six points from 2021 to 2023, from 59 to 65 percent.[11] The biggest increases were among non-mainline Protestant blacks and Hispanic Catholics.

Numerous polls in 2023 found mass voter awareness—and dislike—of "efforts to expose children to the transgender movement using things like drag queen shows, school curriculum, and social media." In one poll, 71 percent of voters with an opinion said this PR effort on behalf of queer identities made them "concerned."

Forty-one percent said they were not only very concerned but also angry, and 30 percent said they were somewhat concerned and upset.[12] Three-quarters of Americans willing to express an opinion want businesses to stay out of cultural battles and focus on providing quality products and services.[13]

Backlash against queer aggression hits companies that promote sexual identities. In June 2023, Bud Light and Target heavily promoted transgender spokespersons and products. Their "trans visibility" prompted boycotts that soon had Bud Light unable to give away its product with 100 percent rebates.[14] Target's stock lost approximately $10 billion in value in ten days, even after many of its stores removed pride-themed clothing and swimsuits that accommodate fake genitals from children's sections.[15] The company's quarterly sales dropped for the first time in six years, along with foot traffic.[16]

The drop in public support for queer behavior accompanied significant amounts of legislation. In 2023, state lawmakers introduced more than 525 bills to protect children and others from queer advances, according to the Human Rights Campaign. Nearly half of these bills were responding to queer exploitation of gender-confused children.[17]

"The backlash is coming because people are lying to children and are using children for medical experiments," writer Douglas Murray, a homosexual, told an Australian news outlet.[18]

Transgender realities horrify people once they get up close. Slicing off the skin from an entire forearm to construct a fake penis is grotesque. And most people don't want to see mentally ill cross-dressers wandering about streets where children play. School policies that keep gender and sex secrets from parents are wildly unpopular.

The significantly higher rates of queer identification among Generation Z—those currently in their teens to mid-twenties—will only increase this backlash. The culture wars over sex in the public square will only escalate.

The Queer Movement Is Self-Devouring

Cultural Marxism forces participants into a zero-sum power game in which all Americans lose, including LGBT citizens. Queer people who comply are dupes for a corrupt regime. Politicians distract queers with special legal carveouts that obscure what is really going on: erasing queer people's natural rights and pitting them against their fellow citizens. It's a weaponization of their identity, using their sexual behavior to divide them from their natural rights and the American way of life that protects them on an equal footing with their non-queer neighbors.

When there is no respect for the objective boundaries of natural law, or the objective realities of nature (men and women are different, and their bodies fit together sexually), the rulers can switch out government-privileged groups as they please. LGBT people may have the upper hand now, but the system of government-defined unnatural rights that many of them are embracing undermines their interests long-term.

Unlike equal natural rights, the identity rights that queer Americans claim now can be taken from them at any time with a public opinion shift (spontaneous, or manufactured). And the government their activism creates is totalitarian. Is gay marriage worth putting one's society on course towards approximating Communist China?[19]

That country promotes queer politics abroad to destabilize foreign competitors while curtailing LGBT activities at home, occasionally detaining and questioning LGBT people,[20] banning Grindr and mentions of same-sex activity from entertainment, and criticizing "sissy men."[21] Why couldn't the United States eventually do the same if leftist activism erases the legal and cultural barriers to China-style human rights atrocities here?

Pride is a way for government to steal LGBT people's most fundamental human rights while pretending it's their savior. This bait and switch trades queer people's constitutional rights for worthless trinkets, like Pride merchandise made in China. LGBT people are being used, and they will be discarded. That's the pattern of human history: group rights eventually devour their own advocates.

Black Trans "Women" Dominate Homosexuals

It has already happened to lesbians, who have been accused of "hate crimes" enacted in the name of their identity for not accepting sex with transgender men.[22] It has already happened to homosexuals, whom transgender people immediately displaced just before the Supreme Court's *Obergefell* decision invented a constitutional right to gay marriage, which was supposed to be a big homosexual victory.

That year, American propaganda outlets became awash with transgender imagery and messaging. Olympian Bruce Jenner publicly switched to Caitlyn weeks before the June 2015 decision[23] as part of a massive media blitz that worked to influence the Supreme Court. The words "transphobic" and "transphobia" exploded in US media.[24]

On June 1, CNN trumpeted that the United States was experiencing a "transgender moment."[25] That year the "transgender boy" Jazz Jennings was awarded a TLC reality show and *Vogue* featured a transgender model photo shoot in its May issue. At the moment of the biggest legal victory for homosexuals in US history, homosexuals were shoved aside to make room for transsexuals in the limelight.

Obama's addition of "transgender" to his 2015 January State of the Union—the first time a president publicly uttered the word—was permission for media to open the throttle. Obama later explained to *Rolling Stone* editor Jann Wenner that he pushed queer politics to American political life step by step, starting with hospital visitation rules, then erasing "don't ask, don't tell," then opposing California's Proposition 8 to affirm natural marriage in the state constitution.

"What happened was, first, very systematically, I changed laws around hospital visitation for people who were same-sex partners," Obama told Wenner in a 2016 interview right after Donald Trump's surprise presidential victory. "I then assigned the Pentagon to do a study on getting rid of 'don't ask, don't tell,' which then got the buy-in of the Joint Chiefs of Staff, and we were then able to [repeal] 'don't ask, don't tell.' We then filed a brief on Proposition 8 out in California. And then, after a lot of groundwork was laid, then I took a position."[26]

This section of the interview led essayist Christopher Caldwell to observe, "Obama was not merely a witness to but a field marshal of the litigative strategy that culminated in the Supreme Court's removal of the country's marriage laws from democratic scrutiny."[27]

That alleged victory for homosexuals was immediately subsumed by a massive political and cultural push for transgenderism, reaffirming

the tendency of group rights to displace one identity group with another
once the initial group has served its purpose.

Before transsexuals displaced homosexuals, lesbians often encountered the same dynamic in relation to gay men. "Lesbianism effectively
became a branch of feminism. . . ." in the 1960s, notes Carrie Gress.
"While politically lesbian activists maintained a relationship with activists who were gay men, most considered it a relationship of convenience
to bolster numbers and to fight a common enemy. Lesbians, however,
saw themselves as very different from gay men, for men at large were
the enemy."

Angry that homosexual men led most queer activist groups, lesbians in the 1960s and '70s formed lesbian-only spaces such as music
festivals and record labels, publications, bookstores, bars, and clubs.[28]
When transgenderism exploded fifty years later, lesbians and the infrastructure they built were hardest hit.[29] These precedents for political
cannibalism are good reason to predict that the same thing will happen
to transsexuals one day. It seems likely that those displacing them will
be transhumanists—if our society doesn't fully collapse first.

If you think skinning entire forearms to make fake penises and
constructing oozing "front-holes" for fake vaginas are bad, wait until
this monstrous tech gets deployed against other body parts. We've
hardly seen anything yet.

Chewing Up Lesbians

As transgender became the new tip of the spear in the campaign to
undo the American way of life, that identification cannibalized not
only homosexuals' role as media darlings but their institutions and their
population. As transgenderism has overtaken lesbianism, lesbian spaces
are going extinct. The number of lesbian bars in the United States went
from approximately two hundred in the 1980s to twenty-seven in 2023,

according to Axios.[30] The number of homosexual bars nearly halved from 2007 to 2023.[31]

Axios made the politically correct suggestion that lesbian spaces are constricting because of "a desire for inclusivity with other LGBTQ+ populations." What really seems to be happening is that transgender identity and propaganda are subjugating homosexuals, according to intersectionalism's upside-down hierarchies. As lesbian folk singer Alix Dobkin noted in 2015 in a coauthored essay, "transsexuals have leaped forward on the civil rights agenda and become the latest cause of the LGBTQ community, often to the detriment of Lesbians."[32]

Lesbian bars are the canary in the coalmine. The lesbian population is being thinned by the rush to trans gender-confused kids. "Many detransitioning [formerly trans-identifying] young women have since come to believe they were just young lesbians who had internalized homophobia and been led to believe that not being typically feminine meant they weren't female at all. Nearly all of them struggled with mental health and engaged in self-harm," notes investigative journalist Abigail Shrier in her 2020 book on the transgender craze, *Irreversible Damage*.[33] Forcing lesbians into medical treatments that deform their bodies for life, including ending their sexual pleasure forever,[34] is not the tolerance they were promised—let alone the special rights showered on them when they were more useful to the revolution.

When homosexuals notice this, they're punished. That's the point of using the smear TERF, "trans-exclusionary radical feminists," for women who know men are not women. The freaky, violent, and totalitarian claim is that homosexuals and lesbians are not "inclusive," and therefore are sexual bigots who need thought reform.

Homosexuals' word weapons are being turned on them now that they're less useful tools for erasing natural rights. Anyone taken in by the pretense that this regime cares about "LGBT rights" should consider that it is already coercing homosexuals and transsexuals' speech, beliefs, and behavior. And repression of speech is a fore-runner of totalitarianism; nobody wants to end up at that train's destination.

Internal LGBT struggle sessions have defamed, pressured, and otherwise socially brutalized not only lesbians, but also male homosexuals. As the lesbian BuzzFeed reporter Shannon Keating put it in 2015, "Against the increasingly colorful backdrop of gender diversity, a binary label like 'gay' or 'lesbian' starts to feel somewhat stale and stodgy. When there are so many genders out there, is it closed-minded—or worse, harmful and exclusionary—if you identify with a label that implies you're only attracted to one?"[35]

"Lately, it's become the fashion to declare that cisgender white gay men are not part of the LGBTQ+ community. They are, apparently, too laden with privilege to be considered part of the coalition of the noble suffering," noted Marxist writer Freddie deBoer in 2023.[36]

This is not coming from the last remnants of Moral Majority fundamentalist Christians or the other bogey-men regularly put up by queer organizations and media—it's coming from inside progressivism itself. Gays, lesbians, and transsexuals can ride the cultural Marxist tiger until it eats them; or perhaps they should consider helping fight the common enemy of human and natural rights: Marxist totalitarians.

Pleasure Me or You're a Bad, Bad Girl

In the age of transgenderism, queer activists have embraced a rather rapey position: pressuring people into sexual encounters against their will. Writing in the queer publication *The Advocate*, Navy veteran Brynn Tannehill, a transgender man, explicitly condemns unwanted sexual encounters, yet he uses pressuring language such as "discriminatory" and "transphobic" to slur and pressure lesbians who don't want to have sex with "transgender women"[37] —that is, biological men. That's what groomers and sexual predators do: wear down their targets' resistance to sex through manipulation.

"Some lesbians who don't go full-out TERF are still all too eager to write off dating trans people because of 'genital preferences,' which means they have incredibly reductive ideas about gender and bodies," Shannon Keating argues.[38] Tannehill claims that the "flat rejection of any possibility of dating any transgender people is rooted in an irrational bias against transgender people themselves."[39]

In a video that writer Taylor Fogarty quoted from and linked to at *The Federalist* before it was taken "private,"[40] transgender YouTuber Riley Dennis claimed that lesbians' sexual preferences that exclude men are "discriminatory" and exhibit "prejudice . . . against transgender people" because "some women have penises."[41] The video is still available in a YouTube response in which lesbian Magdalen Berns describes Dennis as "suggesting that lesbians have privilege and therefore they oppress trans women by not sleeping with them or not being interested in them or not including them in their dating pool."[42]

A lesbian woman told the BBC in 2021 that transgender activists had said "they would strangle me with a belt if they were in a room with me and Hitler. That was so bizarrely violent, just because I won't have sex with trans women." Some lesbians have been pressured into unwanted sex with transgender people because they were called "transphobic" after initially refusing, the BBC reported. "I was told that . . . I owed it to my trans sisters to unlearn my 'genital confusion' so I can enjoy letting them penetrate me," one lesbian wrote in a survey of eighty lesbians, 56 percent of whom said they had been pressured to have sex with "transgender women."[43] Frankly, that sounds worse than the "praying the gay away" and "conversion therapy" boogiemen.

The BBC faced a firestorm after publishing this article about the toxicity of queer culture. The article was "probably the first in

mainstream UK media to explore the reported experience of some lesbians of pressure to have sex with trans women."[44] Complaints by LGBT
activists about the article from a reported twenty thousand signatories
led to edits, internal review, a Wikipedia article, and other elements of
a public struggle session.[45]

Public pressure to bully people into sexual experiences they don't
want is a disturbing step down the road to violent totalitarianism. We're
pretty far down that road already, considering that half of the men
in Wisconsin prisons who identify as transgender and then apply for
transfer to women's prisons are in prison for sexual crimes.[46] Few things
could be more like a concentration camp than being locked permanently
into a cell with someone who's in jail for raping people like you.

Sexual Cannibalism

Some people who would formerly have come out as homosexual are
now coming out as transgender—at least partly because of peer and
cultural pressure. "Many of the girls now being cornered into a trans
identity might, in an earlier era, have come out as gay," notes Shrier.
"'You've got a situation where young lesbians are being pressured if they
don't give into this new idea of what it is to be a lesbian,' prominent gay
writer Julia D. Robertson told [Shrier]. That 'new idea' is that lesbians
do not exist: girls with more masculine presentations are 'really' boys."

Sexual malleability is well-established by many studies. The
well-resourced, long-standing, yet fruitless search for a "gay gene"—or
any other hardwired characteristics that predict any non-heterosexual
orientation—implicates psychological, cultural, and social factors in
sexual orientation. "The best scientific evidence suggests multicausal
explanations for how we experience sexual desire and gender, with
environmental and social factors playing crucial roles in their development," explains Nathanael Blake at The Public Discourse. "As one

LGBT-sympathetic writer put it, 'it's likely that our sexualities and genders are textured by a mix of social experience, the firing off of neurons, hormonal swirls and the transcription of DNA.' We are, in short, not born this way."[47]

The largest-ever study seeking to establish genetic links for same-sex attraction, in 2019, found that it's "impossible to use genes to predict someone's sexuality," reported the *New York Times*.[48] The international study was conducted by geneticists and social scientists from prestigious pro-Marxist institutions such as Harvard University. In studying nearly half a million people, they found that more than a thousand genes may predict one-third of people's tendency to same-sex attraction, leaving two-thirds of queer identity to come from "societal or environmental factors."

The pro-queer American Psychological Association notes the lack of a "gay gene" and the complexity of sexual attractions: "There is no consensus among scientists about the exact reasons that an individual develops a heterosexual, bisexual, gay, or lesbian orientation. Although much research has examined the possible genetic, hormonal, developmental, social, and cultural influences on sexual orientation, no findings have emerged that permit scientists to conclude that sexual orientation is determined by any particular factor or factors. Many think that nature and nurture both play complex roles; most people experience little or no sense of choice about their sexual orientation."[49]

Women's sexual orientation, especially, seems to be at least somewhat influenced by context, such as the availability of male partners.[50] A significant number of study participants also reported changes in their sexual orientation. People don't reorient only from heterosexual to bisexual or lesbian over time, but also in the other direction.[51]

If the boundaries between sexual identities are at least somewhat permeable and sexual attractions are largely affected by environmental factors, there are numerous massive implications. "Sexual cannibalism" is one we've been describing: switching one's sexual identity based at least in part on social cues and psychological factors. It clearly happens among some kids who identify as transgender.

If transsexual behavior is, at least for some kids, a social contagion, why couldn't other queer identities be also? If the transgender identity can cannibalize the lesbian identity, why couldn't (and wouldn't) other sexual identities make similar conquests? What's to stop people from adding new identities that claim exclusive legal privileges? Is sexual behavior a legitimate way to dispense legal privileges, such as the power to punish others for speech you don't like?

A key protection against people being pressured into unwanted sexual actions is erasing the source of that pressure. That means protecting all Americans from winning or losing privileges based on their sexual preferences or behaviors, which, after all, change over time. While people's sexual identities and actions may change over time, what doesn't change is their humanity. Human rights should be based on what all human beings share, instead of what we don't.

Sexual Contagion

The malleability of sexual expression appears to be at play in rapid-onset gender dysphoria, according to hundreds of parent reports, some for an explosive 2018 study by the feminist Brown University scholar Lisa Littman.[52] Littman was the first researcher brave enough to delve into a phenomenon that parents were reporting online: groups of teen girls all coming out as transgender at once. That is statistically impossible unless sexuality is affected by social environment.

Littman found evidence that rapid transgender self-identification spread by social contagion. Friends identifying as LGBT, schools and entertainment pushing identity politics, talking with strangers about sex online—all these increased the likelihood kids identified as transgender.

"Parents described intense group dynamics where friend groups praised and supported people who were transgender-identified and ridiculed and maligned non-transgender people," Littman's study noted. "Where popularity status and activities were known, 60.7% of the [children with gender dysphoria studied] experienced an increased popularity within their friend group when they announced a transgender-identification and 60.0% of the friend groups were known to mock people who were not transgender or LGBTIA."

Eighty-seven percent of the 256 children Littman studied had become gender dysphoric after friends did, after increasing their time online, or both.[53]

Their sexual identification was clearly influenced by their peers and culture. Kids at school "are constantly putting down straight, white people for being privileged, dumb and boring," one study participant wrote. Another told Littman, "In general, cis-gendered people are considered evil and unsupportive, regardless of their actual views on the topic. To be heterosexual, comfortable with the gender you were assigned at birth, and non-minority places you in the 'most evil' of categories with this group of friends."[54]

It's no wonder this study was canceled. The journal that published it pulled it from the internet, and eight months later republished it—after a lengthy private and public self-criticism process—with few actual changes except self-flagellating editor's notes.[55] In the meantime, Brown University retracted its press release announcing the study[56] and wavered on whether to stand behind its own professor's freedom to research topics that are taboo to cultural Marxists.[57] Littman lost a consulting job over the ballyhoo and left Brown a year after her mobbed study was republished.[58]

Another study about rapid-onset gender dysphoria by a left-leaning, highly cited sexual orientation researcher received even harsher treatment than Littman's. Northwestern University professor Michael

Bailey's March 29, 2023, study in the allegedly prestigious journal *Archives of Sexual Behavior* was retracted after an online mob attacked it, not for serious errors, but because of what it found.

"There is ample evidence that in progressive communities, multiple girls from the same peer group are announcing they are trans almost simultaneously. There has been a sharp increase in this phenomenon across the industrialized West," Bailey wrote. "But there have been virtually no scientific data or studies on the subject. In part that is because researchers who have touched this topic have been punished for their curiosity."[59]

Bailey coauthored the article with a mother of a rapid-onset-gender-dysphoric child who used a pseudonym to protect her family. The need for that reflects the frightening Sovietization of America's formerly vibrant free speech culture.

The study included the parents of 1,655 young people with rapid-onset gender dysphoria. "Pre-existing mental health issues were common, and youths with these issues were more likely than those without them to have socially and medically transitioned," the retracted article reported. "Parents reported that they had often felt pressured by clinicians to affirm their AYA [adolescent or young adult] child's new gender and support their transition. According to the parents, AYA children's mental health deteriorated considerably after social transition."[60]

Many queer-supportive people have realized that gender-confused children often have major coexisting mental and physical conditions. A woman who is married to a "transgender woman" says, of working in a gender clinic, "The girls who came to us had many comorbidities: depression, anxiety, ADHD, eating disorders, obesity. Many were diagnosed with autism, or had autism-like symptoms. . . . We had patients who said they had Tourette syndrome (but they didn't); that they had tic disorders (but they didn't); that they had multiple personalities (but they didn't). The doctors privately recognized these false self-diagnoses as a manifestation of social contagion. They even acknowledged that suicide has an element of social contagion. But when I said the clusters of girls streaming into our service looked as if their gender issues might be a manifestation of social contagion, the doctors said gender identity reflected something innate."[61]

The same is true of other queer identities. It's well-established that depression, anxiety, trauma, and suicidal thoughts and attempts are higher among homosexuals.[62] Yet after years of searching, scientists have been unable to find any evidence for sexual orientation or gender identity as immutable, inborn traits.

France's National Academy of Medicine notes that no genetic predisposition for transsexuality has been found.[63] In 2019, a "massive study," "the largest to date," of half a million genomes, essentially ended researchers' attempt to establish a "gay gene" or any other immutable evidence for inborn homosexuality.[64] Noting that entire social groups are simultaneously identifying as transgender and an exponential increase in children presenting with gender distress around the globe, the Academy calls transgender identification an "epidemic-like phenomenon" and a "primarily social problem."[65]

Yet, how social factors affect sexual orientation can barely be studied because of severe taboos. Alfred Kinsey could explore toddlers' erections and pedophiles' fantasies and get university "research" centers named after him,[66] but explore evidence for sexual contagions or negative outcomes of queer identification and get ready to be canceled.[67]

Cultural Aspects of Queer Contagion

Cultural saturation, combined with historically high rates of family trauma such as divorce and unwed childbearing, helps explain why queer identification has skyrocketed. For centuries homosexuals have manifested at 1–3 percent of the population. After 2010, suddenly nearly one-fifth of young people in the world self-identified as LGBTQ.

In a 2021 survey of more than nineteen thousand people in twenty-seven countries, 18 percent of those born after 1997 identified as non-heterosexual. That's more than four times the percentage of Baby Boomers who identified as non-heterosexual.[68]

In the extreme leftist environments of liberal arts colleges, students are four times more likely to identify as LGBT than the rest of the US population, and twice as likely as their peers. Nearly 40 percent of liberal arts students in a 2022 survey of 57,000 students identified as some form of queer.[69] This is driven by an explosion in women, 60 percent of whom have only had male partners in the last five years, identifying as bisexual. It looks an awful lot like they're adapting a queer identity due to cultural and peer pressure.

Surveys establish that "there has been a surge in LGBTQ self-identification among young adults who do *not* display homosexual behavior." On every data source from Gallup to the General Social Survey, the percentage of people identifying as queer tripled or quadrupled between 2010 and 2021—all while the majority of people identifying as LGBT tell pollsters they're having heterosexual sex.

"No matter the data source, it's clear that in 11 short years, LGBTQ identification among young Americans *tripled*," writes University of Texas sociology professor Mark Regnerus. "And yet under-30 non-heterosexual *behavioral experience*, while climbing, remains just over half that figure, at 8.6 percent (in 2021)" [emphasis in the original].[70]

If even some youth are identifying as transgender because of social contagion, why couldn't that also be true for other queer identities? In the relatively recent past, queer identification often met discouragement, but today it receives hysterical encouragement. The few studies available indicate that people in politically left environments are most prone to adopting queer identities, and the United States is increasingly saturated with extremist left messaging and government pressure.

All of this suggests that some proportion of LGBT identification today is driven by peer groups and social conditioning. It's the opposite social situation to what many older homosexuals experienced when coming out, even up until a decade ago.

Sex-Based Rights Are Insecure

Given that, it's fair to ask Americans to consider that if today peer pressure pushes queer identities, which secure people social and legal privileges, what if some kids coming out aren't actually LGBT? Or what if at least *some* LGBT identification is malleable?

If that's even possibly the case, should a potentially evolving sexual identity form the basis of assigning Americans privileges, or pushing Americans into life-altering choices like sex at a young age with older partners or HIV-positive partners, or into unrepairable genital mutilation? Or should all Americans be treated equally before the law, no matter how they identify?

Even those who believe that sexuality is fluid, potentially shifting along a wide spectrum over one's entire lifespan, should be able to get behind equal protection of natural rights for all. That basis is unchanging, while sexual activity often does change over people's lifetimes and therefore is an unstable basis for any social and government privileges.

The now-disproven "gay gene" assumption is behind treating sexual behavior as equivalent to race in securing special government privileges. It was key, for example, to Obama Attorney General Eric Holder's promotion of LGBT legal preferences,[71] and to the *Obergefell* decision. Skin color, eye shape, and all the other markers of the "race" social construct come from DNA. They don't change based on environment. But for at least some people, sexual identities do.

That means sexual attraction is an unstable ground on which to build an entirely new American constitution. All Americans, including those who identify as queer, should think about that. Do we want Americans' rights to be tied to Americans' behavior, which does change for some people, or to their *being*?

Would it be right for someone who identifies as a lesbian yet has sex with a man (something lesbians do all the time)[72] to lose the ability to sue an employer for sexual discrimination over it? Would it be right for someone who identifies as transgender who desists in identifying as transgender to lose the ability to get health care over it? That happens, too.[73]

In all these scenarios, and surely dozens more yet to arise, citizens' rights are unstable because their foundation is unstable. Rights must be based on our common humanity and on the objective and unchanging natural differences between the sexes, not on sexual preferences that sometimes change.

Love Doesn't Experiment with Child Torture

If—as seems obvious—even a small percentage of people are identifying as queer due to massive social pressure, the consequences can be horrifying.

The previously mentioned queer surgeon Blair Peters says that "a lot of adolescents are presenting for [transgender] surgical intervention" and increasingly these teens have been taking puberty-suppressing drugs. Because they're so young, some of Peters's patients have had no sexual experiences. So to stop their genital wounds from closing, they need to exercise muscles that haven't begun to develop: "Some of the early challenges are getting someone to successfully dilate [keep opening the genital wound after surgery] that's never had to engage with their pelvic floor musculature and is maybe 17, 18 years old. It's hard," he says, laughing.[74]

Boys who have been taking puberty-blocking drugs "don't have enough tissue to line the [fake] vaginal canal," so Peters has to take a skin graft, usually from an arm, or use a robot to peel off skin from inside the stomach: "You either have to take a skin graft or take skin from elsewhere or use artificial products. The way that we're dealing with it is by using a robot and we're basically performing intra-abdominal components of the surgery. So we're using peritoneum, which is the inner lining of the abdomen, to line most of the vaginal canal."[75]

Some patients, Peters explains, first have their penis cut off and turned into a vulva-like arrangement without a "canal" for "penetration," then can later get a vagina-style hole installed after their sexual preferences for "penetration" express. "Some of our adolescents, for example, who are not sure if they want a [vaginal] canal, we've done a couple of vulvoplasties, just to sort of relieve dysphoria, have them live in that body for a couple of years and make that decision for themselves when they're maybe ready for sexual penetration or dilation and they're at a better place in their life," he says.[76]

He prefers a penis amputation without a surgically created "vaginal canal," because the canal is more like an open wound, more subject to infections, weeping, and closure: "I would much rather do a vulvoplasty and have a small chance someone will want a vaginal canal in the future and do a slightly more complicated surgery, than having the more common thing of a person that isn't really wanting the canal and doesn't use it and isn't doing a good job dilating, and then all of a sudden is having these pelvic floor issues and chronic discharge and infections. And it just becomes a huge mess. So I think it's better to just avoid those things unless they truly need them."[77] "I don't even know how I would do this [surgical practice] if I wasn't queer," he says.[78]

The grotesque nature of such surgeries explains why multiple European nations have recently limited them, especially for children.

International medical organizations including the Australian College of Physicians, the Royal College of General Practitioners in the United Kingdom, and the Swedish National Council for Medical Ethics have concluded that cross-sex hormones and puberty blockers are "experimental and dangerous."

Sweden's Karolinska University Hospital banned hormone blockers in 2021, on account of their experimental nature.[79] France's National Academy of Medicine recommended extreme caution with hormone blockers because of "side effects such as impact on growth, bone fragility, risk of sterility, emotional and intellectual consequences and, for girls, symptoms reminiscent of menopause."[80]

Peters says genital mutilation accounts for 80 percent of his practice. A few months after this interview, the *New York Times* labeled Peters "among a handful of young, social media-savvy doctors" who are researching female genitals.[81] In 2023, Nike featured Peters at a Pride month event where he was scheduled to discuss doing double mastectomies on healthy young women.[82] How is it pro-queer for any person to be put on a conveyor belt to this?

A 2023 poll found that 71 percent of likely voters with an opinion on this issue "believe that pharmaceutical companies and doctors who promote puberty blockers and cross-sex hormone treatments for underage children seeking gender transition should be legally liable for any harmful side effects that arise."[83] Such lawsuits have begun, boosted by state attorneys general.[84]

Gays against Groomers

Plenty of queer people don't want their private lives used to erase the Constitution and other basic facets of human decency, such as not talking to other people's kids about sex and not putting male rapists into women's prison cells. Several queer-run organizations oppose many policies enacted in the name of their identities. Establishment queer figures and institutions who are on board with identity politics, seeing such organizations as a threat, have worked successfully to ban them from social media.[85]

Those include Gays Against Groomers, Genspect, the Society for Evidence Based Gender Medicine, Our Duty, and LGB Alliance. They show courage in refusing to accept pedophile-adjacent behavior and the erasure of fellow citizens' natural rights simply because that's what "good" gay people must do—or else.

"The overwhelming majority of gay people are against what the community has transformed into, and we do not accept the political movement pushing their agenda in our name," says the Gays Against Groomers "About" page. "Gays Against Groomers directly opposes the sexualization and indoctrination of children. This includes drag queen story hours, drag shows involving children, the transitioning and medicalization of minors, and gender theory being taught in the classroom."[86]

Many queer people do not support the policies pushed in their names. But many others are willing to let their sexual identity be weaponized by extremists not just to allow these atrocities but to give them government privileges. All Americans need to put our citizenship and our nation's good above our personal identities, and seek the common good that benefits us all.

Father-Deprived Kids Destroy Society

Bari Weiss has been waking up for three years. The liberal columnist famously quit the *New York Times* in 2020 over its venom against free speech, then started The Free Press, which has more than 630,000 readers, making it the No. 1 publication on the Substack platform.[87] Subscriptions are $8 per month or $80 per year.[88]

Weiss, who attended Columbia University as a "theater kid," can't unsee the reality that intersectionalism creates "a caste system" that labels Jews like her "oppressors" on account of their race.[89] Her lifelong positioning among the US ruling class has allowed Weiss to see, earlier than many others, that cultural Marxism's doctrine of intersectionalism is not only incoherent but totalitarian.

Being targeted as an oppressor for her race prompted Weiss to argue publicly for "ending DEI"[90] and for people from all political persuasions to "fight for the West."[91] Not only religious and ethnic minorities like Jews but also sexual minorities should do the same, she argues, because cultural Marxism threatens us all.[92]

On October 7, 2023, Hamas terrorists entered Israel and beheaded babies, raped women, captured two hundred hostages, and murdered fourteen hundred people. Weeks later, Weiss gave a speech to the Federalist Society, an organization of non-leftist lawyers. Leftists openly joining Islamists in celebrations of terrorism all over the globe motivated a stirring speech. Weiss noted the crude Cultural Marxist calculus that slots people into groups based on sex, sexual behavior, and race, then labels people "oppressed" and "oppressor" based on membership in those categories.

"Their moral calculus is as crude as you can imagine: they see Israelis and Jews as powerful and successful and 'colonizers,' so they are bad; Hamas is weak and coded as people of color, so they are good. . . ." she said. "This is the ideology of vandalism in the true sense of the word—the Vandals sacked Rome. It is the ideology of nihilism. It knows nothing of how to build. It knows only how to tear down and to destroy."[93]

Referring to her sexual preferences, Weiss recognized that some in the audience "do not believe my marriage should have been legal," but she brushed that disagreement aside for a greater purpose. "In the fight for the West, I know who my allies are. And my allies are not the people who, looking at facile, external markers of my identity, one might imagine them to be. My allies are people who believe that America is good. That the West is good. That human beings—not cultures—are created equal and that saying so is essential to knowing what we are fighting for. America and our values are worth fighting for—and that is the priority of the day."[94]

These are stirring and true observations. Weiss's journey of discovering the truths to guide her actions surely mirrors that of many other Americans, queer and not. Yet, like all of us, she has a lot further to go.

Some aspects of Weiss's personal life suggest that she doesn't fully understand what "ending DEI" and "fighting for the West" require. In 2016 she divorced her husband of three years, and in 2021 she obtained a marriage license with a woman.[95] In the Federalist Society speech, Weiss celebrated speaking in a series dedicated to the wife of a man who fought for homosexual licenses at the Supreme Court.[96]

Parallel to libertarian pundits Guy Benson and Dave Rubin, Weiss and her female partner bought reproductive parts to generate a child in 2022.[97] That means she chose to create a fatherless child, although lacking a father is perhaps the chief risk factor for almost every disadvantage in life. That's not just because fathers provide revenue. It's because fathers provide a sex-specific form of parenting that every child needs and deserves in order to thrive.[98]

Since bringing a child into existence is impossible without sperm, which only men can generate, it also means that Weiss has made use of a man's reproductive parts and functions without an intimate relationship with—or acknowledgement of—the person attached to them. She has excluded this man from his child's life. An outspoken feminist, Weiss might question someone who exploited a woman in exactly the same way that her journey to motherhood exploited a man.

Or she might not. When the Free Press published an article on "the surrogacy boom,"[99] Weiss tweeted it with this quotation: "'I'm not a handmaid,' said Ashley Mareko, who has given birth to three surrogate babies and is about to do it again. She's made $200,000, which has enabled her to pay off student debt, cover a mortgage, and buy a camper. 'I'm a businesswoman.'"[100]

It was unfair to take baby Weiss's father away before she was born, and that injustice will matter to her for her entire life. No amount of money can make up for this deliberately inflicted primal loss. The same is true of the motherless children Benson and Rubin acquired to fill the deficit created by their failure to commit to their children's mothers through marriage.

A father or mother deficit is one of the chief causes of systemic American social problems including crime, addiction, poverty, depression, early sexual activity, low achievement, and susceptibility to predators. Indeed, the decline of marriage and the Marxist denigration of men are chief sources of our culture's decline. You only have to name any effect of cultural Marxism to see almost instantly that stronger and better men and women would end or reduce it.

So while she speaks true and admirable words repudiating Marxist politics, in her own life, like other alleged anti-Marxists Rubin and Benson, Weiss enacts those same politics. Despite spending her entire professional life chronicling sexual politics, like most in our society Weiss is still blind to the full implications.

Weiss is clearly open to changing her mind and adopting counter-culture positions. So can others who share her current sexual preferences, and those sympathetic to them. If we truly want to save Western civilization, which protects us all, we must refuse to perpetuate Marxism no matter how much we want a child in our arms.

Only Heterosexual Sex Makes Babies

Marxist sexual politics invert natural male-female relations. The natural order is obviously that men and women are different and must commit their complementary capacities in a lifelong marriage to perpetuate human life. Marxists turn this upside down, making heterosexuals the oppressor class who must be overthrown and subjugated to homosexuals and transsexuals.

While Weiss publicly rejects subjugating one identity group to another, her own actions do exactly that. The manufacture of children for those in naturally infertile homosexual relationships subjugates heterosexuality to homosexuality. It steals the fruit of a heterosexual marriage without committing to such a marriage, even though such marriages clearly provide the best environment for raising a child to be happy.

Obtaining a child through a sperm donor also negates the humanity of men. It erases their right—and their duty—to act as fathers to the children their bodies are necessary to generate. It turns fathers into mere sperm donors. The same is true of homosexual men paying to obtain children without engaging in the act of love with their own children's mother. All this subjugates heterosexual relations to homosexual desires, enacting sexual Marxism.

Marriage depends on the same sexual dimorphism that lesbians appeal to when declining sex with transgender men. It's incoherent to reject that dimorphism in one case and demand respect for it in the other. We should all respect the basic realities, our own bodies' capacities, the need for another human being of the opposite sex to procreate, and the fundamental natural right of every child to the daily in-home presence of his or her father and mother together for life.

All adults need to put the good of children and of society above our wounds, appetites, and insecurities. That is what it will take to preserve the West against Cultural Marxism: we must take a stand for reality—for the givenness and complementarity of the sexes against the negation of their mutual powers.

With one voice we must all affirm that men and women are different, that only men and women together can reproduce, and that that unique procreative relationship is what marriage means and is for. Other things adults may do in private are their own private business, and they will not be attacked for it in their private homes.

Weiss is a strong and needed voice for millions of Americans seeking a halfway house from the violent chaos of cultural Marxism. But halfway houses are not fortresses against invaders.

Natural Rights Protect *All* Americans

If we affirm Weiss's exploitation of male body parts to procure a child without a father, in the end there can be no security of free speech and or of the other natural human rights she prizes. People who live as she does are not, on the whole, as tolerant of differing views as she is.

The overlap of support for totalitarianism with LGBT expression is very strong. Approximately 70 percent of "very liberal" women who support shouting down speakers they don't like on college campuses identify as LGBT.[101] Glenn Greenwald, Guy Benson, Douglas Murray, Andy Ngo, and Dave Rubin are notable exceptions among LGBT people in being friendlier to freedom of speech and religious exercise.

Yet you can't have the protections of Western society without the boundaries Western society enforces on your choices. Those who don't accept a society's basic rules are incompatible with that society. Western society, for example, has traditionally excluded women, children, and noncombatants as targets of war. Clearly, Islamists don't agree with that exclusion, and they are therefore incompatible with Western societies.

For there to be a West where homosexuals are not imprisoned or thrown off buildings, queer people need to respect the Western understanding of natural law, which creates unprecedented tolerance for them and secures their natural rights equally. It also requires drag shows to be held discreetly in the corners of adult-only establishments, not in kindergartens. LGBT people have to give up their attitude of entitlement, their demands for special rights nobody else has, like to wag naked butts at children.

Securing a free society costs all of us something. Just like heterosexuals, who sacrifice a lot to form the families that keep our society going, homosexuals need to be willing to sacrifice something to get something more in return.

The truth of the matter is that aggressively public LGBT identification hurts society. People who do not support securing every child's natural right to his own biological father and mother are destroying Western culture. Western culture did not create legal protections for inherently sterile sexual activities, because sterile sex acts cause cultural suicide. Western culture could never have been built in a society so decadent and detached from nature, because building a strong society requires millions of acts of directed self-sacrifice of the kind that do not habitually come from people whose main motivation in life is self-pleasure.

This is not an argument for punishing private activities between adults. It's an argument for keeping adult sexual activity private, and for publicly promoting heterosexual marriage and procreation as the norm.

Yes, this would curtail homosexual privileges. But it would also secure homosexuals' equal rights, based on our common humanity, that government can never take away.

Cultural Revolutions Eat Themselves

The extremism of gender ideology is creating a backlash against the entire alphabet constellation. The power mongers cynically manipulating sexual identitarians subject queer people to the same loss of freedoms that they're imposing on other Americans currently in the name of special rights for queer people. That's the pattern we saw in China's

Cultural Revolution, Soviet Russia, and East Germany: struggle sessions eventually devoured those who originally egged them on.

Queer Americans are trading in the American birthright of equal rights for the pottage of special rights granted by the government, with other citizens forced to pay the bill. If the government can give "trans" Americans special status at the expense of "cisgender" Americans, it can take that status away from "trans" people at the behest of any other group that becomes powerful enough to displace them on the intersectionality hierarchy.

For example: Could transgender medical interventions take research, attention, and energy away from better treatments for AIDS? What about the lifelong costs of transgender medical interventions, with which we have essentially zero long-term experience? Is it just for government to force people who aren't transsexuals to pay for transsexuals' lifelong high medical costs incurred for entirely elective procedures? How would you like to be on the hook for someone else's $100,000, $200,000, $500,000 in elective medical bills? American governments are already forcing Americans to pay for these interventions through Medicare, Medicaid, military health systems, and insurance mandates.

What's the limit on people racking up medical bills they can force others to pay? Consider that confiscating the wealth of all the United States's billionaires would only fund the federal government for eight months—at *current* rates of expenditure.[102] The US national debt is $187,000 per household and escalating fast. And America's unfunded liabilities—the entitlements promised minus projected intake—currently amount to *$1.2 million per household*.[103]

LGBT people lose big when they decide that government should determine what gay people are allowed to think and say. Our government should secure homosexual and gender-dysphoric Americans the exact same rights as it secures for all other Americans, because queer people benefit from free speech, self-defense, equality under the law, robust due process, being innocent before proven guilty in a court of law, and the free exercise of religion, too.

Culture critic Camille Paglia, a self-described "queer" woman, accurately notes that queer "conspiratorial ambushes unleashed on small bakers" are not only "illiberal and intolerant," but also indicate "a strange lack of confidence in gay identity."[104] LGBT Americans need to be confident enough in their identities to stop weaponizing them to destroy equal rights for all Americans.

No decent emotionally stable person forces others to associate with him or say nice things about him on pain of job loss or government oppression. Queer people don't have to be the manipulative, sex-crazed, child-thirsty egomaniacs they're cast as in today's regime-approved forms of queer expression. They can join with other Americans in demanding equal rights for all, and special privileges for none.

CHAPTER 5

Domestic Color Revolution

"The Declaration is saying that government's main job in foreign policy is to defend the nation while refraining from interference in other nations."

—Thomas West, The Political Theory of
the American Founding[1]

Formerly, the Pride flag was a symbol of American occupation abroad. Now it is a symbol of domestic occupation as well. On behalf of this flag, US military officers and soldiers have openly defied their oaths to the Constitution, betraying the American people.

To enter military service, all American soldiers swear to "support and defend the Constitution of the United States against all enemies, foreign and domestic," and "obey the orders of the President of the

United States and the orders of the officers appointed over me."[2] But there is growing evidence of military leadership carrying out an insurrection against the Constitution and the people it protects to advance sexual and other identity politics.

This chapter will show that not only have top US military officers admitted to lying to elected officials including the commander-in-chief about military policy and personnel on behalf of sexual politics, they have also acted contrary to law and denied evidence of the US military promoting this rainbow insurrection. These betrayals have gone unpunished.

To many top American military leaders, homosexual privileges exemplify America. The US Department of Defense (DoD) pledged allegiance to identity politics in 2020 in a statement declaring, "We are committed to making the DoD a workplace of choice that is characterized by diversity, equality, and inclusion."[3]

Democrats fully back that stance. A telling example is a 2023 letter signed by 154 House Democrats—two-thirds of their House of Representatives members—opposing Republican proposals to withdraw federal funds for LGBT porn in military kids' school libraries, for genital amputation for transgender soldiers, and for genital amputation and sterilization for soldiers' transgender children.

That coalition also opposed Republican efforts to stop drag queen shows on military property and to stop flying the pride flag as an emblem representing the American people.[4] In September 2023, every House Democrat and eighteen Republicans voted to continue using military funding for Pride month celebrations that include drag queen shows.[5] The 2023 annual military bill funded essentially everything Democrats wanted—transgender mutilation procedures for soldiers and their kids, abortions and travel to them, and military drag shows. House Republicans merely got an upper limit on increased funding for civilian "diversity, equity, inclusion" (DEI) personnel.[6]

The Trump administration began dismantling the DoD's identity politics politburo in 2020, but in 2021, Joe Biden revived and expanded it.[7] Biden ordered all military entities, plus the rest of the federal government, to create diversity, equity, and inclusion (DEI) offices.[8]

The executive order singled out "lesbian, gay, bisexual, transgender, and queer (LGBTQ+) persons" for federal privileges these new DEI departments would secure. It required federal agency heads to "identify the best methods, consistent with applicable law, to assist agencies in assessing equity with respect to race, ethnicity, religion, income, geography, gender identity, sexual orientation, and disability."

The military swiftly implemented this order. A few months into the Biden administration, Deputy Defense Secretary Kathleen Hicks met with LGBT activist groups. The Defense Department issued a press release three months later showing that it had obeyed these groups by ending the previous DoD policy of removing troops with gender dysphoria from service and by "fully implement[ing] policies" to force taxpayers to pay for transgender troops' medical mutilation.[9]

In addition, "a 2022 letter from Joint Chiefs of Staff Chair Army Gen. Mark Milley estimated that the armed forces dedicated nearly 6 million hours and about $1 million in additional expenses to DEI training sessions in 2021," reported the *Epoch Times*.[10]

As numerous investigative reporters and scholars have documented, DEI in practice privileges women above men, homosexuals above heterosexuals, darker-skinned people over paler-skinned people, and gender-dysphoric people above those who honor their natural sex.[11] In short, "equity" policies systemically discriminate against Americans based on their skin color and sexual behavior. This is not unifying or strengthening; it is divisive and anti-American. It is also flatly unconstitutional.

Top Military Leaders Push DEI Regime Change

Yet top leaders of the US military—especially those Biden's administration has elevated—believe the opposite. They prefer the identity politics constitution to the real American Constitution.

A prime example is the Biden Pentagon sidestepping Congress to force American taxpayers to pay for abortions in 2023. The Pentagon announced it would use taxpayer funds not only to pay for abortions but also for travel and up to three weeks of taxpayer-paid time off for soldiers to get abortions, implying that killing tiny American citizens is a necessary cost of admitting women to combat.

Congress had never appropriated funds for abortions or travel to them. Service members usually have to take unpaid leave and pay their own travel expenses to attend events such as family funerals, pointed out Senators Tom Cotton[12] and Mike Lee.[13] This was a wildly political move, made without congressional authorization and against federal law.

Since 1977, the public-supported Hyde Amendment has prohibited taxpayer funding for abortion.[14] Since 1984, 10 US Code § 1093 has prohibited DoD funding of abortions except if the mother's life is at risk.[15] As *Wall Street Journal* columnist Kimberly Strassel noted, "federal law doesn't authorize these payments, and the Hyde Amendment prohibits the use of federal funds for most abortions. At worst this is a flagrant violation of statute, another example of the administration evading congressional power and the rule of law."[16]

Alabama Senator Tommy Tuberville objected and began requiring the Senate to vote on individual military promotions instead of mindlessly approving them in batches, as had become the norm. This—not the Pentagon's defiance of Congress—kicked over a hornet's nest.

The Pentagon quickly showed it was willing to disregard elected civilian authority in defense of sexual politics. Biden's diversity hires Navy Secretary Carlos Del Toro, Air Force Secretary Frank Kendall III, and Army Secretary Christine Wormuth went on CNN to demand that Tuberville end his military holds.[17] The three also signed a *Washington Post* op-ed targeting Tuberville and insisting the military needs to kill small Americans.[18]

"Pentagon launches media blitz to combat Tuberville blockade," *Politico* reported[19] of these Cabinet officials' use of their offices and enormous public resources to fight an elected official. It's as if the US military's decades of regime change abroad have helped develop habits, mentalities, and tactics in its leaders that are now being imported for domestic use.[20]

The US Army commander in Europe and Africa, Lieutenant General Andrew Rohling, called Tuberville's use of his legal authority "reprehensible, irresponsible and dangerous."[21] Biden's appointee to head the Marines, General Eric Smith, trashed Tuberville before a public audience.[22]

The *Politico* article shows that the Pentagon's media push amplified Democrat messaging, meaning the Department of Defense was essentially using its public resources and power (constantly expanded by Republicans) to serve one political party. The Senate's Democrat caucus published a letter, signed by seven former secretaries of defense, demanding that Republicans stop objecting to the military breaking the law.[23]

If rank-and-file soldiers behave the way these generals did—using public resources to oppose a sitting senator and the Senate prerogatives that give him the options he exercised—they would be punished. US military personnel are legally and ethically prohibited from politicking *even when not in uniform*, because that may imply military involvement with politics.

The reason is serious. The brass rebelling against elected officials is a mark of military rule. The immense power militaries wield must be controlled by the representatives of the people who give them this power, or the military rules the people rather than the opposite. That alternative is called a "military dictatorship" and its rollout is called a "coup."

These insurrectionary officials accused *Tuberville* of being a traitor for exercising the authority of his office while they abused theirs. Del Toro claimed Tuberville was "aiding and abetting communists" for demanding the Pentagon obey laws banning Sexual Revolution-sanctioned murder.

Elevating Identity Politics above National Defense

Tuberville's hold illuminated that Biden's military promotions are often made, as he has stated, on the basis of sex, sexual orientation, ideology, and race—a very good reason for examining and denying many of them. This starts at the top, with Defense Secretary Lloyd Austin. "When Secretary Austin was sworn into office, he shifted the Pentagon's priorities away from the National Defense Strategy and towards issues that can be perceived as political. . . ." testified Army veteran Jeremy Hunt to a House committee in 2023. "These include climate change, domestic extremism, and diversity, equity, and inclusion (DEI)."[24]

An investigation showed that making "climate change" a top "national security priority" distracted top US military officials during the Afghanistan retreat that left eight hundred Americans and thousands of US allies stranded, US war materiel in the hands of the Taliban, and the United States launching drone strikes that killed innocent children instead of enemy combatants.[25]

In July 2023, the Biden administration nominated Admiral Lisa Franchetti to lead the Navy.[26] She was not just the first woman (a meaningless qualification) selected for that position, but a wholesale supporter of DEI policies. "Today's theme of ally-ship is a key enabler for building inclusive teams," Franchetti told 330 sailors and their guests at a November 2022 Navy diversity, equity, and inclusion summit.[27]

Hunt noted that the US military recently replaced "longstanding Equal Opportunity programs with a new DEI bureaucracy." Some recruits now have to spend eleven weeks at an in-person DEI training class. The Navy also implemented a new "gender sensitivity" training that commands soldiers to police each other's use of pronouns.

The DEI Officer Corps

When Tuberville required Congress to pass the pending list of military promotions one at a time, it allowed more information about top military officers to surface. Investigative groups like the American Accountability Foundation found that numerous military nominees support extremist DEI policies.

Among these was Captain Michael Donnelly, the commanding officer of the USS *Ronald Reagan* when seaman Joshua Kelley performed on board in drag.[28] The Biden administration nominated Donnelly for promotion to rear admiral, while military PR scrambled to downplay the extent of Kelley's military-promoted drag activities to the public and Congress.

Another nominee was Army Colonel Monty Montague, in line for promotion to brigadier general. On his Facebook page, he had praised a movie about pederast Harvey Milk[29] and claimed "there is a general advantage to being white in this country."[30]

Biden renominated Craig A. Clapperton as vice admiral and assigned him the US military representative to the North Atlantic Treaty Organization. Clapperton was a featured speaker at a US Navy Pride month event in 2018, when he was a captain.[31] Military public relations photos show him, beaming, with junior service members in front of a Pride flag and behind a cake decorated with a rainbow and the words "LGBT pride."[32]

Biden nominated Air Force Brigadier General Scott A. Cain for promotion to major general. A military PR video shows him calling establishing a diversity, equity, and inclusion office his "most long-standing and significant accomplishment."[33] In the video, Cain says the military pushed DEI harder in response to the George Floyd insurrection of 2020.

Biden nominated Air Force Lieutenant Colonel Kevin Schneider for promotion to general and the next commander of Pacific Air Forces. In a military video, Schneider says the Air Force needs "diversity, equity, and inclusion" to become part of its "DNA."[34] "When we can stop having meetings about [DEI], or stop having specific, focused discussions on it, and it becomes part of our DNA, then we have achieved success," he says.[35]

Biden's politicized military has also punished military leaders for supporting the Constitution. Biden's nominee for Space Force commander, Lieutenant General Stephen Whiting, "played a role in the firing of Lt. Col. Matthew Lohmeier" because Lohmeier criticized the US military teaching Marxism to soldiers. "Our diversity, inclusion, and equity [DEI] industry and the trainings we're receiving in the military via that industry are rooted in critical race theory which is rooted in Marxism," Lohmeier had said. Whiting fired Lohmeier for that statement, and then the Biden administration put Whiting in line for a promotion.[36]

"I Had to Change the Rules"

Until Obama's last months in office, it was military policy to discharge soldiers who contracted gender dysphoria, to protect unit readiness and cohesion. When Donald Trump became president, he reinstated that policy. Then Biden axed it again.

While the policy was in place, myriad military personnel and institutions worked to undermine it, using public resources. A 2015 military press release touts Navy Pride Month speaker Amanda Simpson, the earliest known transgender presidential appointee. A division of the Naval Surface Warfare Center hosted Simpson in its base theater to "create a culture of inclusion." At the event, Simpson told soldiers, "To be authentic to who I am, I had to change the rules."[37] The military requires efficiently obeying orders, not challenging them.

Simpson is right, however, that queering the military reverses its traditional mores. Effective soldiering demands habits antithetical to queer ideology, such as self-discipline, controlling strong desires, following rules, and subordinating one's preferences to authority for the good of the whole. This means military leaders are absolutely wrong about "diversity" helping assemble a lethal force. In fact, to the extent the military pushes for sexual chaos among soldiers, it undermines its core mission of defending the United States. "It's very simple. If you want a certain type of people in your service, market your recruiting to them," Navy veteran Paul Gagney told the *Epoch Times*.[38]

Open Secrets

In 2011, President Obama appointed Simpson to an Army procurement position in the Pentagon. While a defense contractor for more than a decade before that appointment, Simpson publicly promoted LGBT policies. He served as the "grand marshal" in the 2005 Tucson, Arizona, Pride Parade and received a "Woman on the Move" award from massive defense contractor Raytheon in 2001.[39] Back in his test pilot days, Simpson's first name was Mitchell.[40]

Obama appointed Simpson to this Army position five years before ending the military's policy of discharging troops who publicly identified as transgender. The appointment was publicized all over queer, leftist, and corporate outlets, including the Huffington Post, NBC

News, and ABC News. In 2015, Obama promoted Simpson to deputy assistant secretary of defense.

Simpson was present at the military promotion of another transgender individual in September 20, 2015, days after the Obama administration implemented its transgender expansion of the illegal[41] "don't ask, don't tell" policy.[42] Navy officer Blake Dremann was promoted from Navy lieutenant to lieutenant commander three months after the Obama administration lifted the alleged ban. "To top it off, everyone on his [sic] promotion stage was transgender," NBC News reported breathlessly in September 2016. Amazing how quickly they were able to fill a promotion stage with transgender soldiers just three months after transgenderism had—supposedly—been a cause for military discharge!

In fact, that was no surprise at all. Transgender soldiers served in direct contradiction to the alleged ban on their military eligibility, with the knowledge and support of their commanding officers. As the *Army Times* reported in 2017, to construct its pro-transgender policies, the Obama administration consulted military doctors who were giving transgender treatments to active-duty soldiers despite the "ban."[43]

Defiance of official military policy saturates this issue. More than five hundred gender-dysphoric troops openly formed an advocacy organization, SPARTA, to protest the ban while violating it. Rather than applying the government's stated policy of discharging these troops, SPARTA was not just tolerated but encouraged by military leadership. Numerous profiles of LGBT soldiers include their statements that their commanders repeatedly expressed full support of their sexual behavior.

This includes Major Jamie Lee Henry, a transgender military doctor who was charged with promising to spy for Russia in 2022.[44] He is the first known American transgender military officer, because in 2015, while gender dysphoria was still cause for discharge, he petitioned to have his pronouns and sex marker changed in military records.

Instead of following the policy and starting the separation process, Henry's officers defied military policy to accommodate him. As Henry told BuzzFeed in 2015, the Army "used female pronouns in the document" granting his request.

"One of the key people who helped her [sic] through the period was her commanding officer. He provided Henry with housing, helped her continue her military career, and advocated for her family interests—all while knowing she [sic] was transgender," BuzzFeed reported. Henry's superior told him to abide by male appearance regulations and not talk to media, so that higher officers wouldn't hear about Henry defying military rules.[45]

Henry came out as transgender amid a contested divorce that included a custody dispute and brief period of homelessness. His first military rotation was in the psych ward at Walter Reed. After he came out, he joined SPARTA and there met "hundreds" of other LGBT troops also defying the military orders they had sworn to follow when they signed up.

Insurrection against Military Orders

Before it pushed for ending the discharge of mentally unwell and medically unfit transgender troops, SPARTA advocated for declaring men sexually attracted to men eligible for military service. Dremann was president of SPARTA when the military promoted her in 2016, apparently for being transgender. Air Force Major Bryan Fram, a "transgender woman" who had worked in the military for nearly fourteen years—for almost all of which time military policy was to discharge gender-dysphoric troops, at least officially—emceed Dremann's promotion.[46] Fram now goes by "Bree" and has been promoted to lieutenant colonel.[47]

Dremann and SPARTA's founding president, Sue Fulton, had both been among the first women to enter certain military roles. Fulton, an

Army officer and lesbian, was part of West Point's class of 1980, the first to admit women.[48] Dremann was one of the first women to be stationed on a Navy submarine, where soldiers are in close quarters for many months and sometimes share beds.[49] (Not surprisingly, "according to a 2010 survey, two of every three enlisted female sailors became pregnant during their tenure in the Navy.")[50]

It's pretty insurrectionary that hundreds, if not thousands, of soldiers with publicly acknowledged gender dysphoria continued to work in the military while legally ineligible to do so—at a time it was against official military policy to employ transgender soldiers. That means that dozens, if not hundreds, of military officers also knowingly defied military policy—and therefore their oaths to obey their commanders, especially their commander in chief, as prescribed in the Constitution.

Corporate media and Hollywood publicized stories of transgender soldiers while US policy still stated that gender dysphoria disqualified a person from the military. An early instance was a 2016 *Business Insider* profile of an Army soldier who came out as transgender after his divorce and while deployed to Afghanistan. The article notes that transgender affiliation was a "dischargeable offense" at the time and reports he was openly flouting that regulation. Patricia "King is overwhelmingly positive about how the US army treated her [sic] after coming out as transgender," *Business Insider* reported. "She [sic] said that by coming out after having built a long and respected career, her peers, subordinates and leaders met the news with 'an outpouring of support.'"[51]

In 2015, the *New York Times* website published a short documentary about two cohabiting transgender soldiers who were also publicly flouting military policy. "Remarkably, after telling his [sic] leaders and some peers that his sex was assigned female at birth, he [sic] received their support—despite military policy that prevents transgender people from serving openly," the *Times* article accompanying the video notes.[52]

In 2017, the *Army Times* published an empathetic profile of a twenty-two-year-old Army soldier, Alex Ketchum, who "started her [sic] transition" more than a year before the Obama administration decided to use US military coffers to pay for mutilating transgender enlistees. "Though trans service members were officially banned prior to 2016, many troops were able to take hormones and begin their transitions while serving," the *Army Times* noted.[53]

The article also disclosed that Ketchum's commanding officer, Captain Tony Nguyen, told Ketchum he could serve while transgender as long as he met Army fitness standards for men. Nguyen "ran his plan up the chain of command" and that command approved—again while the military officially banned transgender soldiers from service. Nguyen also disclosed that his commanding officer didn't tell his own senior officers about the breach of policy "until the Army policy came out" allowing actions that they had taken a year before.

Ketchum even disclosed that his transgender status had damaged his unit's cohesion: "Ketchum took exception to a discussion between two other soldiers [about his gender dysphoria], and it escalated to throwing fists. A similar thing happened at their battalion Christmas run."

The 2018 documentary *Transmilitary* won the audience award at the South by Southwest festival (SXSW).[54] The film focuses on four transgender soldiers: Senior Airman Logan Ireland, Corporal Laila Villanueva, Captain Jennifer Peace, and First Lieutenant El Cook. Its IMDB page claimed that at the time the film was made, "Around 15,500 transgender people serve in the US military (notably the largest transgender employer in the US)." Even presuming that was exaggerated, along the lines of other data inflation from leftists,[55] that still suggests a large number of insubordinate soldiers and supervising officers.

SPARTA felt comfortable enough to publish profiles of at least ten transgender soldiers—including their names and commands—in 2019, while the policy was still in effect.[56]

Promoting Incompetent Liars

Many of these insurrectionary soldiers were rewarded instead of sanctioned. Biden's administration, for example, nominated SPARTA founding president Brenda Sue Fulton to be an assistant defense secretary in 2021. Fulton was part of the first homosexual couple to marry in West Point's chapel, in 2012.[57] After, she was a "key figure" in pushing Bill Clinton to violate federal laws banning homosexuals from military service, she had been appointed the "first openly gay" member of the West Point Board of Visitors, says the *Military Times*. Fulton's nomination to Defense stalled because of tweets in which she called the Republican Party "racist" and Christian ideas "twisted." So the Biden administration installed her at Veterans Affairs in a PR position not subject to Senate confirmation.[58]

Perhaps the most ridiculous example of failing liars upward is Rachel Levine, a transgender health official. In 2021, Joe Biden swore Levine in as a four-star admiral in the federal health bureaucracy, the highest US position ever held by a transgender person. Levine left a troubled health agency in Pennsylvania responsible for sending COVID-positive elderly people back into nursing homes—potentially the riskiest possible COVID policy.[59]

USA Today named Levine "woman of the year" in 2022.[60] Two Republican senators—Susan Collins and Lisa Murkowski—voted Levine's confirmation across the finish line.

Levine never served in the real military.[61] He now leads the Public Health Service Commissioned Corps. No average American would consider that a branch of the US military (and most have probably never heard of it). The federal government claims PHSCC as one of the "eight uniformed services," but this section of the US Department of Health and Human Services consists entirely of noncombatant commissioned officers, with no enlistees or warrant officers. As an "admiral," Levine commands no ships.

Four-star is currently the highest rank in the US military. While General George Patton was kicking tail and taking names in World War II, he was a three-star general. So Levine outranks Patton at the height of the latter's world-saving warfighting. As retired Army Ranger John Lucas wrote of Levine, "promotion to the four-star level normally indicates decades of military service, often in dangerous and life-threatening circumstances, and military achievements of the highest order. Levine does not remotely merit any comparison with these or any of the other accomplished four-star officers, whether admirals or generals."[62]

Just as Levine is not really a woman or an admiral, PHSCC is not really a branch of the military. Like Levine, it just engages in stolen military valor and military cosplay. What a fitting branch to be run by a man pretending to be a woman, a licensed physician who believes that mutilating children equals health care.[63]

How can anyone take seriously any health directives from people who so deeply subordinate reality to political lies? And how deeply offensive to rank a mentally unstable and professionally incompetent man above soldiers who have endured multiple deployments for their country.

This is a humiliation ritual. Promoting a man like Levine above soldiers who bled for their country gut-punches the people who put their lives at risk defending America. It is a display of hierarchy, a clear signal that the Pride regime rewards sexual decadence above competence, dedication, sacrifice, honor, and truth-telling—in short, prefers vice above virtue.

A nation that rewards vice and punishes virtue is a weak nation. And our enemies know it. Russian propaganda videos have used leftist insanity in its attempts to demoralize Americans. A 2022 video shows a Russian couple immigrating to the United States. They are made to bow to a black man because of his skin color, stop eating meat because it offends vegetarians, and sit next to a transgender female who says she's married to a woman.[64] The video ends with the couple parachuting out of a plane back to Russia.

Chinese-owned TikTok is also known to push gender-confused content on children. It's a font of pro-transgender videos that trans kids credit with pushing them into this destructive identity.[65] The Chinese are well aware transgender content destabilizes American culture and weakens our families.[66]

It's not clear which American leaders also know this, and which are simply dupes and narrative-obeying midwits. It often seems the two coincide.

Lying to Congress about Military Drag

In 2023, Biden Defense Secretary Lloyd Austin told Congress the US military does not sponsor drag performances. That is false. And it's a crime to lie to Congress.

"Drag queen story hours is not something that the department funds," Austin told the House Armed Services Committee in a March 29 hearing. Representative Matt Gaetz immediately replied to provide evidence that the testimony was false, citing multiple drag events that had occurred on bases and with US military approval. Yet Austin continued to deny military support for the events. [67]

The US Navy also allegedly misrepresented its sexual programming to elected officials. Representative Jim Banks says Navy officials lied to him about their "digital ambassador" program hiring a homosexual, "nonbinary" soldier who performs in drag for military PR.[68] Banks, a Navy reserve officer and combat veteran, serves on the House Armed Services Committee. After the Navy told lawmakers they weren't promoting drag, in May 2023 the X account Libs of TikTok posted videos of Joshua Kelley posing in drag as a Navy "digital ambassador."[69] In the ensuing firestorm, the Navy claimed it was a pilot program and canceled it.[70]

As "Harpy Daniels," Kelley had performed in drag for US troops on the carrier USS *Ronald Reagan* in 2017 and 2018—years before Navy officials and Secretary Austin told their overseeing members of Congress that the US military wasn't promoting drag.[71] Kelley performed in drag again in 2022 at a US air base, an event base commander Colonel Gregory Beualieu paid for with taxpayer funding, according to Gaetz.[72] According to *Daily Wire* reporting, some of these military drag events advertised "bouncy houses and face painting for the children" and promised "the first 25 children will be gifted goodie-bags."[73]

"My command alone has given me the most support," Kelley told the *Navy Times*.[74] In multiple media interviews, Kelley said the Navy has fully supported his public sexual displays.[75] "The amount of support the Navy has given me is spectacular," he said in a glowing profile for the USS *Constitution* Museum, which rents its facilities from the National Park Service.[76] As a soldier, Kelley headed PR for the Reagan carrier's Gay, Lesbian and Supporting Sailors activist group and won $1,000 in Navy Exchange dollars in a lip sync competition[77] in which he performed in drag with the approval of his commanding officers, he said.[78]

The head of Navy recruiting, Rear Admiral Lex Walker, puts his pronouns in his email signature and has told soldiers that the Harpy Daniels events are part of US military "diversity, equity, and inclusion" efforts.[79]

According to the pro-transgender site Military.com, "In the US military, the first on-base drag show is believed to have been held at Kadena Air Base, Japan, in 2014."[80] In 2021, Nellis Air Force base in Nevada held a drag show featuring performers from Las Vegas.[81] That base includes the US Air Force Warfare Center, the world's largest advanced air combat training center.[82] According to base communications, "approximately 180 people" attended the show. Base leadership defended the drag performance as "providing and championing an environment that is characterized by equal opportunity, diversity and inclusion."[83]

Go Woke, Get Smoked

The Navy experimented with the drag "ambassador" amid its worst recruiting year in all-volunteer US military history. In 2023, officials testified to Congress that all branches of the US military, except the Marines, were projected to be significantly short of recruiting targets that fiscal year.[84] Before that, 2022 had been the toughest recruiting year since the ending of the draft in 1973, military officials and analysts said.[85]

In 2022, the Navy met its active-duty targets but failed to meet officer and reserve targets, even after upping potential enlistment bonuses to $50,000 and student loan payoffs to $65,000,[86] ending its ban on recruits with proven marijuana use and tattoos, lowering intelligence test standards, and raising the entry age to forty-one.[87]

The Army missed its recruiting target by 25 percent in 2022 despite also lowering standards. In February 2024, the Army announced cutting forces by 24,000 soldiers on account of ongoing failures to recruit to full capacity.[88] This locks the US military into a catch-22 that endangers national security: dangerously low numbers of recruits, or dangerously low standards.

"I've been studying the recruiting market for about 15 years, and we've never seen a condition quite like this," a DoD official told the *Wall Street Journal* in June 2023.[89] These dramatic recruiting dives followed lockdowns that damaged Americans' physical and mental readiness for military service, military purges of conservatives using the COVID vaccine mandate, the devastating US withdrawal from Afghanistan, a new US war against Russia—and a dramatic increase in military branding efforts touting the Pride flag.

In June 2023, Gallup reported only 60 percent of Americans polled expressing either "a great deal" or "quite a lot" of confidence in the US military.[90] It was the lowest level that Gallup had measured since 1997. The largest decline in confidence occurred among self-described Republicans. Their confidence declined from 91 percent in 2020 to 68 percent in 2023.

Vilifying the Top Category of Combat Recruits

US military leaders have openly vilified white heterosexual male soldiers, a practice that would be vociferously criticized as bigoted if applied to black or homosexual recruits. Air Force recruiting head Major General Ed Tomah stated in 2020 that the branch would "concentrate our efforts in traditionally underserved communities," and if a recruiter was getting too many white males, that recruiter would target places there aren't as many.[91] In 2022, amid the recruiting crisis, the Air Force set goals of reducing white officer candidates from 80 percent to 67.5, and male officer applicants from 72 percent to 64.[92]

The Biden administration said it would only promote officers who support identity politics.[93] In 2023, for chairman of the joint chiefs of staff, Biden nominated the Air Force general who was pivotal in increasing identity policies. General Charles Brown has many times publicly endorsed using race, sexual preference, and sex as key criteria for military promotions.[94]

These efforts at "diversity" demonize and alienate the majority of current troops and the historically best source of US military recruitment. Nearly 80 percent of US enlistees are family of current service members or veterans. Most also come from the conservative-friendly American South. The families that compose the vast majority of troop recruitment, the *Wall Street Journal* reported, increasingly believe the US military has betrayed them and will betray their children.[95]

Pride messaging fuels that feeling of betrayal. A 2023 survey of active-duty soldiers found 80 percent agreed that "the changing of policy to allow unrestricted service by transgender individuals" decreased their trust in the military.[96] Sixty-eight percent said this kind of military politicization would "somewhat" or "significantly" affect whether they'd encourage their children to enlist.

In 2023, the Army's assistant secretary blamed recruitment problems on those *publicizing* the military's morale-killing identity policies instead of on the policies themselves. Christine Wormuth told reporters, "That drip, drip, drip of criticism about a 'woke military,' I do think is having some counterproductive effects on recruiting."[97]

Identity politics repels the very people who make up the vast majority of combat enlistments: conservative, white, heterosexual men. Identity politics treats the straight white male as the source of all evil and the very bottom of its oppression matrix. Unfortunately for all who benefit from the world's best military, the men we rely on to keep American safe are being demonized by the very armed forces that cannot function without their skill, readiness, competence, and willingness to sacrifice.

"It would, candidly, be entirely rational for conservative families to tell their children not to enlist in the current ideological climate," says Aaron Renn. "Particularly for the young white male, who is the bête noire of our elite today, it's not clear why he would want to sign up to get killed or maimed to advance the agenda of those who think he's the problem in our society."[98]

Military Propaganda Pushes the Rainbow

Military public relations have promoted queer troops since the Obama administration ended President Clinton's contrary-to-law[99] "don't ask, don't tell" policy in 2010.[100] Corporate media have promoted queer troops since the 1950s.[101] The US Department of Defense has publicly observed pride month since 2012.[102]

These PR efforts include cutesy profiles of homosexual and transgender troops, written by military communications staff and published on US military websites, complete with photo shoots. These PR efforts promote virtual and in-person military Pride Month events,[103] profiles of transgender servicemen telling their coming-out stories,[104] and complaints against the US military for "discrimination."[105] It amounts to taxpayer-sponsored activism on behalf of non-heterosexual sexual encounters that have nothing to do with military service.

The title of a notorious 2023 US Army public affairs article was, "Living Authentically Saves Soldier's Life." It opens, "Coming out as a transgender female saved Maj. Rachel Jones' life." The article explains that Jones struggled with mental illnesses for years, but now that he's "living her truth" as a transgender woman, he is "no longer battling depression or suicidal thoughts."

"Once the ban on transgender service members was lifted, Jones was finally able to come out publicly as transgender. She was met with nothing but acceptance by her peers and fellow ASC Soldiers," wrote Sarah Patterson,[106] an award-winning civilian Army communications specialist.[107] The article is accompanied by a photo shoot showing a man with an aging square male face under a balding pate holding two rainbow flags while wearing his Army uniform.[108]

These PR efforts celebrate LGBT messaging and events on military properties as central to command's desired military culture. A prominent example is the 2021 christening of the Navy fleet oiler USS *Harvey Milk*, named after a San Francisco homosexual who abused underage youth.[109] Milk served in the Navy in the 1950s.[110]

Secretary of the Navy Carlos Del Toro said that naming a warship after the pederast "helps right the wrongs of the past and shows a commitment to current and future LGBTQ service members," reported NPR.[111] In June 2023, the X account @realtrmlx posted pictures of large rainbow-filled displays celebrating Harvey Milk and the USS *Harvey Milk* at Fort Novosel in Alabama. The display was stamped with the words "Department of Defense Pride Month Celebration June 2023" and the insignia of every service branch.[112]

In June 2023, @realtrmlx also posted pictures of the children's section of the library at Laughlin Air Force Base in Texas. The wall was decorated with the slogan "Find your Pride!" and the books set out for children included *Bad Gays: A Homosexual History, This Book Is Gay* by Juno Dawson, *Queer As All Get-Out*, and *It Doesn't Have to Be Awkward*, by Dr. Drew and Paulina Pinsky.[113] Remember, in 2023 every Democrat in the House voted for this.[114]

The US National Guard featured a transgender spokesman in 2023. In a recruiting ad, Captain Nicole Wiswell, a man, says he joined the Guard after "Don't ask, don't tell" was repealed. "Gender doesn't matter," he says in the video. Wiswell is a diversity officer in Minnesota's National Guard.[115]

The 2021 Army recruiting ad featured Corporal Emma Malonelord. As the face of the US Army, Malonelord narrates her childhood as a girl "raised by two moms" over a cartoon showing her beaming at their wedding. She likens LGBT activism to "fighting for freedom" in the Army by manning (irony intended) Patriot Missile Defense Systems.

The Army disabled public comment on the YouTube ad after it received more than 36,000 dislikes and only 775 likes.[116]

Woke Military Academies

The military is flush with identity indoctrination, and it has been for decades. That's where these woke generals get their start, promotions, and confirmation in cultural Marxism.

When the US Supreme Court ruled in 2023 that selecting college students by race is unconstitutional, it irrationally exempted US military academies. Biden's Solicitor General Elizabeth Prelogar had argued to the Court that military academies needed to discriminate to ensure a "racially diverse" officer corps.

Not only do the academies openly employ racist criteria to select officers,[117] they also teach students to worship the entire pantheon of identity gods. Take the Air Force Academy as a case study. Air Force Academy recruits have reported that their DEI trainings on American taxpayers' dime included prohibitions on calling their parents "mom" and "dad." The Academy told cadets that was "divisive language because everyone might not have a mom and a dad."[118] After these reports became public, the military began marking its DEI training materials "classified" so that cadets would face legal and military penalties for disclosing them.[119]

The US Air Force Academy offers a "diversity, equity, and inclusion" minor to cadets studying to become the nation's next generation of military leaders. The academy's DEI office "resources" include a White House video telling kids how to come out as LGBT, featuring Air Force Lieutenant Colonel Bree Fram,[120] a trans man with a curly bob wearing a female dress uniform in the propaganda video.[121]

In a leaked video of a 2023 DEI conference at the Air Force Academy, a cadet asks a presenter how to keep the DEI instruction he's receiving at public expense from being exposed to the public and elected oversight: "Can cadets and service academies safeguard the teachings of these topics, or, if we get a particularly bad batch of Congressman, are these teachings like screwed?"

As Representatives Mike Waltz and Jim Banks noted, "The apparent failure of any senior officer to correct the highly inappropriate behavior of scorning lawful, civilian authorities amounts to turning a blind eye to conduct that could be a violation of Article 88 of the UCMJ [Uniform Code of Military Justice]."[122] It is no wonder that a cadet like this would come out of an academy that forcefully promotes DEI ideology.

Several Air Force Academy professors have a record of sexually extreme scholarship.

Assistant sociology professor Joseph Currin's research interests include "how people explore their sexuality," according to his Air Force Academy bio.[123] His recent "research" includes journal articles titled, "'Horny and Wanting to Watch Something': An Exploratory Qualitative Analysis of Heterosexual Men's Pornography Viewing Preferences" (2022);[124] "'That Was Fun, I Gotta Run': Comparing Exit Strategies of a One-Time Sexual Encounter to Buyer–Seller Relationship Dissolution" (2021)[125]; and, in the *Journal of Homosexuality*, "Sex-Ed without the Stigma: What Gay and Bisexual Men Would Like Offered in School Based Sex Education" (2020).[126]

None of these "studies" meets high-quality standards for social science research—starting with their abysmally small sample sizes. One might be forgiven for concluding that they're not really research, but simply taxpayer-funded propaganda for sexual extremism being laundered through the US military.

Currin's "studies" also include several on how to facilitate HIV-positive sex through government payments for a drug called PrEP, which reduces the likelihood of HIV transmission during sex with HIV-positive people. In September 2018 the Association of LGBT Issues in Counseling gave Currin its "Outstanding Contribution to Public Health" award.[127]

In her coauthored chapter on "Sexuality in the Military" in the 2013 book *International Handbook on the Demography of Sexuality*, current Air Force associate professor Karin De Angelis complained about "a military culture that privileges heteronormative masculinity" and pushed for increased female and homosexual recruitment.[128]

De Angelis also coauthored a chapter on "Lesbian and Gay Service Members and Their Families" for the 2017 book *Inclusion in the American Military: A Force for Diversity*. The coauthors praise military observances of Pride month, President Obama appointing an "openly gay man" as Secretary of the Army, and adding sexual orientation complaints to federal nondiscrimination investigatory powers.

"The military has generally attempted to reproduce itself demographically as heterosexual, white, and male while also preventing equality of opportunity and service for other minority groups," De Angelis and her coauthor write, providing no citations for this smear.[129]

A study by military academics published in 2023 found that 49.7 percent of the military academy and ROTC students sampled already opposed a military ban on transgender soldiers.[130] The study by taxpayer-funded academics also explored how to change other service members' minds to support trans soldiers.

"[O]ur military sample represent the future leaders of the military," the study noted. "Those who advance to flag rank will serve into the 2050s. If they retain these inclusive attitudes, the future integration of transgender people into active duty will be eased."

The study concluded that the young soldiers' patriotic support for the concept of civil rights should be harnessed to manipulate them, by telling them transgender people's civil rights are damaged if they're prohibited from military service. Nobody makes this claim about people with poor eyesight or ADHD, whose pre-existing health conditions also disqualify them from military service. But who needs facts and reason when you're deploying propaganda?

Diverting Military Resources
to Mutilating American Soldiers

Under Joe Biden's presidency, US military resources are being diverted from national security to deform the bodies of American troops. A transgender Air Force soldier stated on TikTok, "Long story short, if I get top surgery through the military, it's free."[131]

That soldier changed her name to Emmett Connell and uses her TikTok account to "document" her transgender mutilation facilitated by the US military. She wears her uniform while giving social media updates about the body changes she's experiencing while on high doses of taxpayer-funded testosterone.

The military has a "really, really nice" gender clinic in San Antonio, Texas, where it sends soldiers for taxpayer-paid genital mutilation, she explains. Military medical staff create plans for gender-dysphoric soldiers that include placing them on opposite-sex hormones for several months before scheduling sometimes multiple genital-mutilation surgeries, according to Connell: "Some things are recommendations as far as surgeries go and some things are necessary . . . hysterectomy or bottom surgery [attaching a fake penis], I need to wait at minimum twelve months on hormones and with 'real-life experience.'"

"By the time you get to the clinic, things move fast," Connell says.[132] She was on testosterone starting in March 2023 and scheduled for a double mastectomy eight months later, on December 6. In between, Connell showed on her channel, she went to dozens of medical appointments, including several for which the military flew her to Texas for pre-operative assessments.[133]

Military policies from 2023 define as "medically necessary" the surgical removal of healthy genitals and construction of genitals that somewhat appear like those of the opposite sex.[134] Gender-dysphoric soldiers can also get taxpayer-provided "facial feminization surgery," voice coaching, and laser hair removal.[135] Even before getting mastectomies, hysterectomies, and vaginoplasties, dysphoric soldiers are granted an "exception to policy" that allows them to sleep, shower, and defecate in opposite-sex facilities while retaining their original genitals.[136]

In approximately a year and a half after Obama okayed transgender troops, taxpayers paid $8 million for "22,992 psychotherapy visits, 9,321 prescriptions for hormones" and "103 breast reductions or mastectomies, 37 hysterectomies, 17 'male reproductive' procedures and four breast augmentations," according to *USA Today*.[137] These few surgeries, from July 2016 to February 2019, cost more than $2 million, the paper said. Since then, many more troops have sought taxpayer-provided transgender interventions.

Insulting and Harassing Female Soldiers

In 2017, the Army told female soldiers in trainings to get used to sharing showers and bedrooms with transgender men. That included men who retained male genitals, as most transgender people do not amputate their original sex organs or construct fake ones.[138] The military now houses and bathrooms people according to their gender identity, not their sex.[139]

The training informed women soldiers that they might have to observe half-naked men peeing into a cup or allow a man to watch them pee into a cup for mandatory drug screenings. The trainings informed soldiers that any objection to men watching women urinate could make them liable for harassment charges.

In 2023, under President Biden's orders, the scenario in this training session became real. In a July 2023 hearing, Senator Mike Rounds of South Dakota entered reports of an eighteen-year-old female National Guard recruit who had been forced to shower and sleep next to transgender men at basic training.[140] The young woman had to sleep between these men who had penises, Rounds said.[141]

In that same hearing, Joint Chiefs nominee General Charles Q. Brown Jr. pledged allegiance to the "diversity, equity, and inclusion" initiatives he forwarded as head of the US Air Force. In 2022, Brown had signed memos dedicating the Air Force to recruiting people based on their sex, sexual orientation, and race.[142] Senators noted that Brown had also publicly stated in 2020 that he hires and promotes staff based on "diversity"—which means their sexual preferences, sex, and race.

Not only is this unjust; it's dangerous. Choosing and elevating military personnel according to non-professional metrics such as sexual behavior, instead of their competence, endangers US national security.

Assisting in the Mutilation of US Soldiers' Kids

Under Biden, the US military appears to be making every effort possible to promote transgenderism. This even extends to hijacking a program for soldiers with special needs children. In 2022, the Air Force began altering duty assignments to keep soldiers' kids' transgender treatments flowing.[143]

The program was created to reduce the turnover in medical teams for special-needs kids whose parents are soldiers. Absent any act of Congress authorizing this, branches of the US military began to categorize transgenderism as a disability in order to bestow these privileges on service members with trans kids. This keeps soldiers with transgender kids from deploying or following their units to states that do not facilitate transgender interventions, further damaging military readiness in service of LGBT politics.

US taxpayers not only lose the availability of soldiers with transgender kids through this carveout, they also pay for transgender interventions for soldiers' kids through TRICARE military health care.

"In 2017, when TRICARE began offering sex change interventions, at least twenty-five hundred children of military parents put in for gender dysphoria benefits through TRICARE insurance, according to a study published in JAMA Pediatrics. About nine hundred received the puberty blocker GnRH-a or sex change hormones," reported *The Daily Caller* in 2023.[144]

Clear Damage to US National Security

Like putting women on the front lines, allowing transgender soldiers reduces US military readiness and effectiveness. "Once a woman becomes pregnant she is lost to the command for 20 months."[145] The same is true of gender-dysphoric soldiers, who are unable to deploy for eighteen months to two years as they phase in opposite-sex hormones and undergo genital amputations or construction.

Even after they phase in hormones, transgender recruits may not be deployable, because of mental illness and because their prescriptions can't be administered under battle conditions. Some of those medicines, for example, require constant refrigeration.

Extremely high rates of mental illness among gender dysphoric people are well-established. That fact is even accepted by trans activists, who claim it's because of social disapproval. Military data released in February 2018 "showed that from October 1, 2015, to October 3, 2017, 994 active-duty Service members diagnosed with gender dysphoria accounted for 30,000 mental health visits. . . . More importantly, service members with gender dysphoria were found to be eight times more likely to attempt suicide than service members as a whole (12% vs. 1.5%)."[146]

Gender dysphoria usually has comorbidities, or coexisting mental disorders that include suicidal ideation, trauma, and depression[147]—conditions that make a soldier ineligible for service. The reason is simple: people with poor mental health are not capable of serving well in the military, which can be a highly stressful job. Transgender soldiers can be indefinitely released from meeting military fitness standards through a waiver they can renew every six months without limit, reported investigative reporter Jordan Schactel in 2023.

"Service members who identify as transgender will be considered 'non-deployable' for up to 300 days while taking hormones for their 'transition' period," Schactel reported, based on military documents. "Again, given that these hormones are often required for life, this may render the transgender identifying service member as permanently unable to deploy."[148]

After their medical procedures, commanders are required to give transgender soldiers up to twelve months of paid time off and periods of "light duty," as another military document that Schactel published shows.[149]

Since the Biden administration publicly welcomed transgender people into the military, the number of transgender soldiers has increased exponentially. According to military records, 19 troops identified as transgender in 2016. In 2020, it was 124. In 2021, after Biden repealed the transgender ban, that number was 284. Then in 2022, it was 436.[150] That's a nearly 2,300 percent increase from 2016 to 2022. In lawsuits, activists claim one in five US transgender people are veterans.[151]

Transgender soldiers' mental and physical problems affect entire units. One person who commits suicide increases the likelihood that people who know him will also. Units need every member to perform his carefully trained functions for optimal battle readiness. When one soldier is lost to pregnancy, serious illness, or gender reassignment, it affects the entire unit for one to two years.[152]

This is why militaries enforce exacting mental and physical standards. People who have asthma, diabetes, or heart conditions, for example, are at a much higher risk of serious physical damage and therefore of setting back their units. All are ineligible for the US military.[153] And nobody is complaining about their exclusion or ridiculously claiming it violates these Americans' civil rights.

Biden administration military documents confirm the level of privileges afforded to transgender soldiers, all on taxpayers' time and dime. US tax dollars are paying for transgender soldiers to get cross-sex hormones, laser hair removal, voice alteration therapy and surgery, facial and body contouring, breast and penis amputation, and psychological therapy.[154]

"Precious time and money are being poured into woke programs and projects that would be better applied towards making the military more capable," explains Thomas Spoehr, a retired Army lieutenant general who now runs the Heritage Foundation's Center for National Defense.[155]

Weakening units and low recruitment can develop into an existential threat to US national security. As the *Wall Street Journal* reported, of recruiting struggles, "Readiness shortfalls can be masked when units aren't headed into war, but a full-scale response, such as what would be needed in the Pacific, could expose undermanned units that can't be deployed or aren't effective, and ships and aircraft that aren't combat ready due to a lack of personnel to maintain them."[156]

Absolutely, every American should serve his country. But every American is not eligible to do so in the military. Why are transgender recruits an exception? It's simple: politics. America's leaders are damaging our national security for the sake of power.

A "Category One Insurrection"

US military installations and embassies all over the world have been flying the Pride flag alongside the American flag since 2011. US embassies and military bases had never flown flags for other special interest groups or voting blocs, such as Orthodox Jews, Southern Baptists, or the Black Panthers.

But the Pride flag, for some reason, gets to sit beside or even fly in place of the American flag every June over US embassies across the world. In 2021, Biden Secretary of State Antony Blinken authorized embassies to fly Black Lives Matter flags alongside Pride flags.[157] Flying these flags symbolically indicates a transfer of allegiance from one flag's ideals to the other's.

It's not just symbolic. What the Pride flag stands for has provoked decades of unlawful and unseemly defiance against the US chain of command. According to The U.K. newspaper *The Independent*, US embassies have "been raising the rainbow banner during Pride Month since 2011. In 2019, [when Trump's administration required LGBT flags to be flown separately from the American flag], many US embassies defied or found a way around the new policy, something one anonymous diplomat called a 'category one insurrection.'"[158]

The Trump administration did not even ban Pride flags. Several US embassies and military sites sported enormous Pride flags during the Trump administration. With administration approval, US Ambassador to Germany Ric Grenell, a homosexual, marched in Berlin's Pride Parade and flew Pride flags on US diplomatic property, he told NBC News.[159]

The Trump administration merely stipulated the Pride flag could not fly *on the same pole* as the official emblem of the United States. The American flag was to be paramount. That wasn't good enough for some military and diplomatic officials, who publicly defied their commander-in chief over the flag policy. There's more insurrectionary behavior.

So is the behavior of California's National Guard, which defied the Trump administration's policy to separate gender-dysphoric troops from service. A few weeks after the US Supreme Court ruled that the commander-in-chief does have the right to set military policy, the California Guard's No. 2 told a state legislative committee it would not obey that order. "Nobody's going to kick you out," Major General Matthew Beevers said to California transgender troops.[160] California Governor Gavin Newsom also defied the Trump administration's military policies, both on transgender troops and helping protect the US southern border.[161]

The National Guard is jointly run by states and the federal government. Members of the National Guard are also members of the US Army or Air Force, and they can be called up by the president.[162]

Endangering International Relations and Americans' Safety

America's adversaries constantly assess US strengths and weaknesses. When US military officials defy their chain of command, America's foes see that, accurately, as a sign of weakness. Military weakness provokes disrespect and invites foreign aggression.

Obedience to the nation's highest law and the military chain of command strengthens the United States' soft power. Soft power is a way of diffusing disagreements that could lead to hard conflict—in other words, war. It is in *everyone's* interests to avoid war whenever that's truly possible, because war means dead and traumatized people. Sometimes war is a necessary evil, and when it is necessary it should be executed resolutely, but it should be avoided whenever possible. Yet damaging foreign relations, and thus increasing the risk of international conflict, is apparently a price US military leaders are willing to pay for flying the flag that stands for erasing the constitutional rights our soldiers swear to protect.

Under the Biden administration, US embassies fly Pride flags in locales where they offend and repulse the local population, including in Vatican City,[163] multiple Muslim nations,[164] Russia, and Singapore.[165] In 2023, the American ambassador to Poland marched in Warsaw's Pride Parade to make a statement against the Polish government, a US ally.[166]

In 2020, Vladimir Putin "mocked the US embassy in Moscow for flying a rainbow flag to celebrate LGBT rights, suggesting it reflected the sexual orientation of its staff." People in many foreign countries consider the Pride flag extremely offensive to their cultural values. The head of the Women's Union of Russia, Ekaterina Lakhova, told the RIA news agency, "Even indirectly, such things make our children accustomed to that . . . flag, the one that was hung up by the embassy."[167]

Russia is out of favor as a warmongering country run by a dictator. Even so, it's an extremely arrogant posture to tell other nations what their culture should value. The United States used to respect foreigners' prerogatives to rule themselves because we wanted the same respect from them.

Just as we Americans wish to run our own affairs, make our own culture, and choose our own government policies, so we should extend the same to other nations. US diplomats are rudely disregarding this basic human courtesy by flying offensive flags in an arrogant display of cultural imperialism. This harms our ability to work with other countries to achieve mutual goals. That works against American interests, the whole goal of diplomacy.

Formerly, the Pride flag was a symbol of American occupation abroad. Now it is a symbol of domestic occupation as well. It is a flag of humiliation, of repudiation and punishment for the Americans who still cling to the original American creed, our Constitution. We are now subject to an occupying anti-American force that runs our own military.

CHAPTER 6

Feeding on Family Dysfunction

"Contemporary gays who try to distance themselves from this issue of boy-love are in effect committing cultural suicide. They're cutting themselves from all the highest achievements of gay men."

—*Camille Paglia*[1]

On the muggy evening of August 25, 2021,[2] fourteen-year-old Sage Blair cut the screen out of her bedroom window, climbed outside, and ran into the clutches of a rapist. Two weeks into her freshman year[3] at Appomattox County High School in rural Virginia,[4] the ninety-eight-pound girl was past her breaking point. School staff following LGBT protocols to divide vulnerable children from their parents contributed to her anguish, her parents say.

While an infant, Sage went through six foster homes before her grandmother, Michele, could take custody and then eventually adopt the little orphan.[5] Michele says Sage thrived in loving family care, but when puberty hit things got rough again. As she headed into high school, the slim, shy Sage was dressing "goth," skateboarding, and dyeing her forelock blue with help from her grandfather.

Peer pressure and anxiety to fit in played a part in Sage's conformist self-expression: "She started a public high school and she told me that all the girls there were bi, trans, lesbian, emo. And she wanted to wear boys' clothes and be emo. Because I saw it as just a phase, it was fine with me," Michele said later.[6]

That summer before she started high school, Sage had been hospitalized for eight days for self-harm. The 2020 lockdowns undoubtedly played a part. In fall 2021, the kids went back to school in person and didn't have to wear masks in Appomattox County public schools, but they did have to wear masks on the bus.[7] The schools distanced students' desks, staggered school pickup times, and sent home kids with coughs.[8]

The teenagers were on edge after two school years of switches between virtual and in-person learning,[9] government-demanded isolation, parents' employment uncertainty, social media bingeing that fed depression and anxiety, and extreme social discord. Amid all that, the pixie child with a history of self-harm entered a high school with approximately seven hundred other adolescents.[10]

Michele says she didn't know until after Sage ran away that in just the first twelve days of high school Sage had been called into the school counselor's office eight times, mostly about the consequences of the school affirming her gender crisis while allegedly keeping Sage's gender struggles from her adoptive parents.[11]

In a lawsuit, Michele says she didn't know Sage had tried out a gender-neutral first name, Draco, in those first few days at school. Nor did Michele know that Sage was using the boys' bathroom, allegedly on the advice of school staff.[12] According to Appomattox counselor Dena Olsen, sealed counseling notes "indicate that Olsen did not instruct [Sage] to use the male restrooms,"[13] but Michele's attorney says witnesses could testify she did.[14] The case is scheduled for a jury trial at this writing.

The Blairs say the boy's bathrooms are where a group of boys shoved Sage and threatened her with rape. School staff told Michele about none of these incidents, she alleges in a 2023 lawsuit, and Sage therefore lacked family oversight and support in her struggles. Michele's legal complaint lays out the details, which can be hard to read.

On August 25, the day Sage ran away from home, the school counselor pulled Sage into her office again to talk about groups of boys on the bus and in school bathrooms threatening to sodomize Sage and murder her and her family.[15] In that meeting, the lawsuit says, Olsen and School Resource Officer Daniel Gunter told Sage she could be prosecuted for responding to the assaults by saying that "all boys are rapists."[16] Sage's guardians were not notified of this meeting and the school failed to protect Sage from these violent sexual threats, Michele alleges.

Sage became so distraught in this meeting that the school called Michele to pick Sage up. Later that day, her mother found a hall pass listing Sage's first name as "Draco." That's when Sage told her that she was identifying as a boy, that the counselors had told her to use the boys' bathroom, and that she had been assaulted in the bathroom.[17]

Michele, a court-appointed special advocate with professional training in helping extremely distressed children, told Sage to get some sleep and they'd "figure it out in the morning." Instead, a wildly upset Sage cut her window screen out and ran away. She left a note saying she had run so schoolboys would not follow through on threats to harm her grandparents.

The lawsuit's claims are shocking. As is common with runaways, a predator picked Sage up that evening. He proceeded to rape away her virginity. She was then drugged and raped by multiple men for eight days, until Baltimore police and the FBI found her in Baltimore, Maryland, in the home of a sex offender. Yet what should have ended her victimization instead led to more trauma, all because the people who were supposed to protect her reportedly followed LGBT protocols.

After she underwent a rape exam alone, law enforcement placed Sage in solitary detention instead of releasing her to her waiting grandparents or giving her any form of post-rape care, says the lawsuit. She was held in solitary for five days while a Maryland public defender assigned to her case worked to prevent her grandparents from taking her home because they didn't "affirm" Sage's gender confusion, the lawsuit states. Michele says she couldn't affirm something she hardly knew was happening because school staff didn't disclose Sage's transgender behavior to her legal parents.

In court on September 3, public defender Aneesa Khan worked to keep Sage from going home with her grandparents after a severely traumatizing ordeal. She succeeded.

"I love you, Sage!" Michele cried when she finally saw Sage on a Zoom screen in the courtroom for the first time after her rescue. Sage responded, "I love you too, Nana!"

"She is a he, and his name is Draco, not Sage," Khan interjected.[18] To Judge Robert Kershaw, Khan accused the Blairs of physical and emotional abuse, including by "misgendering" Sage—which means calling Sage a girl. Sage later told her grandparents that Khan had told her to lie and say that they had yelled at her for being transgender, punished her in other ways for her gender identity, and made her make her own food since age eight.[19]

"We were willing to use any name and pronouns just to bring her home," Michele testified to the Virginia state legislature. But her seventy-one-year-old husband "was so tearful he kept forgetting the new pronouns," so the judge had the bailiff remove him.[20]

The judge ultimately placed Sage—a sex trafficking victim with no criminal record—in a Maryland detention center for *male* juvenile offenders. She spent two months there after her trafficking with almost zero contact with her family. Sage later alleged that she was assaulted and given illicit drugs by the juvenile offenders in the boy's home.[21]

She also "was not provided with any trauma therapy or medical care for the physical consequences of the many rapes she had suffered while being abused by sex traffickers," the lawsuit says. Khan allegedly added to Sage's abandonment and distress by lying to Sage, telling her that "her parents no longer wanted her, and Ms. Khan was going to arrange for [Sage] to live with a family in Maryland who would affirm her as a boy. [Sage] later told her mother that she missed her but tried not to think about it because she believed her mother did not want her anymore."[22]

That wasn't true, the lawsuit says. Sage's grandparents were working furiously to find lawyers and other assistance in getting Sage home. Meanwhile, they were sending her notes, stuffed animals, and other gifts, which Michele and Sage say Khan withheld from Sage, as the young trafficking victim continued to be assaulted in the male juvenile offenders' home.[23]

On November 12, 2021, Sage cut her ankle tracker and fled the group home to meet someone she thought was a sixteen-year-old boy who liked skateboarding. He turned out to be another sex trafficker. This time, Sage was trafficked to Texas and raped, drugged, and otherwise tormented in captivity for almost three more months.[24] Michele testified tearfully to the Virginia legislature that she was told Sage might be dead given how long she had been missing, but a social media tip she found finally led Texas marshals to her girl.[25]

Texas law enforcement finally reunited Sage and her grandparents, in compliance with an interstate child runaway compact that Texas, Maryland, and Virginia have all signed.[26]

"Don't Tell Your Parents" Is What Predators Say

Except for the law enforcement who rescued her twice, Michele's lawsuit charges that Sage was betrayed by essentially every public employee and institution whose moral and legal responsibility it was to protect her. Consequences like these can directly result from people and institutions adopting LGBT policies that separate children from their parents. LGBT extremists are working hard to expand these policies, with potential effects as terrifying as Sage's story for countless other children.

The very same White House whose current occupant called it "outrageous" to separate foreign children illegally entering the United States from adults they were traveling with[27] also enacted LGBT policies that divide young Americans from their own loving parents. The Human Rights Campaign's "wishlist" that the Biden administration has followed includes directives to hide children's medical care from their parents. These include requiring health insurers and Medicaid to correspond with kids about their medical treatments, not with parents.[28]

In model LGBT policies, called "Schools in Transition," from the American Civil Liberties Union, National Center for Lesbian Rights, Gender Spectrum, National Education Association teachers' union, and Human Rights Campaign activist group, schools are told to put gender-dysphoric kids in opposite-sex school bathrooms, locker rooms, and sports teams. HRC's "wishlist" also demands placing gender-confused youth in opposite-sex rooms in foster care, shelters, and youth homes. When Sage used such facilities, she was repeatedly assaulted. The "Schools in Transition" model policy recommendations

from these organizations also support schools hiding kids' gender identities from their parents,[29] a key claim of the Blairs' lawsuit.

"Any decision to raise the topic with parents must be made very
carefully and in consultation with the student. In some instances, a
school may choose not to bring the subject up if there is a concern that
parents or caregivers may react negatively," the report says.[30] "Processes
like enrollment, taking attendance, assigning grades and communicating with parents and caregivers can all easily compromise the student's
privacy and undermine an otherwise supportive school environment,"
it also notes.

"Schools in Transition" also encourages schools to give
gender-confused kids LGBT "resources." Michele Blair's lawsuit
notes counselor Avery Via, who worked at her school, directed Sage
to "pro-transgender resources including websites, social media platforms, and apps which were frequented by men who sought to harm
and traffic vulnerable girls." It's not clear if Sage encountered any
of her traffickers through these pro-trans websites, some of which
predators prowl, especially the comments sections on pro-trans social
media.

LGBT policies work to create a direct relationship between children and the government, bypassing children's parents. Common and
American law classically refrain from intruding into family matters
except in the most egregious (and rare) incidents such as incest or
violence, precisely to preserve familial autonomy and privacy. This is
why, for example, spouses cannot be compelled to testify against each
other in court. To even ask is considered abusive given the unparalleled
intimacy of the relationship. As law professor Helen Alvare notes, the
"traditional family law presumption" is "that a fit parent acts in her
child's best interests."[31]

LGBT policies flip this, starting with the opposite assumption, that
parents are likely abusers. Like totalitarianism, they seek to make even

the most intimate and private of interactions, the private sphere inside one's home and mind, subject to government micromanagement and interference. By separating children from their statistically and historically most likely protectors and advocates, totalitarian-style government always most heavily brutalizes the most vulnerable, like orphaned children struggling to emerge into adulthood. Like Sage.

Separating Kids from Loving Parents

Sexual identity politics separates children from their parents, making all children—not just orphans—effective wards of the state. This dramatically increases state power by destabilizing society. Family instability is not an accident of totalitarian government, it is its direct goal.

Demonstrating the deep commitment of pride politics to separating kids from parents, California's Attorney General Rob Bonta filed a lawsuit in August 2023 to prevent San Bernadino County schools from notifying parents if their children express gender dysphoria at school. Bonta argued that telling parents about their children's mental and medical needs violated California's constitutional equal protection clause and right to privacy.[32]

The state superintendent also publicly criticized the policy at a school board meeting while parents booed him down.[33] A judge granted the state a preliminary injunction pausing the school policy while the attorney general's lawsuit proceeds.

This is a preposterous position, morally, practically, and legally. It pretends schools have a right to keep secrets about children from their own parents.[34] It's based on the assumption that children belong to government, not to their families. That's a totalitarian idea voiced in, among other seminal texts, Karl Marx's "Communist Manifesto" and Black Lives Matter position statements.[35] Marx calls "abolition of the family" an "infamous proposal of the Communists."[36]

California's Democrat-controlled legislature worked to codify this totalitarian stance into state law, pausing its passage to do more polling on how to lie to the public about this policy after parents went ape in local school board meetings.[37] The legislature also passed bills to secretly expose kids to sexual information, including to require every public school to stock explicit gay sex books and to allow children twelve to eighteen to seek "mental health care" without their parents' knowledge or consent. That "health care" could include removing themselves from their parent's homes for "residential shelter."[38] The Democrat-controlled legislature and governor passed both into law.[39]

Eyeing a presidential bid, Gov. Gavin Newsom vetoed AB 957, which a California school board president told media "would make any parent who doesn't affirm transgenderism for their child guilty of child abuse under California state law."[40] The bill says "the health, safety, and welfare of the child includes, among other comprehensive factors, a parent's affirmation of the child's gender identity or gender expression." Every Democrat in the state Assembly and Senate voted for the bill except one Democrat state senator.[41]

In January 2024, Oregon banned a mother from adopting children because of her Christian beliefs about sex. Oregon considers prospective parents child abusers if they cannot promote transgenderism to children.[42] In 2023, while more than 1,500 Massachusetts children couldn't find foster homes and were therefore housed in hospital wards, the state denied a Catholic couple a foster care license because of their traditional beliefs about sex and gender.[43] Vermont implemented a similar policy in 2020.[44]

In fall 2023, the Democrat White House released a similar nationwide policy, stating it would consider foster families child abusers if they do not use false pronouns and assist in transgender mutilation, even of very young children.

"[T]o be considered a safe and appropriate placement, a provider is expected to utilize the child's identified pronouns, chosen name, and allow the child to dress in an age-appropriate manner that the child believes reflects their self-identified gender identity and expression," the proposed regulations state. As Nathanael Blake noted, "Once they have set this point, they'll expand it to everyone else—after all, if it's abuse for foster parents, it's abuse for biological parents as well."[45]

The proposal estimates it would cost more than $40 million over its first three years to recruit foster families who will comply with the requirements.[46] This amid pre-existing shortages of foster families nationwide due to open borders furthering family-destroying addictions.

"If it is legally established that not affirming a child's LGBTQI+ identity constitutes 'mistreatment' or 'abuse,' this standard could have massive ramifications for families seeking to adopt, biological parents of children both in and out of foster care, and individuals who work with children," wrote lawyer Rachel Morrison in an analysis of the rule.[47]

While the rule technically would exempt religious families and foster agencies, it would result in government discrimination against Christians while also reducing the homes available to desperately needy children, say foster care advocates: "While some governments may continue to place some children in families through these [Christian] agencies, it seems likely that the new two-class system would promote both implicit and explicit bias against these agencies," says the Christian Alliance for Orphans.[48]

Loving Parents Lose Custody for Not Hopping aboard the Trans Train

In his veto message on AB 957, Newsom noted that courts are already taking kids from parents who don't enable their gender confusion: "a court, under existing law, is required to consider a child's health, safety, and welfare when determining the best interests of a child in these proceedings, including the parent's affirmation of the child's gender identity."[49] Because courts are already charging child abuse based on whether a parent assists his or her own child in living as the opposite sex, Newsom concluded a new law wasn't necessary to get that outcome.[50]

Perhaps the most famous case of this is of James Younger, a Texas twin boy his mother began dressing in girl clothes at age six. James's father, who says James chose boy clothing when visiting him,[51] lost custody of James because he didn't want his six-year-old son put on track for chemical and possibly surgical castration. A Democrat judge made the ruling.[52]

More than a thousand US school districts' LGBT policies state they'll keep a child's gender dysphoria secret from his parents, according to data from Parents Defending Education. Those thousand school districts teach 10.7 million American kids.[53] PDE notes their list is not exhaustive, meaning it's likely many more districts do the same.

The Michigan Department of Education trained its employees and school employees around the state to conceal children's gender confusion from their parents. Black lesbian presenter Amorie Robinson tells teachers to erase kids' understanding of two sexes and replace it with the falsehoods that "gender is fluid" and "nonbinary."[54]

Of US school districts that oversee more than one hundred thousand students, 79 percent employ a "chief diversity officer" and have installed "diversity, equity, and inclusion" programming, the Heritage Foundation documented in 2021.[55] Such districts also likely hide children's gender confusion from their parents. In fact, it's common in public schools to hide not just LGBT identification but also related curricular materials from parents.

A Maryland court told families they cannot opt their children out of reading obscene materials as part of sex and gender identity instruction in public schools. The lawsuit arose after parents discovered their children were being given queer books that teach kids about topics including transvestites and oral sex as early as preschool.[56]

"With respect to familial material presented outside of sex education courses, lower courts have held that parents who send children to public schools are subject to state decision-making about educational content," notes law professor Helen Alvare.[57]

The Democrat-controlled state of Washington passed a law in 2023 that would hide runaway children from their parents in the state's foster system if the children sought an abortion or transgender mutilation and their parents disagreed. "No allegation of abuse in the household is required" now for the state of Washington to hide children from any state in the union from their own parents, says legal analyst Sarah Parshall Perry.[58]

These are called LGBT "sanctuary state" or "trans refuge" proposals. California's senate also passed one[59] that is likely to become law.[60] According to ABC News, so have the legislatures of New York, Minnesota, Colorado, Connecticut, and New Mexico.[61] Several LGBT activist organizations announced in 2022 that homosexual and transsexual lawmakers have introduced such legislation in nineteen states: California, Colorado, Connecticut, Florida, Georgia, Illinois, Kansas, Kentucky, Maine, Michigan, Minnesota, New Hampshire, New Mexico, New York, Oregon, Rhode Island, Vermont, Washington, and West Virginia.[62]

Washington's "sanctuary state" law provides up to $7.5 million to get these runaway kids transgender mutilation. Its lead bill sponsor was Democrat state Sen. Marko Liias, a homosexual and the co-chairman of the state senate's LGBTQ Caucus.[63] Like Sage, many runaway kids are quickly snapped up by sex traffickers.[64] Media telling these kids another state is a "sanctuary" for them dangles a lure that will get many trafficked into a living hell.

The bill received more than 4,700 public comments, 98 percent of them opposed. It still became law. Republican state lawmakers pointed out that at the same time Democrats worked to assist kids in obtaining transgender mutilation without their parents' knowledge, they were also pushing bills to reduce sentencing for juvenile offenders because teens' decision-making capacities aren't fully developed.[65]

Family Dysfunction Causes Identity Distress

Identity politics both separates families and results from separated families. As scholar Mary Eberstadt demonstrates, identity politics is one consequence of dysfunctional families.

Relationship trauma and other forms of familial chaos such as divorce often results in an affinity for identity politics, Eberstadt points out in her 2019 book, *Primal Screams*. This indicates feminism's push for no-fault divorce and erasing public acknowledgments that men and women are different have helped spawn the queer tsunami.

"Western politics is increasingly transformed by deep emotions that lie outside of politics itself,"[66] Eberstadt notes, arguing identity politics' origins are *"prepolitical."*[67] Identity politics originates and amplifies in the dramatically increased proportion of homes where children have lived without one or both of their biological parents. Because divorce and fatherlessness harms even those who don't inflict them,[68] this is now all of us.

Eberstadt identifies sexual politics as a grandchild of the sexual revolution, noting that our society's decision sixty years ago to detach sex from marriage has expanded psychic chaos among each subsequent generation. Three generations are now into their adulthoods since the advent of the Pill and widespread no-fault divorce, which separate sex from marriage and childbearing.

"Not only in the United States, but around many parts of the world, the [sexual] revolution has included the de-stigmatization of nonmarital sex in all its varieties, and a sharp rise in behaviors that were formerly rare or stigmatized or both," she notes.[69]

Primal Screams notes the sexual revolution's unprecedented damage to human societies' traditional relational ecosystems. Through reducing fertility and dividing homes, the feminist sexual revolution has deprived almost all Western people of relatives such as children, husbands, wives, fathers, mothers, siblings, uncles, aunts, cousins, grandfathers, grandmothers, and grandchildren. Eberstadt argues this massive relational dislocation causes psychic shocks by making the question *Who am I?* unanswerable.

"[P]ost revolutionary havoc has given rise to new social survival strategies, as people unmoored from kinship identity seek substitutes that will do what organic families exist to do (i.e., protect the individuals included in them)," Eberstadt posits.[70] In short, identity politics arises from people seeking substitute "families" to replace their missing and chaotic biological families. As with government attempting to replace fathers, however, dysfunctional people devising their own—mostly virtual—group homes usually goes very badly.

Identity politics is rife with immature social strategies, such as the toddler-like shrieks of "mine!" that Eberstadt suspects underly intersectional anger at, for example, "cultural appropriation." Like toddlers, identity activists throw tantrums, steal, assault, scream, and cry. Identity politics also reek of middle-school relational aggression. Regardless of what exact developmental stage a particular outrage incident foregrounds, it's all arrested development.

Trauma can cause a person to "get stuck" in behaviors from the age at which the trauma occurred. A child whose mother dies when he is in middle school or whose father leaves when he is in early elementary school often holds onto the emotional patterns and core beliefs of that age for life. Some pedophiles have told researchers they believe their sexual orientation is due to this kind of arrested development—they got stuck in sexual attractions that started in childhood.[71]

This means parents' accelerating lack of sexual self-control holds back entire generations' collective maturity. Many people who cohabit, for example, say they do so because their parents divorced and they want to avoid that suffering.[72] It's a reasonable response—for a child. Any adult, however, can see that breaking up with someone you share a home and often a child with is effectively also a divorce.

Mature adults seek the truth through conversation, maintain their own principles while seeking to understand where others differ, negotiate, listen, explain, and demonstrate with evidence. None of these is part of the identity politics movement, partly because it arises precisely from childhoods that lacked these things due to broken families. As Eberstadt notes, "great swaths of humanity are more socially illiterate than our forebears were, because the pool of those from whom we learn earliest and most naturally has diminished."[73]

Our entire society is regressing due to decades of cumulative anti-family sexual decisions endorsed and encouraged by our leaders. Sexual politics has directly caused this doom loop.

Identity Distress Causes Family Dysfunction

Identity politics also amplifies relationship dysfunction. People who buy into identity politics worsen their relationships, which affects them, their families, and society. Casting oneself as a victim based on characteristics one can't change damages people's ability to get along with others and each person's moral duty to take responsibility for his own life. For good reason, psychologists label as mental problems multiple aspects of the Left's victim complex.

These include, for example, apocalyptic thinking, a lack of agency, projection, inflexible thinking, catastrophizing, narcissism, and emotional manipulation. All these mental habits degrade people's lives rather than build them up. These mental illnesses are built directly into intersectionalism, another word for cultural Marxism. The next chapter will also look at this, but here let's note the correlations between leftist affiliation, mental illness, and family dysfunction.

The women who consider themselves the farthest left politically also report the highest rates of mental illnesses, according to a 2020 Pew study.[74] Fifty-six percent of white women ages eighteen to twenty-nine who considered themselves "liberal" instead of "moderate" or "conservative" also reported a mental health diagnosis. Conservative women in the same age group were least likely to report a mental health diagnosis, at 27 percent—or approximately half the rate.

Men are less likely than women to report mental health problems, but those identifying as the farthest left in the survey reported the highest rates of mental illnesses among men, at 33 percent for ages eighteen to twenty-nine. That means conservative young women are less likely to report a mental illness diagnosis than are young liberal men. Perhaps when mental illnesses and therapy were more stigmatized one could suggest this large gap was partly a reporting problem, but among millennials and Gen Z, therapy is practically a rite of passage instead of embarrassing,[75] so that seems less likely.

The farthest-left women are also the least likely demographic to be married.[76] Marriage has long been a predictor of political patterns, with married women as a group voting Republican and unmarried women as a group voting Democrat.[77] Marriage is also a key predictor of happiness, especially among women: "a combination of marriage and parenthood is linked to the biggest happiness dividends for women."[78] It is correlated with dozens of benefits including longevity, nutrition, resilience, and financial security.

Social science has long documented that females are far more susceptible than males to social pressure and conditioning.[79] A November 2023 AEI poll found 31 percent of Generation Z women—today's teens and twenties—identify as some form of queer. Two-thirds of that group identified as bisexual, an identification that, as explained earlier, often results from pro-queer peer pressure and conditioning, including exposure to queer pornography. Half the number of young men as young women identified as queer,[80] again indicating at least some queer identification is driven by social conditioning, which is more effective on women.

Conversely, marriage and childbirth open special windows of opportunity for repairing an adult's attachment traumas.[81] All this reinforces that adopting identity politics both reflects antipathy towards forming family bonds and reduces people's ability to heal that antipathy and trauma by forming new healthy relationships.

Political beliefs are "one of the strongest predictors" of quality parenting, itself the "most important factor in the mental health of adolescent children," writes Jonathan Rothwell, a Gallup researcher, summarizing a 2023 Gallup/Institute for Family Studies study on teen mental health. The study asked both parents and their children to report their relationship quality based on measures such as frequency of conflict and warmth.

"Conservative and very conservative parents are the most likely to adopt the parenting practices associated with adolescent mental health," he writes. "They are the most likely to effectively discipline their children, while also displaying affection and responding to their needs. Liberal parents score the lowest, even worse than very liberal parents, largely because they are the least likely to successfully discipline their children."

The study also asked whether parents support marriage by disagreeing that it is an "outdated institution," agreeing it improves relationship commitment, and hoping for their own children to marry someday. The parents who "embraced a pro-marriage view on all three" were the most effective parents, the study found.[82] They were the most likely to monitor their kids, set limits on them, proactively work through problems, and engage in family activities.

Rothwell notes that more than one thousand studies find a strong correlation between neglectful, harsh, and permissive parenting and mental illnesses among children. "Authoritative parenting," which combines both warm responsiveness and limits on negative behavior, produces the happiest children. Conservative parents are the most likely to exhibit those beneficial parenting habits.

In short, conservative views and lifestyles are correlated with happiness and social cohesion. People from broken families are more likely to adopt identity politics, and adopting identity politics worsens people's relationship health. It's a vicious cycle in which family wounds can amplify across generations.

Separating Sex from Parenting Breeds Trans Kids

Look up the life story of any transgender person. Every time you can find this information, the person has experienced serious trauma such as rape or parental abandonment including through divorce, as a Catholic pastor who ministers to transgender people also notes.[83] In a sobering illustration of the reality, sociologist Brad Wilcox notes, "children who are exposed to divorce are two to three times more likely than their peers in intact marriages to suffer from serious social or psychological pathologies."

The growth of divorce and unmarried childbearing in the United States is directly responsible for the psychological suffering contributing to increasing numbers of Americans identifying as queer. Compared to their parents, Americans born after the 1960s sexual revolution were twice as likely to have experienced four or more "adverse childhood experiences" by age eighteen.[84]

ACEs are a sociological term for childhood traumas such as abuse, severe family dysfunction, neglect, divorce, witnessing violence, and going hungry for long periods. Studies have established a long list of lifelong damage inflicted by ACEs, including prolonged sadness and distress, poor health outcomes, and increased crime rates. Researchers also consistently find correlations between higher ACE scores and LGBT affiliation.[85]

The most likely source of child abuse is a mother's unmarried sexual partner.[86] Therefore, the dramatic increase in unwed childbearing since 1960 is one of the prime drivers of the increase in child abuse. This means the sexual revolution has inflicted on millions of individuals depression, drug use, suicide, domestic violence, and other horrors, as well as major costs to society such as foster care, crime, and family courts.

It's also inflicting gender dysphoria on kids struggling to cope with the traumas such as their parents' divorce and failure to marry. Searches into trans kids' backgrounds often show this is part of their story.

Queer policies that erase sexual differences, notes Boise State University professor Scott Yenor, have "coincided with the amazing rise in non-monogamous relationships, a public acceptance of alternative lifestyles even among conservative Americans, cohabitation, the sexualization of childhood, and the consumption of pornography. It has also coincided with the decline of marriage rates, marriage stability, the priority of marriage, the character necessary to sustain marriage, and birth rates."[87]

If Americans had as few unmarried mothers and divorces today as we did in 1960, estimates sociologist Paul Amato, 600,000 fewer kids would be seeing therapists, 1.2 million fewer would be suspended, 70,000 fewer would attempt suicide, and there would be 500,000 fewer acts of juvenile crime.[88] Taxpayers spend an estimated $112 billion per year, or $1 trillion per decade, to mitigate the damage of divorce and unwed childbearing, such as increased child abuse, foster care placements, theft, domestic violence, welfare programs, and family court infrastructure.[89]

"Isabel Sawhill at the Brookings Institution has concluded that virtually all of the increase in child poverty in the United States since the 1970s can be attributed to family breakdown," Wilcox notes. "Meanwhile, the dissolution of marriage in working-class and poor communities has also fueled the growth of government, as federal, state, and local governments spend more money on police, prisons, welfare, and court costs, trying to pick up the pieces of broken families."[90]

The simple fact of less time to spend with their children makes it harder for divorced and single parents to create the strong bonds necessary for their children to grow up happy. In itself, lacking a father or mother in the home traumatizes children, who are far less likely to grow up functional and happy without married parents.[91]

Eradicating unwed partnering would, then, dramatically decrease not only child abuse, but its severe social and individual effects. Those include a dramatic increase in mental illnesses that are expanding into sexual psychoses such as gender dysphoria.

Lisa Littman's Brown University study found that nearly half of children with rapid-onset gender dysphoria (48 percent) had "experienced a traumatic or stressful event prior to the onset of their gender dysphoria," such as parental divorce, a death in the family, a romantic breakup, rape or attempted rape, school bullying, family relocation, or a serious illness. Nearly half (45 percent) had been harming themselves before coming out trans.[92]

The study was based on parent reports. That means it's likely some of these kids experienced traumas their parents didn't know about, such as pornography exposure or severe bullying.

People with unstable families are at far higher risk for dysfunctional behaviors that impede their ability to run their own lives. Family dysfunction creates a demand and justification for government tyranny. As James Poulos notes, the dysfunction of the sexual revolution obliterates ideals such as marriage and its reflection of sexual differences, fostering the "age-old affinity between decadence and authoritarianism."[93] Erasing sex distinctions and marriage protections in law is directly responsible for incalculable amounts of American suffering.

"We sacrificed the happiness of children for the freedom of adults," writes blogger Rob Henderson. "And because every adult starts out as a child and carries their experiences with them, we get to live with the consequences."[94]

Extramarital Child Trafficking Erases Parental Rights

In 2023, the *Wall Street Journal* profiled a man who, through selling his sperm, has fathered ninety-six children—that he knows of. Dylan Stone-Miller quit his job and spent a year trying to find his kids through Facebook and DNA banks after he saw one of his daughters and recognized himself in her face: "He got tears, he recalled, and unexpected feelings of kinship."[95]

Some of the mothers of his children "want nothing to do with him," *WSJ* notes. They paid him $100 a pop to masturbate in a cup, not to father his children for their entire lives. Several of the single and lesbian mothers who bought Stone-Miller's formerly anonymous sperm instruct their children to call their dad "Donor," telling them, "You don't have a dad."

The article depicts a man who deeply feels his biological connection to these children whose mothers he will never love. The children feel that connection, too. They look like him and have his mannerisms, pieces of his personality. Some of them call him "Dad." But all they get of his presence in their lives is, at most, a few days a year. Stone-Miller has 96 kids and, thanks to selling his generative body parts, he can never be their dad.

"He said he tries to be fair about splitting his time with the children. He keeps a spreadsheet for their names, ages and birthdays and when he last saw or spoke with them," *WSJ* says.

Research indicates that as Stone-Miller's kids grow, lacking a connection to their father will become even more important to them, inflicting a primal loss they will feel for their entire lives. It's a fertility industry horror story.

Non-heterosexual partners and single mothers by choice must purchase children from companies that employ surrogates and sperm banks. That requires contracts and inevitable legal disputes governing this severance of parenthood from natural sex. These legal precedents and structures inevitably affect those who haven't chosen to buy children to masquerade as a natural family. They create legal precedents and attitudes in courts that assume babies do not naturally arise within a marriage and create a family without and preceding state involvement. They create a license and legal ecosystem for treating every family as if their children are born as wards of the state, rather than natural wards of their parents until the children reach adulthood.

Can you imagine what family court proceedings will look like, and the precedents they will set for all families, when "throuples" of three-person polyamorous couples and "polycules" of up to twenty concurrent sexual partners—with children between some of them—become more normalized through profiles in publications like *New York Magazine*[96] and *The New York Times Magazine*?[97] Beyond these torturous situations for children and those who concoct them outside marriage, legalized baby trafficking creates precedent for inserting government enforcement into private life, thereby potentially subjecting all relationships to government control and separating all children from their parents. It's yet another totalitarian component of queer policy.

Only one-man, one-woman encounters autonomously produce children. All non-heterosexual sexual encounters are infertile. Natural families are self-creating. Any other relationships depend on government permission to perpetrate human rights abuses to look somewhat like a natural family through unnatural means. This means self-creating families decentralize power and state-manufactured families centralize power. [98] Naturally created families promote constitutional, limited government. Artificial families promote unlimited, totalitarian-trending government.

Adoption doesn't make an artificial family, because it repairs family bonds broken *by accident*. Nobody, however, should ever destroy those family bonds *on purpose*, including through trafficking in wombs, eggs and sperm, and children. Erasing sex and parenthood from its just and natural context of male-female marriage—queering family law—is the main driver of this atrocity. Children should not be manufactured intentionally motherless or fatherless. Doing so is a crime against humanity.

Abusing Procreation Affects Even Natural Parents

Child trafficking to compensate for infertile coupling also inflicts totalitarianism in creating a demand for government licensing of parents. Currently, people who buy children from surrogates and fertility companies do not have to pass the same background checks and home studies as adoptive parents. [99] This is how pedophiles and seriously mentally ill adults have been able to purchase children. [100]

Some leftists would address this with government licensing of all individuals for parenthood, instead of solely adoptive parents. This would convert all parenting into an adoptive relationship in which the state is the true "owner" of all children. In 1980, University of Florida professor Hugh Lafollette wrote "Licensing Parents," a highly cited journal article that has been republished in academic collections around the globe more than thirty times. [101] In 2010 he updated the article as "Licensing Parents Revisited." There, he recommended adopting this extremist policy incrementally, due to public opposition.

Claiming sexual activity is a human right, as LGBT activists do in institutions such as the United Nations, effectively allows the state to arbitrate every parent's fitness to raise his or her own children. If sex is a human right that parents don't allow their children to freely exercise, that grants government a pretext for negating parents' natural authority over their children, as writer Stella Morabito has noted.[102]

This also would effectively comprise government licensing of parents because it constitutes government setting intrusive conditions under which parents are allowed to keep their kids. We're not talking government stopping parents from punching kids, an abuse of parental authority that legitimately invites community oversight and restraint. We're talking government redefining as abuse natural parental actions that protect kids, such as preventing sexual exposure. This shifts the presumption of authority over children from parents to the government. Instead of government working as an extension of the household, it displaces the household.

"When we give the state the power to decide—at the outset and for everybody—whether family autonomy and privacy may exist, this means, *de facto*, that the attributes of autonomy and privacy have already ceased," Morabito notes. "This is not a debate about whether child abuse is bad. This is about whether the presumption of child abuse by state bureaucrats justifies the state takeover of the family."[103]

Licensing would treat all parents as if they had obtained children unnaturally, through sterile contracts and purchase agreements instead of natural affection. The same is true of replacing marriage with relationship contracts, as multiple leftist and libertarian scholars have advocated.[104] This would effectively punish and erode all families to patch some of the risks created by people who chose infertile and temporary relationships but don't like the inevitable consequences.

Instead, society should adhere to the most logical, biologically natural, and historically grounded approach: natural parents are the best possible natural guardians of children and the most likely to be motivated by love for their own flesh and blood. That primal family bond should be supported in every possible way instead of destroyed in every possible way.

Why Aren't Children Off-Limits for Queer Sex?

The midcentury philosopher Michel "Foucault's influence on queer theory has been so great than he can be considered one of the founders of queer theory," says Wikipedia. Foucault is a godfather of cultural Marxism. Like queer theory developer Gayle Rubin, Foucault spent time in the San Francisco's 1970s "homosexual bathhouses" and "sex dungeons." There, he pursued sadomasochism, for which he bought various sexual leatherwear, as well as "clamps, handcuffs, hoods, gags, [and] whips."[105]

The last time Foucault visited San Francisco, says a biographer, he knowingly infected younger men with HIV. Biographer James Miller calls it a "potential[ly] suicidal act of passion," ignoring that deliberately infecting people with HIV is essentially murder.[106]

Foucault also "overthrew oppression" by defying "societal conventions" against sexual interactions with children: "Foucault signed a petition in 1977 to the French parliament campaigning for the abolition of all legislation regarding the age of consent. . . . He left Tunisia in the late '60s after allegedly sexually abusing Arab children."[107]

Foucault is the tip of a very dirty iceberg. Many historically prominent queers infamously pursued and obtained sexual encounters with minors—some teens, some as young as babies. Those include Simone de Beauvoir,[108] André Gide, Paul Goodman, Alfred Kinsey,[109] Harvey Milk, Jean-Paul Sartre,[110] Oscar Wilde,[111] and Walt Whitman.[112] The gay writer Chad Greene believes this isn't outlier behavior, but "common": "gay men seem to hold a generational view that sex with teenagers is a rite of passage and a necessity."[113]

Harvey Weinstein would like a word. Or perhaps he, too, will one day be rehabbed with dozens of cheerful children's biographies making him into a secular saint.

Thousands of exhibits form a very long parade connecting queer sex and children, to the point it's at best super-freaking suspicious. An eleven-year-old transgender boy led Orlando's two hundred thousand–person pride parade in 2023 as its "youngest-ever" grand marshal.[114] The massively popular online multiplayer game Roblox offers unsupervised kids access to LGBT chat rooms that include a "hide from your parents" panic button.[115] An Indiana reporter whose articles vociferously supported publicly sponsored porn in libraries was outed as a convicted child molester and child porn consumer.[116]

Nine-year-olds throbbing their rear ends and catwalking in sparkly clothes for stripper tips[117] are universally condemned—except if their prepubescent sexual displays can be coded as queer. Why should queers get a pass for *any* attempts to connect sex and kids? Why are we told it's pro-queer for children to see strangers' breasts, rear ends, and penises in public?[118]

If the queer movement doesn't support pedophilia, why does it work to expose kids to pederasts like Milk in schools and on social media? It's demeaning to homosexuals—and, more importantly, dangerous to children—not to apply the same sexual standards to them that we rightly apply to heterosexuals.

Yet these efforts are blatant, occurring right out in the open today under the rainbow flag, as if that flag legitimizes anything done in its name. Besides the rampant and well-publicized pornification of school curricula and library shelves, consider US efforts to lower the age of sexual consent and reduce legal penalties for sex with minors, right in line with Foucault's advocacy.

State Sen. Scott Weiner, a gay man, was the lead sponsor of a law Gov. Gavin Newsom signed to let California's far-left judges keep adults off sex offender registries after having sex with someone up to ten years younger, as young as age fourteen. The new law also makes oral or anal sex with a minor fourteen or older a misdemeanor instead of a felony. Democrats cast the law as pro-queer.

"I challenge everybody: Give me a situation where a 24-year-old had sex with a 14-year-old, any kind of sex, and it wasn't predatory," Democrat state Assemblywoman Lorena Gonzalez said in remarks opposing the bill her colleagues quickly made law.[119]

Also the lead author of California's "sanctuary state" law protecting parents against prosecution for cutting off their children's genitals,[120] Weiner argued higher ages for statutory rape laws are anti-LGBT. Weiner also insists the word "groomer" is an anti-gay slur.[121] There's no reason to think the word "groomer" is specifically anti-gay—*unless* gay people are more likely to target children for sex. That makes Weiner the one suggesting homosexuals are uniquely interested in underage sex, while insisting nobody be allowed to talk about that.

"We're Coming for Your Children"

In 2021, the San Francisco Gay Men's Chorus released a song titled, "A Message from the Gay Community." It rejected multiple bases on which homosexuals won public acceptance and legal privileges, including the claims that bedroom activity doesn't affect anyone outside it and that queer people are "born this way."

The song openly celebrates queer exploration dividing young people from their families: "We'll convert your children, happens bit by bit, quietly and subtly and you will barely notice it," the lyrics say. ". . . They'll change their group of friends, you won't approve of where they go at night (to protests). And you'll be disgusted when they start learning things online that you kept far from their sight."[122]

After right-wing outlets picked up on the song, the choir claimed it was a joke. The organization then quickly hid its video of the song. In 2023, however, queer activists went on to publicly defend the same sentiment.

In June 2023, NBC News reported, "The 'coming for your children' chant has been used for years at Pride events, according to longtime march attendees and gay rights activists, who said it's one of many provocative expressions used to regain control of slurs against LGBTQ people."[123] NBC's article was prompted by podcaster Tim Pool circulating a video clip of people at a pride march chanting, "We're here, we're queer, we're not going shopping."

"But one voice that is louder than the crowd—it's not clear whose, or whether the speaker was a member of the LGBTQ community—is heard saying at least twice, 'We're here, we're queer, we're coming for your children,'" NBC says. Pride marchers told NBC they use the "coming for your children" chant all the time. In 2022, *Gothamist* reported that Drag March participants chanted, "Ten percent is not enough: Groom! Groom! Groom!"[124]

Grooming is definitely going on—and evangelization. Multiple studies have found that the vast majority of children expressing gender dysphoria as teens affirmed their natal sex as an adult if they received psychotherapy instead of sex-mutilating medical interventions.[125] Depending on the study, the percent of children who lose their dysphoria naturally over time without medical intervention is between 98 and 73 percent.[126] Transgender identities are artificial, and they need constant reinforcement from social pressure.

Several pride march organizers told NBC these boisterously chanted "groomer" sentiments were ironic, jokes, a way to spin back criticism. *Post-Millennial* editor Libby Emmons commented: "This is part of an ongoing cycle where the leftists do something crazy and bizarre, the right calls it out, the left says it isn't even happening, and then pivot and claim that not only is it happening, it's good to have it happen. . . . The response from conservatives has been, essentially, when someone tells you who they are: listen."[127]

Using Social Contagion to Expand the Rainbow

Indeed, one cannot wave away the words and actions of famous queer individuals and founders of queer theory that openly target children for homosexual and transsexual behaviors. Through the rapidly spreading Drag Queen Story Hour, says a 2020 academic journal article, transvestites "position[] queer and trans cultural forms as valuable components of early childhood education."[128] Drag story hours for preschoolers comprise "a way of bringing queer ways of knowing and being into the education of young children."

Transsexual authors Harper Keenan and Lil' Miss Hot Mess argue for shifting the modern idea of the purpose of education as training children for adulthood. Instead, they argue, education should be about "broadening" children's "interests, abilities, and eccentricities."

Keenan trains public school teachers through an organization she founded, the Trans Educators Network. Keenan earned her doctorate in education from Stanford University[129] and now teaches on the education faculty of the University of British Columbia.[130] Lil' Miss Hot Mess is a PhD student at New York University and founding board member of national Drag Queen Story Hour.

Queerness, as they define it, represents "our desire to practice an embodied political resistance to confining constructs of gender and sexuality as they are produced by the institutions and social relations that govern our lives." They want to train *all* children to, like them, "upend the binaries," to "subvert the genders," to "live queerly." As discussed here and earlier, this works. It can encourage statistically impossible events such as twenty of thirty-two fourth graders in a Texas classroom identifying, according to their teacher, as queer—*before* they hit puberty.[131]

The "Drag Pedagogy" article is so clear that anyone pretending its authors believe the goal of queer education is not creating a children's crusade is incapable of reading or lying.

Pornography Changes People's Sexual Preferences

One of the world's largest pornography companies works to "convert" heterosexuals and children to queer sex using its videos and algorithms, an undercover interview revealed in 2023.

"Let's say you're 12 years old, you're still figuring out your sexuality, maybe even your gender. Wouldn't it be helpful to see, not a celebration but just maybe a normalization of something that you think is what you want?" says a "senior script writer" for a transgender porn company owned by PornHub.[132]

Script writers explained they deliberately insert transgender partners, children, and opposite-sex partners into pornography aimed at children and heterosexuals, in order to "see if you can convert somebody, right? Like maybe somebody who's never looked for anything like that."

The new ubiquity of smartphones and internet access has exploded porn consumption and addiction, including among children. Phone viewing accounts for 86 percent of PornHub's traffic.[133] New state laws requiring porn sites to verify that their users are eighteen or older cut 80 percent of their traffic.[134]

"Kids today are as savvy about online porn as they've been for years about nicotine and alcohol. We know how to get around web blockers and site filtration. I did, and so did my friends, even though our moms did everything they could to protect us," writes sixteen-year-old Isabel Hogben in *The Free Press* in 2023.

Hogben says she first watched porn at age ten. Eleven is the age researchers estimate the average American first encounters porn.[135] Thanks to her parents providing her a smartphone, and with her mom in the next room, Isabel "found myself on Pornhub, which I stumbled across by accident and returned to out of curiosity. The website has no age verification, no ID requirement, not even a prompt asking me if I was over 18. The site is easy to find, impossible to avoid, and has become a frequent rite of passage for kids my age."

Most of the public are intuitively aware of what plenty of research has backed up: early sexual exposure is highly damaging to children. Sixty-one percent of voters polled in June 2023 who expressed an opinion thought exposing young children to "ideas like transgenderism, drag shows, and LGBTQ+ themes" hurts the children's emotional and psychological development. Including the 14 percent of likely voters who weren't sure still left a majority—51 percent—willing to say that sexual exposure for small kids is harmful.[136]

The kind of porn available today is not pre-internet porn, like 1970s *Playboy*. Porn viewers today demand stronger stuff to feed their addictions. Today's porn is unfathomably violent and twisted. In fourth grade, Hogben says, "I saw simulated incest, bestiality, extreme bondage, sex with unconscious women, gangbangs, sadomasochism, and unthinkable physical violence."

Pornography today is so exceptionally stimulating and addictive compared to pre-internet pornography that internet porn consumers now don't even get sexually aroused by pre-internet porn.[137] This has changed the sexual marketplace for everyone. Among other things, it has dramatically increased sexual violence. A U.K. study of men ages eighteen to twenty-nine in 2020 found 71 percent had "slapped, choked, gagged or spat on their partner during consensual sex."[138] The earlier girls are exposed to pornography, an Indiana University study found, the more they accept rough treatment in sex like choking and "aggressive fellatio."[139]

Sexual predators expose victims to porn to get them to accept not only sex but also violent and degrading forms of it.[140] Due to widespread porn exposure, kids today often think sex is supposed to be violent.

The dramatic increase in porn consumption and addiction has also fed queer sexual experimentation. Just as the porn script writers noted, searching for a dopamine hit pushes pornography users to try out various forms of "kink"—like videos of transgender people, the opposite sex, and kids.

A 2016 study found that many men view homosexual pornography, even if they don't identify as gay. When they stop watching porn, they stop reporting homosexual attractions.[141]

In a book[142] and a paper[143] delivered at a Columbia University conference, transgender writer Andrea Long Chu says pornography that depicts men behaving like women rewired his attractions into transgenderism. Chu quotes multiple online commenters disclosing the connections between porn addictions and gender dysphoria.

Chu makes the same point as "no-fap" groups of men who swear off porn because it emasculates them: "porn *feminizes*," he writes (italics original). A "a great number of heterosexual men" consume porn, "not to have power but to give it up." Chu is infamous for a 2024 *New York Magazine* cover essay arguing that children and mentally ill people should be able to mutilate themselves simply because they want to, not for any medical necessity: "We must be prepared to defend the idea that, in principle, everyone should have access to sex-changing medical care, regardless of age, gender identity, social environment, or psychiatric history."[144]

So, if porn teaches kids that choking is sexy and desirable, why could it not also teach kids (and adults) that cross-dressing is sexy and desirable? If porn leads people to lose their minds in desire, as Chu writes, that's obviously applicable to queer identities, too.

Pornography presents an extremely strong stimulus attached to specific scenarios. Of course it can rewire people's attractions. It seems especially likely to do so among porn addicts, who search for different kinds of kink to get their sex high. This is another explanatory factor in the explosion in queer identification that happened at exactly the same time that increasingly extreme, strange, violent, and disgusting porn became easily available.

Not surprisingly, the pornography explosion also contributes to queer identification by breaking up families. Porn addictions delay and prevent marriage by partially satisfying the sexual desires that contribute to marriage, as well as completely distorting each sex's expectations of the other.

As Pascal-Emmanuel Gobry writes in a comprehensive overview of the porn epidemic, a study of thousands of representative American couples between 2006 and 2014 found "beginning pornography use between survey waves nearly doubled one's likelihood of being divorced by the next survey period."[145] That means porn increases kids' risk for growing up traumatized by divorce, which can also lead them to express their distress in gender dysphoria. It's a hellish sexual revolution cycle.

Seeing pornography also inflicts trauma, especially on children. Dozens of young people have publicly testified that accidentally seeing porn led to obsessive viewings that hijacked their still-developing understandings of sex. Being exposed to porn at age eleven and then getting addicted to it scarred singer Billie Eilish so much she wore baggy clothes for almost her entire adolescence so people couldn't see—and therefore pornify—her body.

"It really destroyed my brain and I feel incredibly devastated that I was exposed to so much porn," Eilish told Howard Stern in 2020. "The first few times I, you know, had sex, I was not saying no to things that were not good. It was because I thought that's what I was supposed to be attracted to."[146]

It's not at all surprising after such traumatizing childhood experiences that Eilish later reported she's bisexual. Her experiences exemplify those of her generation.

The Goal Is to Queer Everyone

Queer theory, journalist Christopher Rufo writes, became an "academic discipline" in 1984 when an academic journal published "Thinking Sex: Notes for a Radical Theory of the Politics of Sexuality," by the lesbian Gayle Rubin. Like Foucault, Rubin was a frequenter of San Francisco "sex dungeons" in which people practice violent and degrading sex similar to that depicted today in pornography. In her "academic work," Rubin described an existing "hierarchy" of sexual orientations, with married heterosexuals at the top and pedophiles at the bottom. She then advocated, as critical theorists do, for inverting this hierarchy. That would *place the pedophiles on the top*, and the married heterosexuals on the bottom.

"Rubin denounces fears of child sex abuse as 'erotic hysteria,' rails against anti-child pornography laws, and argues for legalizing and normalizing the behavior of 'those whose eroticism transgresses generational boundaries.' These men are not deviants, but victims, in Rubin's telling," writes Rufo. ". . . Rubin wrote fondly of those primitive hunter-gatherer tribes in New Guinea in which 'boy-love' was practiced freely."[147]

Using the frameworks of child rapist[148] and leftist philosopher Foucault, queer theory applies the Marxist approach of "inverting the hierarchy" to sex, thereby subjugating heterosexuals to those who engage in all manner of non-heterosexual practices. The child molester Foucault is one of the key philosophers driving cultural Marxist beliefs that all power imbalances represent oppression and therefore social Marxists must "subvert hierarchies."

That means, for example, subverting men to women and replacing natural sex with non-procreative masturbation, sometimes in pairs and groups. It's all an expression of Marxism's opposition to all authority, including God and nature.

Sexual Marxism also works to erase entire categories of thought, eerily enacting the dystopia "1984." In 1990, key queer theorist Judith Butler began formulating and disseminating the now-pervasive ideas that gender is "fluid" and therefore there's no such thing as a woman.[149]

Butler, Rufo notes, "argues that even the word 'woman,' though it relates to a biological reality, is a social construction and cannot be defined with any stable meaning or categorization. There is nothing essential about 'man,' 'woman,' or 'sex': they are all created and re-created through historically contingent human culture; or, as Butler puts it, they are all defined through their performance, which can change, shift, and adapt across time and space."[150]

These people are serious, and they're reshaping our world. *The Daily Wire*'s Matt Walsh interviewed dozens of current gender academics and found them all defending this incoherent, anti-human, and totalitarian position.[151] The House of Representatives under Democrat leadership erased all references to males and females in congressional rules.[152] During her confirmation hearings in 2022, Supreme Court Justice Ketanji Brown Jackson said she couldn't define what a woman is, because "I'm not a biologist."[153]

Ending "heteronormativity," as queer theorists openly demand, would require making at least half of citizens non-heterosexual. The norm is what the majority does. So ending the norm of heterosexuality means queering at least the majority of the population. Yet the ultimate goal is not just the majority. "Overturning the gender binary" means making *everyone* queer. Erasing the sexual binary erases marriage. The explicit goal is to de-sex *everyone* and everything.

The average person may not know or like these implications, but they're not a secret.

Queer Activists Pushing Pedophile Politics

Like a number of Democrats today and perverts like Foucault before, admitted pedophiles support reducing the age of consent and eliminating penalties for sex with minors. In the 1990s, Pat Califia, a lesbian and Rubin collaborator who later became transgender, explained that to "liberate children and adolescents," the Marxist sexual project must "disrupt[] the entire hierarchy of adult power and coercion and challeng[e] the hegemony of antisex fundamentalist religious values."[154]

Dutch pedophiles arrested for a child sex hotel in Mexico in 2023 publicly posted a political platform in 2006.[155] *Harper's Magazine* published an English translation.[156] It included eliminating the age of consent, showing children pornography, publicly broadcasting pornography at all hours, sex ed "starting in kindergarten," alcohol consumption starting at age twelve, "anyone will be allowed to walk around outside naked," and eliminating marriage.

Except for the alcohol, these are all active parts of the pride program in the United States. That program is almost unanimously supported by Democrat politicians, half-supported by Republican politicians, and deliberately ignored by most of the rest of Republicans.

At pride parades, participants often walk down public streets naked, violating public decency laws and fulfilling pedophiles' political platform. LGBT programming and books in schools include showing children pornography. They describe and depict naked people performing a wide variety of sexual acts, including between adults and minors. LGBT ideology is taught to children as young as three in schools and daycares. And queer politicians are working to decriminalize sexual contact with minors and lower the age of consent.

Such policies also accomplish political goals of the North American Man-Boy Love Association, a pedophile group for years adjacent to LGBT activism driven underground by FBI stings. One of the organization's goals was eliminating the age of consent for sexual encounters. In 2016, the "historian and pederasty advocate" William Percy, a longtime homosexual activist, told *Vice* magazine that NAMBLA should have pursued this goal incrementally, starting with, for example, lowering the age of consent to something like fourteen.[157]

Right out in the open, top queer organizations like Human Rights Campaign and GLSEN and their politician allies are at the forefront of pedophilic acts like transgender strip shows for kids, showing kids porn, and reducing age of consent laws. The Dutch pedophile party included only three members. But the people enacting the same policies these pedophiles favor are in control of nearly the entire lawmaking infrastructure of the West.

Is Pedophilia a Sexual Orientation?

Admitted pedophiles use the same language and arguments as LGBT activists for inclusion in the government-sanctioned gender alphabet. The "unrepentant pedophile" Thomas O'Carroll has been imprisoned twice for pedophile-related activities, including his vast collection of child pornography depicting the rape and torture of mostly boys as young as age six.[158]

In 2018, O'Carroll's argument for ending the age of consent appeared in an academic journal on whose board sits more than two dozen US taxpayer-funded professors.[159] He says consent is not necessary for adult sex with children or animals, and insists pedophilia is "a sexual orientation like any other."[160]

In 2017, an American academic published two articles in the respected journal *Archives of Sexual Behavior* arguing that homosexual adult sex with minors as young as thirteen doesn't harm the minors. Hardly any academics criticized the studies or their conclusions.[161]

Today, some pedophiles call themselves "boylovers," "girllovers," and "minor-attracted persons" (MAPs).[162] "[T]he term 'boylover' is most commonly used as a term for a sexual preference analogous to 'gay' or 'homosexual,'" says an online pedophile wiki.[163] Pedophiles distinguish between people with sexual preferences for boys ages six and under and teen boys. They call the former "little boy lover" and the latter "teen boy lover,"[164] using the acronyms MAP, LBL, and TBL on social media.[165]

The now-deleted Substack of a user who named himself "MAP for life" says one pedophile "was aware of his attractions from age seven" and later "went through the rare process of coming out."[166] Pedophiles "did not ask to be this way" and "are all born as non-offending," says the Association for Sexual Abuse Prevention.[167]

ASAP refers pedophiles struggling with their attractions to VirPed, an organization that advocates for "virtuous pedophilia," which to them means not acting on their attractions to children. Its website features eighteen academics supporting this mission with arguments mirroring those made on behalf of queer people, including, "No one chooses their sexual preferences" and "sexual interest is far from immutable and new sexual interests, including non-pedophilic interests, can be discovered and enhanced."

"There are still scientists who would like to argue that adult sexual contact with children is no more than mere 'inter-generational intimacy,'" notes sociologist Sarah D. Goode in her endorsement of VirPed, a stark statement about the state of academia.[168] Certainly, a number of academics and institutions fund research on so-called MAPs, perhaps most prominently the 2021 book by PhD Allyn Walker, "A Long, Dark Shadow: Minor-Attracted People and Their Pursuit of Dignity."

A transgender woman, Walker was a criminal justice and sociology professor at Virginia's Old Dominion University before resigning amid public outcry after the University of California Press published her book. The Johns Hopkins University school of public health almost immediately hired her to work in its child abuse prevention center.[169]

In the book's introduction, Walker notes that John Jay College and the City University of New York funded her research for the book with graduate awards and travel funds, and that she wrote the book while working for the University of Utah, Penn State Wilkes-Barre, and ODU. She thanks multiple colleagues at these institutions for their help with her research on pedophiles who claim to never have abused a child personally, although several admitted they view child abuse images and even travel abroad for that purpose to avoid US law enforcement.

Walker came to advocating ending the "stigma against people who are attracted to minors" through a desire to abolish prisons and police, a top political goal shared by Communist Black Lives Matter muse Angela Davis. One obstacle to that goal is nearly universal agreement that child molesters should be in prison. Because Walker wants to fully abolish prisons, and won't consider the death penalty, she has to figure out what to do with the strongest case for prisons: child rapists. She condemns "sexual abuse against children," but believes it can be prevented through "support and understanding" of people tempted to sexually abuse children.

That's the reason for calling such people "minor-attracted persons" instead of "pedophiles": "to decrease stigma against this group." Because this sexual orientation can't be changed, Walker argues, shaming MAPs "is an ineffective method of keeping children safe." Instead, she says, showing such people "empathy" and "support" is the best way to keep children safe because distress and alienation makes pedophiles more likely to offend.[170] Love the sinner, hate the sin.

In the book, "Walker traces the obvious and pronounced parallels between MAPs' experience of dealing with their identity and queer people's,"[171] writes Bly Rede, VirPed's "strategy coordinator." Walker cites several academics who argue "there is evidence showing that attractions to minors can be considered a sexual orientation."[172]

Psychologist Michael Seto, Walker says, "shows that MAPs' attractions and trajectories mirror those of other sexual minorities in terms of the age when individuals first became aware of their attractions, their sexual history, endurance of attractions over time, and experiences of romantic feelings in addition to sexual attraction."[173]

To the argument that pedophilia isn't a sexual orientation because children can't give informed consent to sex, Walker points out that doesn't negate some adults' attraction to children: "A person's sexual orientation does not determine their behavior—it only determines their sexual interests."[174] "As a queer person myself," Walker says, she understands strong concerns among LGBT-identified people about calling pedophilia a sexual orientation. It appears to link their cause with the criminals most detested by society, even by other criminals. Yet, she notes, "unfounded and reductive historical claims of queer individuals' supposedly predatory behaviors mirrors today's assumptions about MAPs."[175]

The majority of the pedophiles Walker interviewed—twenty-seven out of forty-two—identified themselves as sexually attracted both to adults and children.[176] The same number also expressed homosexual attractions, including to children.[177] Several also identified as gay or queer. Attractions to "younger-looking" men are "normalized within gay culture," Walker notes, which allowed some of her interviewees to refer to their sexual orientation publicly without being clear that they meant minors.[178]

Walker says one interviewee, "Neil," "liked to use the term 'queer' for himself because its meaning was flexible enough that it allowed him to openly and accurately identify as such, without creating suspicion that he was attracted to minors."[179] Others said they avoided identify-ing as gay to protect homosexuality's "reputation" from associations with child rape.[180]

Not surprisingly, many of Walker's interviewees said their sexual orientation formed in relation to childhood traumas, such as the death of a father or sexual rejection. Twelve disclosed they viewed child por-nography, a likely underreported disclosure because child abuse images taken of real children are illegal to make or possess.[181]

Contrary to Walker's claims that ending the social shame of pedo-philia would help children, several study participants disclosed that the fear of imprisonment for possessing child pornography reduced or ended their consumption of it.[182] Consuming child abuse images, of course, encourages child abusers to make more.

While the bias in academia makes it difficult to research connec-tions between child molestation and pornography, studies do document such a connection.[183] Child pornography has grown "exponentially" in the internet era, to the point authorities can hardly keep track of it, the *New York Times* reported in 2019.[184] From 1998 to 2018, reports of child abuse images skyrocketed from 3,000 to 18.4 million.

Juxtapose this data with the evidence Walker cites showing that "only" 4 to 6 percent of people convicted of obtaining child abuse images later went on to molest actual children.[185] Five percent of eigh-teen million is *nine hundred thousand* children sexually assaulted in one year alone—atop all the children who were assaulted to create the images that encouraged the molesters of the nine hundred thousand.

That's a loose, back-of-the-envelope calculation. Its underlying point stands: a small percentage of a huge number equals a massive number of children being molested because of pornography that chan-nels sexual appetites towards children. Eliminating parents is how predators usually get access to children. This is perhaps the most evil consequence of queer ideology's total war on family.

CHAPTER 7

Woke Theocracy

"External freedom is only an aspect of interior freedom. Political freedom, as the Western world has known it, is only a political reading of the Bible. Religion and freedom are indivisible. Without freedom, the soul dies. Without the soul there is no justification for freedom."
—Whittaker Chambers[1]

From the beginning, queer theorists have identified their sexual identities as religious. Trans male Susan Stryker, a founder of gender studies, made this quite clear in a seminal 1994 essay: "This trans movement manifesto is intended as a secular sermon that unabashedly advocates embracing a disruptive and refigurative gender-queer or transgender power as a spiritual resource."[2] A "secular sermon" that calls "transgender power" a "spiritual resource." Can one get much clearer? Pride is about much more than bodies and politics. It's about spirits.

Stryker's identity is not just religious, but also Satanic. In the essay, he identifies his transsexuality with the monster in Mary Shelley's "Frankenstein": "I am a transsexual, and therefore I am a monster."

Eerily, Stryker claims the presence of monsters foreshadows divine intervention: "the ancients considered the appearance of such beings [monsters] to be a sign of some impending supernatural event." Speaking of Frankenstein's monster and metaphorically of the monster he's made of himself, Stryker says, "rather than bless its creator, the monster curses him."

Like the "dragon lady" noted earlier, Stryker says he has become a transsexual "monster" as an act of rebellion against nature and its Creator, God: "Transsexual embodiment, like the embodiment of the monster, places its subject in an unassimilable, antagonistic, queer relationship to . . . Nature. . . . Nature exerts such a hegemonic oppression." He says the world's refusal to comply with his attempts to denature it fills him and other transsexuals with rage, a word found in the essay forty-nine times.

Stryker also says transsexuality fulfills the feminist-turned-homosexual project to erase the sexes, even though many people who support partial erasures of sexual distinctions often do not like this outcome of their own ideology: "transsexuality more than any other transgender practice or identity represents the prospect of destabilizing the foundational presupposition of fixed genders upon which a politics of personal identity depends."

Later, Stryker again directly curses God by cursing God's law that made him a man: "I defy that Law ['of the Father'] in my refusal to abide by its original decree of my gender." Few Christians would put things as starkly, but Christianity would have little to dispute in

Stryker's demonic, purposeful, and open rebellion against the human body and the need for two sexes to create life.

Like Satan in John Milton's *Paradise Lost* and Dante Alighieri's *Divine Comedy*, Stryker describes it as a "pleasure" to defy his body's created order, and thus his Maker to His face. Stryker even references Milton in categorically tying his rejection of his male body to his rejection of the Christian God.

He also speaks of using man's technical powers for the spiritual ends of deity-defying "immortality" and "transcendence." "The scientific discourse that produced sex reassignment techniques is inseparable from the pursuit of immortality through the perfection of the body, the fantasy of total mastery through the transcendence of an absolute limit, and the hubristic desire to create life itself."

Stryker ends the essay with more religious imagery, in the form of a "monstrous benediction": "May you discover the enlivening power of darkness within yourself. May it nourish your rage. May your rage inform your actions, and your actions transform you as you struggle to transform your world." The religious connections here are unmistakable, within the Christian frame, and explicit. Yet many still are unaware that's what queer leaders say they are doing.

Identity Politics Marry Church and State

In his autobiography, *Witness*, the former Communist Whittaker Chambers gives a rich account of the ideology that generated today's identity politics. He points out how Communism answered fundamental questions that, following World War I and the Great Depression, many deeply devastated people refused to seek from Christianity. It gave them a false hope.

Yet Communism—an atheist political cult—has some great contradictions, too. Noticing these eventually converted Chambers to

Christianity. Chambers says human beings need religion. If they don't adhere to a traditional religion, they will adhere to a new one—and new ones simply rehash old pagan cults and philosophies, using perhaps new terms for old concepts, and sometimes mixing up old ideas in a new way.

Transgender ideology, for example, incorporates major aspects of the ancient cult of Gnosticism. Gnostics believed nature was an evil illusion. Its distinctions—such as between men and women—were therefore evil. So Gnostics rejected procreation and embraced androgyny.

The Gnostic enlightened save themselves by returning to a "primordial state of oneness, where no distinctions existed," writes Peter Burfeind, author of *Gnostic America*. This process of *gnosis* can be literally translated as "becoming woke."[3] Once becoming aware of the oppressions of nature, the Gnostic rebels, thus saving himself: "Rebellion against the natural order was thus salvific, a liberation of the true Self."[4]

Like sexual distinctions, androgyny has always been religious in nature. It's a reflection of people's spiritual beliefs about the nature of man, the soul, and the deity. These transcend mere technical specification—"females have ovaries"—to meaning: what can those ovaries be *for*? What is their just and moral use? That is a question science can't answer, but religions do.

Identity Politics Exhibits Key Features of a Religion

In his bestselling 2021 book, *Woke Racism*, Columbia University linguistics professor John McWhorter suggests that because identity politics is irrational and religion is irrational, therefore identity politics is a religion.[5] Even though that's a logically invalid argument, he does provide some helpful definitions, arguments, and descriptions that show identity politics does replace religion in at least partially meeting human needs for meaning, absolution of guilt, eternal justice, and transcendence.

The Elect, as the atheist McWhorter calls wokesters, submit to their ideology as religious believers submit to a God.[6] The Elect also religiously believe in myths (such as "hands up, don't shoot"),[7] he shows. McWhorter lists several other overlapping characteristics between cultural Marxism and religions: "The Elect have clergy;" "The Elect have original sin;" "The Elect are evangelical;" "The Elect are apocalyptic;" "The Elect ban the heretic;" and "The Elect supplant older religions."

"[A] deeper look at Wokeism does, indeed, reveal a whole series of mythological and supernatural beliefs, including the idea that white people today are responsible for the racist actions of white people in the past; that climate change risks making humans extinct; and that a person can change their [sic] sex by simply identifying as the opposite sex," write journalist Michael Shellenberger and philosophy professor Peter Boghossian in a November 2021 *Public* article that extended McWhorter's arguments.[8]

Shellenberger and Boghossian provide a helpful "taxonomy" that slots intersectional beliefs into other religious categories. They summarize intersectionalists' understanding of "original sin" as "What happened in the past to make things so terrible today." In sexual politics, the original sin might be "the patriarchy" or "heteronormativity." Intersectionalism's "sacred victims" are "People who continue to be harmed by original sin," such as women, homosexuals, trans people, and so forth.

Shellenberger and Boghossian's taxonomy lists wokeism's "purifying rituals" as "acts perceived to make people innocent of guilt and responsibility." This would include what the Roman church used to call "indulgences:" paying "tithes" to Elect priests, such as government, academia, activist organizations, and people at the bottom of the intersectional hierarchy.

"Purifying rituals" for identity politics adherents include experimenting with anti-heterosexual behaviors, including pornography. As the ancient Gnostic cults and 1970s New Age spirituality would have put it, such exploration "expands one's consciousness" and seeks to unleash one's "true self." How can you know you're not repressing your latent homosexual or pansexual identity if you don't explore a little?

More Like a Cult Than a Religion

While, as these authors note, cultural Marxism does feature many characteristics of a religion, it also has many characteristics of a cult. In fact, it likely is better described as a cult than as a proper religion. *Critical Theories* coauthor James Lindsay is among those who have delved into identity politics' cult patterns at some length.[9]

At least two characteristics distinguish cults from religions: severe ostracism of dissenters and extreme attempts at information control. Both of these are readily apparent in cultural Marxism. Everyone is aware of "cancel culture's" high-octane ostracism. The Left's extreme information control is what the political right used to call "propaganda" and "bias" and now extends to leftist efforts to pull an Iron Curtain around the internet.[10]

All religions—and membership institutions of every kind—keep standards for admittance. Decent people have always refused to associate closely with indecent people. That's normal human behavior, and necessary to enforce societal standards and protect self-restrained people from people who will not restrain themselves.

Yet cults take this normal human behavior to an extreme level. Far beyond things like not inviting drunkards to cocktail parties, a reasonable response to alcoholism, cults attempt to cut off those who reject their ideology from *everything*.

As everyone knows, cultural Marxists do that—with a vengeance. It's in obedience to their ideology that banks are cutting off people and organizations from their own earnings due to political disagreements[11] in the United States,[12] Canada,[13] and Europe.[14] People in Western societies cannot live without a bank account, even on welfare. This means debanking is certainly a poverty sentence, and possibly a slow death sentence.

The whole world is aware of cancel culture's ever-expanding forms, from threatening to imprison J. K. Rowling for insisting men and women are different[15] to physical attacks on libertarian campus speakers like Charles Murray. Indeed, finding ways to damage people who merely disagree with them is practically a full-time cultural Marxist occupation. It's hallmark cultism, another characteristic cultural Marxism shares with Stalinism.

Also like a cult, cultural Marxism seeks total information control, not only over its adherents, but over everyone. That accounts for its dominance over education, media, and technology. The only messages Marxists allow to enter people's minds are those approved by vast networks of leftist information manipulators. Indeed, this is an explicit part of their philosophy.

As Aaron Kheriaty and Emily Burns write in City Journal,[16] the New Left philosopher Herbert Marcuse argued for "repressive tolerance" on the grounds that "the rise of leaders like Hitler could have been avoided had liberals declined to tolerate illiberal and conservative views."

> Marcuse, like Wilhelm Reich before him, argued that right-wing ideas inevitably lead to fascism and genocidal leaders. Thus, according to Marcuse, it was not just prudent but necessary to censor, and even pre-censor, ideas that might find their full and murderous expression in a future neo-fascist regime.

Marcuse proposed targeting exclusively right-wing ideas, while tolerating any left-wing ideas, no matter how violent or base. This line of thinking is the intellectual backbone of "political correctness."

Cultural Marxists sabotage all competing information sources including religious schools, charter schools, non-leftist media, and politicians. Like cult leaders and manipulators of all kinds, Marxists deprive their political enemies of funds, personnel, customers, contracts, and every other life-sustaining connection, often through lies.

Simply given these two hallmarks of cultural Marxism, it seems more apt to describe it as a very powerful cult rather than a religion. That also helps explain why intersectionalism features and amplifies so many mental pathologies, a third key feature of cults.

In October 2023, Boghossian and Shellenberger expanded their taxonomy into psychology, explaining, "Wokeism is a religion, but its religious nature didn't necessarily describe the madness that seemed to grip its most devoted adherents. Many people believe crazy things but don't behave so narcissistically or psychopathically, without regards for other people, in the way that Woke activists do. And so we decided to create a new taxonomy, one focused on Woke psychopathology."[17]

The two applied psychiatric diagnostic criteria for personality disorders to intersectionalism. They show psychological pathologies amplifying the religious impulses of wokeism, making this cult particularly, well, crazy. These traits include attention-seeking, grandiosity, emotional dysregulation, excess of empathy, lack of empathy, victimhood ideology, impaired reality testing, and splitting (refusing to accept any complication or nuance). This analysis is important for reconnecting intersectionalism with its spiritual dimensions, as one's psychology, or mind, is an aspect of the soul.

The two liberal authors also connect intersectionalism with totalitarianism, noting that it is not merely a political outgrowth but also psychological and religious. It is a totalizing ideology that unifies religion, politics, and the soul.

The Rebellious Bastard Child of Christianity

From ancient cultures to today, church and state have always been intertwined, including within the United States. When the Constitution was passed, several US states maintained state churches. Some continued to do so until nearly the Civil War.

Even religions that claim to be disassociated from politics, such as Buddhism, have major political effects (Buddhist sects have fought wars for centuries). So do religions that claim not to be religions while, like identity politics, filling religious roles and answering religious questions, such as atheism and secularism. For example, both are highly correlated with demographic decline and atheism, and the state religion of Communism is highly correlated with totalitarianism and mass murder.[18]

People's presuppositions about the world affect their politics. So it's not at all strange that identity politics should occupy both religious and political space. The successor to secularism, it is a competing religion to the United States' historic Protestant Christianity.

In fact, it can even be thought of as a perversion of Christianity, as it employs many Christian concepts. That's visible even in the taxonomy that McWhorter, Boghossian, and Shellenberger—two atheists[19] and one Christian[20]—apply to cultural Marxism. They use the Christian category of "original sin," variations on the Christian concept of atonement, and a vision of the apocalypse to categorize woke beliefs.

It goes far beyond that. As noted earlier, the early American Progressives distorted Christian theology about global perfection at the end of time into the here and now. They sought not heaven in the afterlife, but heaven on earth—through human, not divine, intervention. They believed their works could create this heaven through government. In effect, they decided to save themselves instead of trusting in God to do it, with government as the means.

That bastardization of Christianity has been very effective at displacing Christianity in historically Christian nations like the United States and Europe. It is the foundation of cultural Marxists' goal of total government control over human life. It's of course highly attractive. Who doesn't want to escape the evils of the human condition for an imminent earthly utopia?

Just like the Progressives, cultural Marxists believe humans are not responsible for their moral choices, but make bad choices because of bad circumstances. Use government to "perfect" the circumstances, and you perfect the outcomes, they claim. Force public affirmation of homosexual and transsexual behavior, for example, to end the "stigma" allegedly causing LGBT people's higher rates of mental illness and intimate partner violence.[21]

This ultimately makes government leftists' god—a category conspicuously missing from Boghossian and Shellenberger's taxonomy. It is the woke cult's all-powerful being that can right all wrongs, wipe all tears away, and bring about world peace. This foundational precept also unites cultural Marxists and their forebears, self-described liberals.

Identity Politics Makes Government God

Those constantly stoking terror of "fundamentalist theocracies" through cultural memes such as *The Handmaid's Tale* never acknowledge that description has for the last century (if not long before) only applied to Islamic and atheist governments. Atheism far dwarfs Islamism in creating efficient totalitarian machines capable of mass murdering hundreds of millions of people. The Crusades have nothing on Communism.[22]

Some liberals have difficulty seeing their ideology leads to cultural Marxism because they have blinded themselves to the reality that atheism and agnosticism are cults that deify government. In deifying government, the woke ultimately deify themselves, who comprise it. This is one reason atheism cannot defend society against wokeness, which is simply mutated Communism. Belief in a god is far stronger than lack of belief in a god.

Atheism is a religion because it makes religious claims: It claims no god exists. That cannot be definitively proven scientifically. It is a matter of interpretation of evidence. The *interpretation* is necessarily religious. Atheism is also a religion because it has religious implications: people believing in atheism cannot also believe in any other religion. It competes for people's religious allegiances.

Atheism also leads to deifying the self through government because, without a god, government is the most apparent lever of power to pull to fix what's wrong with the world. All Communists essentially deify government, including in cult-like religious rituals such as public prayer for the health of the Communist Party leader ("may he live forever").

This means Communism is a logical outgrowth of Progressivism. Leftists believe perfecting humans through perfecting government will eventually create paradise on earth. This is the work of a god. To the Left, government is the solver of all ills, the solution to every problem, the cowbell that must increase until it is all we see and love.

Psychological resistance to this reality has persisted since the Progressive era, as Chambers noted seventy years ago. "Men who sincerely abhorred the word Communism in the pursuit of common ends found that they were unable to distinguish Communists from themselves," he wrote of New Deal supporters. "... For men who could not see that what they firmly believed was liberalism added up to socialism could scarcely be expected to see what added up to Communism." But people's continued dislike of accepting this fact does not negate its truth.

This Insurrection Is Totalitarian

Negotiators for Communist nations originated the "hate crimes" laws that effectively allow leftists to criminalize their opponents' participation in self-government. Soviet Communists fervently pushed for speech restrictions and "discrimination" clauses in post-World War II treaty negotiations. The United Nations' 1948 Universal Declaration of Human Rights is a chief example. "More than any other voting bloc the communists pushed from the very start for the inclusion of clear antidiscrimination language in the Declaration. This nondiscrimination stamp is their mark on the document," explains the philosopher Johannes Morsink in his acclaimed historical account.[23]

The Soviet representative to the United Nations proposed this language allowing governments to criminalize speech: "Any advocacy of national, racial, or religious hostility or of national exclusiveness or hatred or contempt, as well as any action establishing a privilege or a discrimination based on distinctions of race, nationality, or religion constitute a crime and shall be punishable under the laws of the state." Representatives for the free nations rejected that language, stating their unwavering support for free speech as a cornerstone of self-rule. They would only accept language that condemned speech when it comprised an imminent incitement to violence.[24]

The Communists were not truly concerned about injustices based on people's race or ethnicity, as the many Communist "ethnic cleansing" campaigns demonstrate. Instead, says international human rights lawyer Paul Coleman, what they really wanted was to criminalize their political opponents: "That's the plain reading of what they're trying to do: Under the guise of human rights law, how can we find a way to censor our political opponents?"[25]

As Coleman notes, post-war treaties were attempting to address the fact that the atrocities Adolf Hitler's regime had committed were all legal under National Socialist laws in Germany. So those treaties were meant to restrain governments. The Communist nations, however, did not want to restrain governments from atrocities; they wanted to expand government and restrain *citizens*. So they worked to propagate Nazi-like legal tools in the name of anti-fascism. "Hate crimes" and "antidiscrimination" laws were sympathetic facades hiding these true goals.

Lawmakers gradually copied into Western nations' legal codes the language that the Soviets had inserted into these treaties. Now it has been imported into the United States, subverting the constitutional norms of free speech and free association. Today, these totalitarian laws are still used for Communist ends: to prosecute people who disagree with cultural Marxists.

"In many ways the Soviet era ended, but the ideology that drove the Soviet thinking at an elite level, it didn't really end, just the political structures ended," Coleman said. "A lot of the ideology in terms of how they push for speech codes and limitations is either explicitly or implicitly reverberating today."

Marxist philosopher Herbert Marcuse, whose progeny include the "intersectional" Black Lives Matter movement,[26] advocated not only for censorship but also for violence against communists' political opponents. Marcuse's regime would, Christopher Rufo writes, "apply strict censorship." He advocated the "suspension of the right of free speech and free assembly" and "intolerance even toward thought, opinion, and word" for the enemies of communist revolutionaries.[27]

Criminalizing disagreement, denying natural rights, fomenting state-sponsored violence against citizens, manipulating language, isolating people from families, separating children from parents, and fostering snitch culture are all features of Communist Cultural Revolutions and totalitarian governments. All are also central features of the Pride agenda. Call it communist, call it fascist, call it totalitarian, call it a theocracy: what is common to all is the pursuit of total state power over citizens' lives.

Erasing Words, Erasing Thoughts

Pride is totalitarian in every aspect, from erasing natural human ties and dictating people's worship to erasing the connections between words and reality. It is an insurrection against the historic American birthright of government limited to securing citizens' natural rights, leaving the people free to seek happiness through virtuous behavior. Pride is therefore a regime change, not only in the United States but across the Western nations, where limited government is older than the Magna Carta.

It's the same ideology as Progressives' "Living Constitution." These totalitarians suck the original meaning from words and deploy the zombified language as a weapon, transforming words from descriptions of reality to tools of power. The ideology of Pride confuses human language—and thus our minds and souls—by calling things their opposites.

Hatred is love. Mutilation is medicine. War is peace. Negation is affirmation. Sex is fluid. Men are women. All this is Pride. It is also totalitarianism, as works from philosophers to novels like *Darkness at Noon* and George Orwell's *1984* demonstrate. The manipulation of language and the constriction of thought are key planks in the Pride platform.

Ultimately, Pride strips away the crowning attributes that distinguish human beings from animals: language and reason. The philosopher Eric Voegelin "taught us," says ethics professor Aaron Kheriaty, that "[t]he common feature of all totalitarian systems is the prohibition of questions: every totalitarian regime first monopolizes what counts as rationality and determines what questions you are allowed to ask."[28]

This is all not only communist but also diabolical. It is only through language that human beings can reason together, establish relationships, and from those relationships form societies. Confusing language separates each person not only from every other person, but also from his very self. It obliterates freedom of speech and freedom of association, fundamental human rights that limit government, which is the most destructive potential abuser of human rights.

According to biographer F. Flagg Taylor, the famous anti-Communist Czech leader Vaclav Benda saw that "the Iron Curtain had not just descended between East and West, but between one individual and another, or even between an individual's own body and his soul."[29]

That is key distinguishing feature of totalitarianism, says Polish philosopher Leszek Kolakowski: "perfect integration through perfect fragmentation."[30]

This endless splintering creates chaos that threatens not only constitutional government but also the way of life that sustains it. The planting and cultivating of natural families is necessary to for any free nation to survive and flourish. Families cannot function without open communication, the basis of love. Totalitarian forces, which thrive on bitterly dividing humans from reality, threaten the nation's happiness and ultimately its very existence.

"Social Justice" Is the Goal of Leftist Government

Astute commentators such as Chris Bray have noticed identity politics distracts people from basic government failures. While Americans squabble over abortion and trans bathrooms, politicians continue to allow basic infrastructure to degrade and increase the cost of living for everyone.

Homeless people pile up, victims of the narcoterrorists who control the US border and make lots of money trafficking addiction and sex slaves. Health costs continue to rise, Americans' diets continue to degrade, the US military declines, and good jobs continue to be shipped abroad. Politicians make a lot of money perpetuating these structural evils while continuing to get elected waving identity politics in front of the voters their cynical corruption harms.

Yet it's also true that, for the Left, social justice issues are the prime purpose of government. They don't pay attention to the roads and availability of jobs because they're busy focusing government on what they consider higher moral issues. They're putting their religion above their pecuniary interests. They see this as noble, and it might be—if their religion were true.

The ubiquitous cultural Marxist "In this home, we believe" yard signs announce a creed. Creeds are religious statements printed in catechisms. Public school districts teach this catechism in very religious terms, such as requiring students to "confess by word" their "faith" that one can be male, female, or neither.[31] Unlike the Christian catechism, the cultural Marxist catechism announces the merger of church and state, for it specifies politics as its locus of morality.

For those of us who aren't woke, identity politics often does distract from and impede good government, because we believe government's place is limited to what it can do well. That is primarily to maintain public order by restricting man's innate violence. For today's left, however, identity politics is not a distraction from government; *it's the highest purpose of government.*

This is why identity politics' lawless bureaucratic mechanisms insert the federal government as a human resources big brother into all interactions. Like the Aztecs and Egyptians of old, their religion is their top priority, and the state exists first and foremost to serve it, even to the harm of the community.

This is why the Left's god, government, assumes tasks formerly reserved in the United States to faith and family. Their god is all-encompassing. He is totalitarian. He doesn't work through mediating institutions and means, he enfolds the people to himself directly. They are his slaves.

Yes, Department of Housing and Urban Development bureaucrats fining and harassing landowners for not using transgender pronouns would better serve the public good by working in homeless soup kitchens and addiction-fighting hospitals. Why are they not redirected in this fashion that 80 percent of Americans would support? Because those bureaucrats are not merely political figures, they are religious totems. They are the priests and prostitutes of a religious cult.

The old conception was that government exists to protect our natural rights, first among them our lives and liberties with local police, strong borders, and a strong national defense. The new conception is that government exists to provide spiritual direction and affirmation amid a culture that no longer seeks spiritual direction in their private lives from its original source—a true God.

To cultural Marxists, the pride political program is not a distraction from basic government, it's a replacement. It's morphed into not only a new legal regime, but a new spiritual regime. It's an attempt to replace our original Constitution with a pagan theocracy.

A Pagan Theocracy

Paganism doesn't keep the trains running or un-looted, but it does keep people involved in rituals that distract from their dysfunction. Some religious rites resolve dysfunction—penitence, forgiveness, and restitution, for example. Others, such as scapegoating, perpetuate dysfunction.

Through repentance, people take responsibility for their actions and work to improve. Through scapegoating, people transfer responsibility for their actions to uncontrollable entities like the rain god, heteronormativity, white supremacy, global warming, and the patriarchy. It's clear why a society based on the former would have more functioning infrastructure and a society based on the latter would decay.

It's no accident that cancel culture mushroomed in the age of identity politics. Its endless cycles of public shaming are a cultic religious ritual.

Identity politics unites pagan religious impulses with legal structures for enforcement and validation. This intertwined religious and political system—a theocracy—is displacing basic American rights that come from Christianity, like being assumed innocent until proven guilty in a court of law and being legally protected from public slander and libel.

Now our own government endorses this religious impulse and elevates its symbols atop the symbols of our former constitutional order. It's an occupation flag signifying regime change.

It's not surprising, because every government has to operate upon a widely accepted code of morality. Every government is informed and affected by the religion of its people. The basis of culture, as Russell Kirk noted, is the *cult*: a religion. From that religion's philosophical underpinnings flow government, the arts, and all the rest.

So, one wonders: What deity do some believe animates this new religion attempting an American regime change? Some of its adherents have a very honest answer.

Open Worship of Demons

A star fell over Birmingham, England, breaking into shards[32] right before a thirty-foot-tall mechanical bull stormed into the opening ceremonies of the 2022 Commonwealth Games. The ceremony dramatically illustrated the increasing overlap of cultural Marxist expressions with public pagan worship of what look like demons.

Dozens of women chained to the "beast" dragged it into the stadium. Then the fire-snorting, red-eyed black bull furiously broke the chains, and readied to rampage. "This causes pandemonium and, in an act of emancipation, the women break their own chains," says the show's script.[33]

A black woman, the lead character of Stella, approaches the bull, "the guardian spirit of Birmingham,"[34] bearing one of the star shards. She reaches up and "tames" it with an "offering of compassion." The dancers accompanying Stella put one open hand on their hearts and another in the air towards the bull.

The shard-bearing dancers once again raise their lighted pieces of broken star aloft and everyone on the field sits before the bull, then repeatedly rise and bow.[35] After lovingly caressing the bull, dancers lift away his armor and "he is revealed as a symbol of light and love."[36]

"I wanted to create an image of a creature that has been celebrated, used, maybe oppressed, but has enormous power, but we see it revealed as a creature of light," said opening ceremony artistic director Iqbal Khan, the son of Pakistani Muslim immigrants to England.[37]

Khan, a classically trained actor and director, told interviewers he wanted to make the 1 billion viewers of the ceremony first frightened of the bull. Then he wanted to strip their "preconceptions" and their fears so they "fall in love with" and "embrace" what they once feared.[38] It's a use of theater as old as Aristotle: synchronize the audience's hearts and minds with the story to change their beliefs through catharsis.

"A symbol of historical oppression . . . ," Khan told a podcast interviewer. "That symbol that at the beginning is terrifying, but that becomes a symbol of light, the symbol of love, the symbol of inclusion."[39]

Even those not deeply practiced in symbolism were struck by the pagan public ceremony. A YouTuber who uploaded a BBC video of the ceremony labeled it "Baal worship."[40] Baal is an ancient Canaanite and Phoenician god who took the form of a bull. In the Bible, Jesus refers to a demon god as "Baal-zebub," or lord of the demons.[41]

This ceremony is replete with cult imagery. In Isaiah 14:12, the Bible refers to Satan as a fallen star. It was a piece of the fallen star, wielded by the chief dancer, that tamed the bull—for a time.

The people's obeisance to these demons involves their "liberation" from chains such as the differences between the sexes—the women dancers who free themselves through political agitation rather than accepting and creatively working within the limitations of their sex. The "workers of the world" who "unite" "have nothing to lose but their chains," promised Karl Marx, in one of Communism's most memorable slogans. It was in this sense the dancing women enslaved themselves to a demon god while believing they were liberating themselves.

Bull worship at a huge athletic festival is just one of many recent incidents of deliberate mixing of pagan religious themes with cultural Marxism. To pay tribute to feminist icon Ruth Bader Ginsberg's satanic lust for killing babies inside their mothers, another Pakistani immigrant constructed a massive gold image of Ginsburg with demonic curling horns and writhing, tentacled arms.[42]

Sculptor Shahzia Sikander said her work depicts "a fierce woman and a form of resistance in a space that has historically been dominated by patriarchal representation." The statue was lodged atop a Manhattan courthouse. The New York Times summarized a black female judge who chaired a "diversity" commission as saying the statue was part of "a long overdue effort to address gender and racial bias."[43]

Target's Pride collection in 2023 featured the work of a "gay trans" designer who publicly promotes connections between Satan worship and LGBT identification. The U.K. designer's pieces for Target's collection promoted transgenderism on T-shirts, bags, and fanny packs with the slogans "Too queer for here," "We belong everywhere," and "Cure transphobia, not trans people." The designer also publicly supported genocide of people opposed to transgenderism: "to keep transphobes at bay we must eradicate them."

"[M]ost of my work focuses on gothic or dark and satanic imagery juxtaposed with bright colours and LGBT+ positive messages," the designer wrote on social media. In other designs on social media, the designer depicted transgender demons, pentagrams, "gay as hell" stickers, and T-shirts with the slogan, "Satan respects pronouns."

"So for me, Satan is hope, compassion, equality, and love," the designer said in a post explaining the T-shirt. "So, naturally, Satan respects pronouns. He loves all LGBT+ people. I went with a variation of Baphomet for this design, a deity who themself is a mixture of genders, beings, ideas, and existences. They reject binary stereotypes and expectations."

Baphomet, a well-known occult deity, is a symbol of Satan. The idol wears a goat head, another animal "monster." After all this, Target hired a gay designer to desecrate Christians' Christmas holiday in 2023 with images of gay Santas and transgender nutcrackers.[44] Transgender *nutcrackers*. Anyone refusing to acknowledge the transparent meaning of these statements and symbols is willfully blind.

At the 2023 Grammys, a gay man and transgender man dedicated their Satan-themed performance to "the kids." To perform "Unholy," an "Arabic scale" song about a man committing adultery,[45] "artist" Sam Smith dressed up as Satan and sang while witches bowed and cavorted before him. His partner Kim Petras gyrated in a cage in front of several strippers.

"The 'Unholy' performance was unique in being the first time that an erotic ritual of devil-worship was targeted at children on a major network during prime time," noted theology professor Thaddeus Williams in *World Magazine*.[46] It recalled, Williams noted, a 2021 music video by homosexual rapper Lil 'Nas in which he gives Satan a lap dance.

In Strikingly Biblical Terms

All these works of "art" depict sexual transgressions as Satanic. It's amazing how Christian that is. Even when blaspheming, the blasphemers affirm the religion they're trying to desecrate. Even Lil 'Nas's 666 "Satan shoes" that came out with his devil music video were inscribed with . . . a Bible verse.

All of this is so striking, in its openness and its religiosity. These LGBT-identified artists are openly stating that if they have to choose between God and the Devil, they'll take the Devil. They want Satan's sexual activities, not God's, and they know exactly which belong to whom.

This is a far cry from insisting LGBT acts are neutral private pleasures that should be accepted and tolerated. That remnant of Christian culture, which developed a broad respect for the private conscience and for the gracious delay of God's judgment on sinners so they might repent, is of course where things started. But, Toto, we are not in Kansas anymore. The face of LGBT-ism has shape-shifted right in front of our eyes.

It's not the Bible-thumpers but prominent queer figures saying they're taking off their mask and demons are under it. Of course, they briefly pop the mask on again to risibly claim all of this is just ironic "art," but that's an insult to our intelligence. The fact is, these artists are finding inspiration and resources in identifying their sexuality with a religion—a religion that worships Satan.

Symbolically and theologically, Satan is the figure of subversion and inversion. That's exactly what gender theorists want: the inversion of the heterosexual norm through pervasive homosexuality.

Also uncannily biblical is many gender-queer people's use of plural pronouns, such as referring to an individual as "they." In Mark 5:9, Jesus asks a demon-possessed man, "What is your name?" The man answers, "Legion, for we are many." Adherents of the gender cult not only use plural pronouns to identify themselves, they insist others participate in their demon-suggestive act of plural self-identification, on pain of state punishment.

Indeed, on TikTok and other social media apps, people with dissociative identity disorder, which used to be called multiple personality disorder, say they are occupied by a "system" of personalities. In videos they post to social media, people who claim to be afflicted with this disorder morph personalities, adopting different patterns of speech, facial expressions, interests, and gender identities. Judging from social media, most DID sufferers include at least one queer personality.

Not surprisingly, people contract DID from sustained abuse, during which they psychically separate themselves from violence inflicted upon them. A new personality enters to deal with the trauma. A *Vice* article quotes one afflicted person eerily referring to her body as a "meat car. The nine members of her system simply take turns driving it around."

"The multiplicity community [sic] insists on being seen as healthy—even normal," *Vice* says. "This is our reality, they argue. Why are you imposing your reality onto us?"

Some "systems" claim one of their personalities is a serial killer or pedophile. They refer to revealing their personalities as "coming out of the closet." Sufferers of this affliction demand societal acceptance of their manifestations rather than admitting the need for resolving their traumas. Like queer activists, they use plural pronouns, support the separation of body and mind ("boy brain in a girl body"), reject normality as a concept, insist the individual's perception determines reality, and insist it's bigotry and oppression to say they have a psychiatric malady.[47]

Again, this is flatly religious. In the Bible, when the Apostle Paul delivers a young woman from a demon, the civil authorities beat him and his companion Silas and throw them in prison. Their crime was depriving the girl's masters of money from her demon-driven fortune telling. The Christians "teach customs which are not lawful for us to receive," the girls' masters tell the city rulers.[48] The religious was the political then, as it is now.

Self-Described Pagans Center Queer Sex

In 2021, a *Washington Post* profile of the growing practice of Wicca and other self-described paganisms claimed that contemporary witches, mediums, and other would-be consorters with false gods and demons strongly support leftist politics. The TikTok hashtag #witchtok has 19.4 billion views, the *Post* notes.

Washington Post religion reporter Michelle Boorstein also openly connects these witches' rejection of God with rejecting distinctions between the two sexes that He created. These pagans are predominantly drawn into Wicca through their allegiance to abortion and queer identities, Boorstein says. Child sacrifice, child mutilation, ritual self-mutilation, and sexual abuse are, of course, ancient rites of idol worship.

Witches the *Post* profiled organized fundraisers for the Lilith Fund, which pays women's abortion expenses.[49] Lilith is the name of a demon from ancient Jewish mythology "who is sexually wanton, and who steals babies in the darkness."[50]

While they are described benignly as seeking "forgiveness," "spiritual power," and "peace," these practitioners of witchcraft do hate something: Christians. Again, a bit on the nose, isn't it?

Sexual license is also at the core of the Satanic Temple. This claims to be a secular humanist outfit while also performing satanic rites such as "Black Masses featuring ritual bloodletting and the desecration of potentially consecrated hosts," notes Jacob Adams in *First Things*.[51] In its efforts to erase Constitutional protections for competing religions, the Satanic Temple claims abortion is one of their religious rites. It also sets up "Satan Clubs" at K–12 schools and colleges, raises money for abortion, and files lawsuits that attempt to erase religious freedom for people of any religion but theirs.

"The Satanic Temple has become the primary religious Satanic organization in the world with congregations internationally, and a number of high-profile public campaigns designed to preserve and advance secularism and individual liberties," the organization states on its "about" page.[52] The organization's cofounder says the majority of its members are LGBT and that chapters are regulars at local Pride parades.[53] The Satanic Temple performs a "pink Mass" that inserts homosexual acts into the central Christian religious rite.

"[T]he Satanic Temple has become a haven for queer folks," a lesbian member writes. "At the first meeting I attended, nearly everyone I talked to was confidently queer, gay, pansexual, transgender, bi, polyamorous, or something in between."[54]

While the Satanic Temple describes itself as "inspired by 18th Century enlightenment values," all this seems a far cry from scientific rationality. There's a lot of demonic overlap, and it's not all irony, either. These Satanists see Satan as the quintessential rebel. They're right about that.

The Culture War Is a Religious War

All these are clear signs the culture war is not merely about "social issues" or "politics." It goes right into the deepest parts of our beings and of the universe. Its core divide is whether a person will acknowledge any authority over the self, such as things that are true for all people in all times regardless of their feelings or "experience." That's what worship is: An acknowledgment that one is under an authority.

For Christians, that authority is Christ, the Word of God and Creator of all. For Satanists—and leftists more broadly—that authority is the Self. In literature and religion, Lucifer defines himself by denying all authority but his own. While Jesus was defined by His submission to God the Father, Lucifer was defined by his rebellion against God the Father.

Our "cultural" divide is spiritual.[55] This is why the leftist project seeks, for example, to overturn a Constitution and society built on natural law, which insists humans can only find true happiness by living in harmony with the created order. Their entire project is rebellion against the created order and therefore the God who made it.

If human beings have rights from God, all men are bound to respect those in an act of submission to God's order. If there is no Christian God, or if we can assume His place by imposing our fantasies on reality, then there are also no natural human rights. It's that simple.

Christianity is waning in the West. Any replacement is necessarily a religious replacement, and that is why all replacements are totalitarian: because no religion but Christianity has developed different (but complementary) roles for church and state. No other religion has developed a template for giving to Caesar what is Caesar's, and to God what is God's.[56]

Every other religion's compulsion for humans to take God's place in shaping human souls turns the governments connected with those religions totalitarian, concerned with what Christians call private family and neighborhood matters such as bullying, language use, bathroom policies, and so forth. This is why the atheist Communist governments are probably the largest mass murderers in world history. They assumed the place of God—which also meant they could do no wrong. As history shows, this tendency even legitimizes genocide.

Including secular humanism and progressivism, every religion but Christianity demands that humans try to save themselves. Instead, in Christianity, God alone completely and fully perfects and saves the soul. This lifts from government its totalitarian tendencies, because a Chrisitan government doesn't need to perfect and save souls. It just needs to serve people's bodies: make the trains run on time and keep poop off the streets.

In discussing her recent conversion to Christianity, the former Muslim and former atheist Ayaan Hirsi Ali explained atheism had led her to despair. Christianity, she told an interviewer, "says human life is worth living because it's in the image of God . . . That's much, much more appealing to me than the story of: there is nothing there, you have no more value than mold."[57]

In leaving Islam, Hirsi Ali said that she thinks she jumped "too soon on the atheist bandwagon and accepted too quickly the proposition that all religions are the same, and equally bad, and equally dark." Rather than reason and religion contradicting each other, like all Christian intellectuals Hirsi Ali sees them as complementary.

During her years as a very public atheist who associated with Richard Dawkins and Christopher Hitchens, Hirsi Ali says that she endured Islamists sending assassins after her, while the Christians she publicly criticized sent letters saying they were praying for her. This caused her to think, "Actually, I'm not quite sure that these two religions are the same or that all religions are the same," she said. Hirsi Ali sees political liberalism as rooted in Christianity and says that without Christianity free societies will die.

"We should stop being shy and inhibited and coy about who we are and who we have to thank for all of these [civilizational] successes," Hirsi Ali said. She took responsibility for "my part in advancing the erosion of the building blocks of this Western civilization that, as I say, I love so much."

"You've got to put in the same level of effort, if not more, into winning hearts and minds over to the broader story of Christianity," Ali said. "It can be done if we want to. It's a matter of will."

CHAPTER 8

Strategies for Counterrevolutionaries

"There will be a reckoning. . . . Ultimately, critical theory
will be put to a simple test: Are conditions improving or not
improving? Are cities safer or less safe? Are students learning
to read or not learning to read? The new regime can only
suppress the answers for so long."
—Christopher Rufo, America's Cultural Revolution[1]

Our time is not one of mere political disagreement, but of a religious cold civil war. Therefore, counterrevolutionary tactics—not "agree to disagree" or "split differences down the middle"—are required to combat America's color revolution. Counterrevolutionary tactics mean understanding Marxists as enemies and taking prudent, tactically intelligent efforts to contain, restrain, and rout them.

Politics is war by other means, and negotiating with cultural Marxists is like negotiating with terrorists. They do not prefer a different route to the same goal. They want Mad Max. We want peace, the natural order, and beauty. Only one of us can win. For the sake of us all, it better be the Americans who still show allegiance to the original Constitution in our hearts and deeds.

In the spirit of the American founders, those who see clearly on sexual politics also need to practice prudence and patience. As illustrated by the stark fact that Roe v. Wade's reversal increased abortion rates in many states,[2] large portions of the American electorate are not prepared for the self-government required to preserve the vestiges of our constitutional republic.

This means those who believe in objective reality must play a long game and take incremental steps that slowly revive habits of self-government among the people. That's not an excuse for leaving advances on the negotiating table or failing to play hardball to get the best deal possible out of political negotiations. But it's a caution that in fighting the extremism of sexual politics, we must not engage in imprudence.

The United States didn't get ruined in a day, and it cannot be restored in one election, either. Backlash does nobody any favors.

That reality can't excuse timidity, because the chances that any politician takes overly drastic actions to challenge sexual politics are about zero. In the current environment, most Republicans are far too timid rather than too brash. That's something conservatives can learn from the Left: they don't believe they have to hold a majority to gain significant wins. Neither did the American founders, and neither must we.

What Executive Branches Can Do

Due to most Republican politicians' cowardice and lethargy and the Democrat Party's consequently unchecked sexual extremism, a lot of low-hanging policy fruit is available. It should be easy for more states to enact the policies of Republicans like Donald Trump and Florida Gov. Ron DeSantis, who are popular with Republicans and attract independent voters.

Waging war on sexual identity politics unites Republicans and attracts independents who see sexual extremism as a threat to kids' safety and adults' rights. An August 2023 survey of a thousand Republican voters found 69 percent selected "transgender activism" as one of "the most important challenges facing America," making it the top item of concern among twelve options.

The poll found most "new right" voters polled wanted politicians to focus on culture war issues including sexual politics, far above the proportion wanting politicians to talk about regulation, taxes, or free trade. Coming in at No. 2 of Republican voters' top concerns was a related issue: "woke corporations."[3] The study also found that groups Republicans traditionally struggle to attract were more attracted to "new right" identity politics issues: women, low- and working-class voters, and self-described moderates.

Incompetent Republican strategists might respond that "social issues" lose elections. That's hard to believe coming from people who cede morality to Democrats. It's fair to suspect Republicans lose on social issues because they don't fight on them, although politicians are sometimes the only voice voters hear arguing against leftist insanity. There's plenty of evidence that Republicans who won't fight obvious issues like child mutilation lose by failing to motivate their own base. People don't get to the polls for a 2 percent tax cut or more tax abatements for politicians' donors. More Republicans need to run on the culture war.

Trump's first term exemplifies what we're up against, what to do, and what not to do. The lessons include: Don't trust the press or the bureaucracy, fire as many bureaucrats as possible, take your message directly to the people, and fire or prosecute everyone who breaks the law.

If elected officials cannot fire insubordinate bureaucrats, they should change policies that ban such accountability. Trump was especially good at communicating support for queer people as fully equal citizens while not supporting the anti-Constitution policies put forward in their name.

Trump's 2024 campaign also illustrates it's long past time for a house-cleaning in the judiciary. Judges keep their lifetime appointments from good behavior. Authorizing the state to mutilate children because their parents won't is evil behavior deserving of impeachment. So is authorizing the state to go after Democrats' opponents and failing to strike down unconstitutional "hate crimes" laws and commissions.

Chris Rufo, who has done extensive policy work, explains what a president and Congress can achieve: "establish ideological authority over the federal bureaucracy in the White House and, in partnership with Congress, decentralize as much of the federal government as possible, with an eye toward gutting the power of the social engineers. For decades, conservatives in Congress have effectively written a blank check to captured institutions, experienced dismay at the subsequent behavior of those institutions, and then continued to fund them. These are all policy choices—and they can be changed."[4]

Rufo also suggests "a new civil rights enforcement office within the Department of Justice. . . . This new office, adhering to a conservative interpretation of civil rights law, would investigate corporations, universities, schools, and other institutions that engage in racial preferences, hostile diversity and inclusion programming, and critical race theory-style scapegoating and discrimination. These practices would all be deemed violations of Title VI of the Civil Rights Act and prosecuted with the full force of the Justice Department. The president can instruct the Secretary of Education to employ a similar method to strike at the origin point of the revolution: the universities."[5] Governors and state attorney generals can do the same.

While legislatures and executives working in concert are needed to fully uproot the DEI regime, Rufo's policy recommendations can also apply both to the national executive and to state executives. He says executive orders should ban every facet of government from promoting critical theory and "abolish the 'diversity, equity, and inclusion' bureaucracy that serves as its administrative vehicle."[6] The executive should replace identity politics with strict merit policies that emphasize equal treatment under the law. He or she should also ban government workers from any sort of political display.

More effective, because it's less susceptible to leftist capture, would be erasing the laws corrupt agencies use to implement Marxism. The United States needs mass deregulation and mass de-bureaucratization. States can do so as well as the feds. This can be accomplished in steps, such as first eliminating duplication among agencies and later consolidating agencies while eliminating many of their anti-Constitutional functions. The US Department of Education not only doesn't need a SWAT team, it doesn't need to exist.

What Legislatures Can Do

Congress's list of possibilities is large, too, if it would ever stop allowing bureaucrats to run the country and start doing real legislative work. Besides defunding every DEI-promoting program, state and federal legislators should make opposing identity politics a litmus test to earn their votes for any executive nominee. That includes judges, military promotions, and administrative positions. Support for disparate impact policies, "implicit bias," and any facet of identity politics should be considered entirely disqualifying for every nominee.

Lawmakers should also defund all identity programs everywhere they exist: higher education, human resources offices, grants, K–12, teacher training, government agencies, the court system, health and child welfare agencies, and so on. Governors and legislatures should also refuse to accept any federal funding that pushes recipients into DEI programming or policies. Where officials are bound by law to run workplace trainings, they should implement trainings in an accurate understanding of the US Constitution and the Founders' thought, perhaps using Thomas West's "Vindicating the Founders" as a study guide and paying for trainings from lawyers and professors loyal to the Constitution as written and understood by its Framers.

In Florida, DeSantis has been extremely effective in wielding both traditional and counterrevolutionary political tactics. He and Florida's legislature have provided trailblazing templates for legislation that other states can copy into their legal codes with minor local modifications.

Examples include DeSantis replacing the board of a state university called New College, banning teachers from talking about sex with small kids, and staring down Disney's identity politics belligerence. Florida also introduced regulations to erase DEI from higher education,[7] which could be extended to K–12. They require schools to designate a person who ensures institution compliance with the state policy.[8]

Florida also passed laws pulling state licenses from any establishment that allows children to see drag, protecting teachers and students from being forced to use false pronouns, banning public school instruction on gender identity until after eighth grade, and banning transgender child mutilation.[9]

Another low-hanging policy tweak: scheduling school board and other local elections at the same time as higher-turnout statewide elections. Lower-turnout spring election dates enable special interest capture of schools and local governments.[10]

States Should Divest from the Federal Government

The risk of the national government's collapse increases with every omnibus Congress passes. It's past time for states to start divesting from federal control created by essentially government bribes. Courts that aren't controlled by Marxists can help.[11]

Many state departments can handle functions currently fulfilled by the feds, such as departments of education and child welfare, workplace safety, and health inspections. The Tenth Amendment reserves such matters to states, yet states allow themselves to be bribed with federal money to give up citizens' constitutional rights. But this federal money costs more than it brings in, not only in compliance costs but also the priceless loss of American constitutional freedoms.

States should be working to disentangle from federal programs, funding this conscious decoupling through local and sustainable economic growth, welcoming of conservative-minded blue state refugees, cuts to unnecessary bureaucracy, and vibrancy among their citizenry. Responsible states will audit their regulatory codes and agencies as well as their legal codes to see what can be liberated from federal micromanagement.

Schools don't need to have windows on only one wall in their classrooms, spindles on staircases don't need to be government-regulated, and foster families don't need to have so many outlets per bedroom. All of this gunk—and the people enforcing it—should go. The savings can be used to replace federal funds.

The largest savings, of course, will be in states making serious changes to health welfare and government pension programs. Just like people getting food stamps should be working if they're able to do so, people getting health welfare should be required to attend classes on how to cook vegetables and to take a daily walk. Illegal immigrants who aren't allowed inside the state or country can't stick their emergency room and other health-care tabs to taxpayers, driving up hospital and insurance costs for all responsible citizens.

States should consider paying families to take care of their elderly who don't need constant medical care instead of occupying much higher-cost nursing homes. They should fix "benefits cliffs" that subsidize antisocial behavior such as making children outside of marriage. They should put Section 8 housing away from decent neighborhoods and police Section 8 areas more. Convert all the state's K–12 dollars to backpack funding that flows through an education savings account that parents control, which will help more children get better educated with less taxpayer outlay. That would save millions over ten years, if not billions depending on the size of the state.

States need to try social entrepreneurship ideas like these to get their citizens doing more for themselves and their neighbors and relying less on stealing others' labor. Not only will this free taxpayer money to replace debt-funded federal "largesse," it will also boost local economies and strengthen families, all of which create a more functional, less expensive, and happier society.

States also should partner with charitable organizations and churches to meet citizens' needs. Unlike the leftists, who drive out these low-cost and high-connection social safety nets, states should celebrate and amplify preferential tax treatment for religious charities. States should support charities that serve tangible human needs over "charities" that function as cultural front organizations for Marxists.

Another way to reclaim money to fund decoupling from federal incompetence would be slashing higher education subsidies. States should start by erasing the diversity, equity, and inclusion staff of every institution funded with state dollars. They should also audit and consolidate state universities with the goal of getting more young citizens into jobs faster and with less debt. All courses, institutes, speakers' series, departments, and professors that teach Marxism should be defunded and the money reallocated to job training and retraining programs.

States should also dramatically raise admissions standards for young people entering non-community colleges to encourage people to enter the marketplace directly. The default post-high school option should be work, not college, and legislatures should work with industries and apprenticeship programs to shift education systems in that direction.

In most colleges, the so-called liberal arts are just fronts for Marxism. As such, they should be eliminated and replaced with concrete and efficient job training. High-level students who need truly liberal education and qualify for its challenges—lawyers, judges, teachers, pastors, doctors—can be served by a few institutions retooled and stocked with non-Marxist professors.

Legislatures should audit all government jobs and eliminate all unnecessary credential requirements that create false demand for college degrees. People don't need a four-year degree to be a clerk or meter reader or many other local government positions; they can be apprenticed for six to twelve months and then take the job. State contracts should require this of private employers as well.

Restore High-Commitment Marriage Options

A divorcé himself, Ronald Reagan said signing the nation's first no-fault divorce law as governor of California was one of his greatest mistakes.[12] It's time state lawmakers acted on his too-late realization to reduce the chaos that no-fault divorce creates. It should be a no-brainer for state lawmakers to create an optional marriage license that includes a state-enforced pre-nuptial agreement protecting both parties in the event of a later divorce.

This state-enforced pre-nup would require those who opt in to this marriage license to prove marital fault to later obtain a divorce. The spouse found at fault in court for violating his vows—such as through adultery, physical abuse, addiction, or abandonment—would be penalized for his breach of the marital contract. This would help deter such crimes against families.

People who want to go into marriage with no-fault divorce as a later option could still choose the standard marriage license, but states could offer an alternative to couples who are interested in more secure vows. Perhaps states could find a way to allow people who are already married to retroactively access this option. Some policy entrepreneurs call this a "covenant marriage."

Discussions about an option like this have been broached in Louisiana and Nebraska,[13] but zero Americans who marry today have the legal protections marriage licenses offered well into the 1980s and 1990s. That's a travesty. Protecting spouses who don't want to divorce and who stayed faithful to their vows should be a no-brainer, especially if marrying couples can choose whether to opt in to stronger marriage protections.

This would open more options to marrying couples, not foreclose any. It would benefit society immensely by acting to protect monogamy and children's natural right to the attention and affection of their two biological parents.

Family scholar W. Brad Wilcox has other good recommendations: "States should combine a one-year waiting period for married parents seeking a divorce with programs that educate those parents about the likely social and emotional consequences of their actions for their children. State divorce laws should also allow courts to factor in spousal conduct when making decisions about alimony, child support, custody, and property division. In particular, spouses who are being divorced against their will, and who have not engaged in egregious misbehavior such as abuse, adultery, or abandonment, should be given preferential treatment by family courts."[14]

Following Arkansas, Florida, and Kentucky, states can also pass "shared parenting" laws that assume in the event of a divorce the child's best interest is to split his time 50–50 between his two parents. Such laws put each parent on equal standing, although judges can alter them based on evidence of a parent's lesser fitness.

Another option for minor marriage reforms includes Florida's recently reduced alimony payments. This also reduces incentives for spouses to profit from destroying their families.[15] In addition, states should ban courts and child welfare agencies from taking children from their homes or otherwise charging child abuse against parents whose only "crime" is supporting their children's real sex.

Boycott, Divest, Sanction DEI

Voters should demand that politicians divest, sanction, and defund the insurrectionists against the Constitution. It's preposterous for any politician to require taxpayers to fund obscene ideologues who endorse child mutilation and put on public pornography shows.

It's not book-banning or censorship to refrain from funding or offering public platforms to pornographers and child mutilators. They're still free to seek out private funding and venues, and to publish smut on their own platforms and dimes. Nobody argues it's "censorship" for libraries to not stock every book available, because that's preposterous. Nobody is censored when government doesn't pay him for his work product.

Government funding is not a civil right. In fact, it's a violation of citizens' natural rights to force us to fund people who hate our country and work to destroy its future. A boycott, divest, sanction campaign against sexual extremists might include:

- Slashing bureaucracy, including erasing the US Department of Education and removing civil service protections that keep abusers in power

- Firing and seeking civil penalties against those who abuse positions of public privilege (such as leakers and doxxers in the IRS, FBI, and elsewhere)
- Ruthlessly cutting all public funds and deposing the leaders of any institution that supplies sex books to children, funds or encourages mutilating surgeries, has pushed DEI, or effectively bans Christians from employment
- Fund intersectionalism escape pods for children by passing full school choice at the state level with full backpack funding that does not include regulations (including testing requirements) that would force critical theory into these DEI escape hatches
- Splitting up the FBI to include an independent federal agency that effectively combats child trafficking and pornography
- Impeaching and shaming judges who do not faithfully apply the US Constitution and historical American jurisprudence, through local pressure campaigns
- And swapping training in the First Amendment and historic American civil liberties for all "DEI" training in every government agency and contractor. Hire local Federalist Society members to perform these trainings.

More Difficult Long-Term Goals

"As the Supreme Court noted in *Bostock v. Clayton County*," I noted in 2023, "more than 100 federal laws now foist Marxist-driven DEI policies into every corner of American society."[16] These are styled "antidiscrimination laws," but they're really *pro*-discrimination laws.

Today it may be a political nonstarter to eliminate the 1964 Civil Rights Act the bureaucracy has turned into a weapon against the Constitution, but so was overturning *Roe v. Wade* until Trump appointed three better-than-average justices to the Supreme Court. Big victories take time, and they take champions ahead of their time. We all can become champions simply by starting to call these laws what they are: discriminatory, bigoted, evil, and Leviathan.

Little victories lay the foundation for bigger ones. Deregulation efforts can include sex discrimination laws that lie to Americans that men and women are completely the same. Surely these 100 federal discrimination laws could be pared down, defunded, narrowed in scope, and eliminated one by one. The incremental argument can be that we don't need 100 laws allowing men to supervise little girls in locker rooms and pose as women in bathrooms; 99 will do. And do we really need 99? Couldn't 98 suffice?

Merely amending the CRA is not ideal because its text explicitly bans the disparate impact and quota systems bureaucrats and judges now use the law to enforce. But it still would be a step forward to add provisions requiring concrete evidence of intentional discrimination for a claim to be successful.[17] And overhauling their enforcement agencies is necessary to end their blatant use of these statutes to engage in what the statutes prohibit.

Focus on States and Localities

Despite all it needs to do, at this point, Congress is largely a lost cause. As detailed by multiple constitutional scholars and investigative journalists, national politics are overrun with special interests with zero incentives for changing the system. Anyone who wants to take necessary actions is hit with attack ads showing him throwing grandmothers off a cliff.

Grifting accompanies many national political efforts on the right and left, as the Tea Party years show. It seems almost anything that gets big gets co-opted by the blob.

States are also overrun with special interests, but those are easier to defeat, especially in lesser-populated red states. At the state level, lawmakers pay much closer attention to constituents, meaning that organizing fewer people can have a larger impact. Aides for state lawmakers told me twenty-five people who handwrite personal letters can get almost anything they want from the state legislature, except on major issues with well-defined positions such as abortion. Conservatives need to stop yelling at their computer screens and enjoying the relative peace of red locales and run for local offices, like the library board, neighborhood association, and town council. If you put more effort into your kid's basketball team than into staving off the Cultural Revolutionaries coming for your family, you need to rethink your priorities.

People who look at national politics and are rightly disgusted give up too easily by retreating from politics altogether. State and local politics are field teams for national politics. As we saw during lockdowns, localities matter a lot. If yours was governed by just a few people whose allegiance to the Constitution was strong, you had far more freedoms.

Local politics require people to meet and persuade their fellow Americans. It requires learning legitimate, real-life leadership skills. It requires toning down the culture war hyperventilation and learning how to practically solve human problems. That is much, much harder than yelling into the abyss of Facebook.

A volunteer team of two dozen people who commit to local politics as much as parents do their kids' soccer team could be highly effective at winning elections outside of big cities. If you want that, start organizing one. You'll find it's a lot harder than you think to motivate people, which will help give you some humility about how "easy" it is to shape national politics. This will also create a group of people around you who can, over decades, transform your local political party institutions, and thereby help transform your state.

Self-Government Starts at Home

To lead others, first you must lead yourself. Leading yourself is the essence of self-government. It's easy, obvious, and accurate to point out everything wrong with tranny twerking in front of children, but it's not easy to reflect on one's own failure to promote the common good.

That's not to draw a false equivalence between people who mind their own business and people who harm their neighbors. But it is to point out that integrity requires self-examination, reflection, then resolute action towards your thoughtfully determined goals. It's also to point out that finding fault with others is easy but fixing your own faults is hard.

If we want a better country, we have to start with ourselves. Leading oneself is the prerequisite for leading a family. Leading a family is the prerequisite for leading a local group. Leading those small groups is a prerequisite for leading larger groups.

One earns authority step by step. Yes, that traditional path is little followed today, and that helps account for why our leaders are so incompetent and corrupt. It's up to us to contribute towards a better society by starting with ourselves, then once we've demonstrated basic competence and integrity, seeking slowly to expand it. All of us who want better leadership should be seeking how we can become the virtuous leaders we're looking for.

With a nod to Jordan Peterson, start by cleaning your own room. Then clean your own house. Then invite people into that house. Marry one. Manage your children. Influence your neighborhood. And grow from there. The nation is counting on you to do your part, and to seek to do as much as you humanly can.

Restore Public Honor for Virtue

Winning status motivates people. Aaron Renn notes, "status seeking is critical to channeling especially young men into healthy and pro-social behavior. When status is not awarded for healthy behaviors, it is probably being acquired through other status systems that are unhealthy."[18]

Mass American culture awards status to the most degenerate people and behaviors: the biggest liars, the biggest cheaters, the Jezebels, the Judases. So anyone in charge of any institution—starting with the smallest and most important: the family—should be prioritizing public honor for private virtue. It's counterrevolutionary to champion full-time moms and homeschooling. It's counterrevolutionary to champion fathers, hard work, humility, and self-sacrifice.

Celebrate everything counterrevolutionary to the highest hilt possible. Write Facebook messages about your mom and dad's sacrifices for you. Award local scholarship money to teens who show true excellence in conduct and intellect. Honor—and assist!—the families who raise their child with Down Syndrome instead of killing him in the womb. Praise pregnant women and celebrate their suffering on behalf of their children and the world. Show up to help with their laundry. Give them free babysitting a few times a year.

Those with large financial and media resources should do the same. Make a powerful documentary about Jack Phillips or someone who faced down the Environmental Protection Agency. Start a business accelerator that prioritizes businesses that employ Americans with living family wages and make things in America. Give an annual prize of $500,000 to an exemplary couple who stayed married for fifty years. Pay off the college loans of a young man with high academic potential who chooses to use it in seminary when he could have earned hundreds of thousands more in his lifetime by instead going into engineering. Fund a local classical school.

These are just a few of the thousands of creative ways to support virtue in America. The media and government will not do it for us, although they should. So we the people should do it in every way possible, and as publicly as possible.

Out-Symbol the Iconoclasts

Imagery is very powerful, especially in a society with declining literacy and thinking abilities. Ad campaigns and artistic works, for example, should depict loving mothers and fathers with each other and their children. These could—and for greatest uptake, probably should—take the form of mini-documentaries, graphic novels, telenovas, YouTube channels, and more that all show what a loving nuclear family looks like and how they confront challenges.

More people need familial and sacrificial ideals. In our world, fewer and fewer people have any mental conception of what sexual restraint and its lifelong benefits look and feel like. Art can help people's minds inhabit homes they've never visited before and teach them what it looks like to fruitfully embody wholeness.

The archetype of a loving, married mother and father caring together for their own biological children is a powerful one, and it needs to be reasserted. So do other ancient archetypes that give people visions of goodness, beauty, and their true place in the world.

Christians own extremely strong archetypal symbols we should deploy. These include the crucifix, martyrs, the clerical collar, angels, the Bible, and prayer. All people with strong religious imagery should be reviving such symbols—and their underlying meanings—and using them in public and private.

Wear that crucifix. Put up a Nativity scene in your yard at Christmastide. Start a YouTube or Rumble channel showing your family planting carrots in your garden, reading beautiful classic books, making handicrafts, and singing folk songs while doing the dinner dishes. Start a Simply Convivial chapter for women, and an exercise club with men from church. People have no idea how to live, and showing the beauty of good ways of life gives them hope, support, and ideas.

Faithful Local Presence

Since this is a religious war, nonphysical spiritual warfare must be deployed. To mark and oppose every instance of anti-American degeneracy such as drag queen exhibitions, locals should hold peaceful prayer vigils, hymn sings, and Bible readings. These should include public prayers for the good of their foes.

People who organize and attend such events should avoid in-person confrontations with opponents and not bring those vulnerable in case of physical attack. They should consider taking trainings on being legal observers in case of a confrontation with police or protesters and understand their constitutional rights to peacefully assemble and express their views.

All churches should work to provide for every child in their congregation to receive a wholly Christian education. Churches don't need to run a school to use part of their budgets to fund a Christian education for parishioners' kids. No Christian child should attend any school where he might be assigned a transgender teacher or exposed to LGBT porn. That's why even families who don't use such schools should strongly support them: because what your neighbors learn to believe will affect you and your children.

Schooling spread as a result of the Reformation's emphasis on teaching every person to read so he could read the Bible for himself. Since then, churches have provided Christian schools to ensure children were educated first in their family's faith and second to serve fellow citizens through intellectual and useful arts.

The church fathers and reformers emphasized this, so that for centuries relocating groups of Christians immediately established a church school right after establishing the church. Today, Christian philanthropists should again make the provision of excellent Christian education a top giving priority. Since Christian schools create far more prosocial, pro-America graduates than anti-God public schools,[19] even non-Christian philanthropists should fund Christian schools.

Churches should spend no money on missions outside their walls until they have provided for the evangelization and spiritual instruction of all the children within their walls. The same goes for religious parents. Charity starts at home, and so does evangelization. Churches that cannot effectively witness to their own congregants have no business with missions anywhere else.

Don't Retreat, Advance

It would be a historical miracle for the US empire to recover its former vitality as expressed in the Founding generation and its laws. Nations almost never come back from running endless foreign wars while a decadent, corrupt ruling class cannibalizes their land and people. No nation in history has ever accumulated as much debt as the United States, nor created such a large portion of fatherless—and therefore at higher risk of being violent and mentally incompetent[20]—citizens.

Decadent nations have, however, encountered periods of resurgent peace and stability. Usually it is presaged by serious suffering: a lost major war, a natural disaster; something that ends the plausible legitimacy of the ruling class despoiling the country. The United States has lost most of its wars since Vietnam and inflicted a disastrous COVID-19 response,[21] and as yet these have sparked no mass repentance that is the prerequisite for a national revival.

That suggests more pain is to come. People who do not heed the evil consequences of their own choices eventually get worse consequences. Although it sounds delightful, Americans are not going to Benedict Option[22] their way out of this. Detroit, San Francisco, and New York City choices affect all of us, whether we like it or not.

For example, the presence of malevolent foreigners capable of terrorist attacks due to open borders threatens all of us even if we didn't vote for Joe Biden. The terrorist attacks such cells are preparing will likely result in further curtailments of all Americans' civil liberties and increases in the US surveillance state.

There is nowhere to hide from this or other problems like the fact that all of us depend on electricity and global food markets. Increased self-sufficiency can certainly boost financial margins, resilience, and health, but statistically zero of us are going to farm our own wheat, milk, vegetables, meat, wood, cotton, and wool. That's what's required to keep people alive, and even the Amish don't do this alone but in communities of several hundred people together. It's humanly impossible for most people to live like Ma and Pa Ingalls.

Homesteading and Benedict Option tendencies, while valuable to the extent they build healthy local cultural ecosystems, can also enable escapism. The point of life is not merely staying alive in your bunker eating acorns, even if soft Westerners could manage that. Conservatives and religious folks need to think a lot bigger. We need to act as groups, not as lone wolves. Not "every man for himself" but "all for one, and one for all."

Certainly, we need many people to build local healthy food infrastructure. America needs more farmers, not fewer. But that's only one part of the larger need for creating parallel healthy societies within our crumbling society, and everyone shouldn't become homesteaders or homeschoolers. Others are needed to build Christian schools, new training systems for lawyers, health-care systems that don't punish

Christians, and businesses that can create hundreds and thousands of jobs.

Still others are needed to staff and build new media outlets, especially outside of politics. Still others are needed to create new political parties and local organizations like Moms for Liberty chapters. Since just about everything in our country is a freaking dumpster fire, that means the opportunities for social entrepreneurship are wide open. Pick something you're good at or could get good at with some practice. Pick something that meets a need in your hometown. Focus not just on retreating to protect yourself and your family, but using your skills to cultivate the community your family needs for high-quality, long-term stability, resources, and companionship.

All of our efforts must not come from a place of retreat, but advancement. Disposition is at the heart of what makes something like freeholding or homeschooling escapism versus prudence. The action might look the same, but the animating factor can be completely different. One comes from despair; the other from hope and faith. We should not be seeking retreats, strategic or otherwise, but advances. Solitary retreat ensures defeat. Institution-building advances are our only hope for survival.

Prepare to Suffer

If you do anything worthwhile, you are going to take incoming fire. That's one way you can know you're over the target: if what you're doing is clearly worthwhile but also really hard.

Building a family, church, business, school, or local political group are all a giant pain in the butt. Accomplishments like these require listening, learning how to persuade and work with different personalities, making budgets, dealing with stupid paperwork and bureaucrats, facing your own rough edges, and all manner of other hindrances. Real achievements take time, money, sleep, and even hair follicles. In short, if you want to do anything real, expect suffering.

Refusing to suffer is destroying our culture. Today most Americans only want to give money, commitments, and time they won't miss, not that they really feel the loss of. But, as history shows, making real sacrifices is the only way to make great advances.

If we want our country to regain any semblance of greatness, we Americans are going to have to sacrifice a lot. A lot of people are going to have to give up comfortable, twenty-year retirements. Others are going to have to give up vacations, child-free quietude, screen-filled pockets of time, their reluctance to marry, and their independence. Too many people don't want to make such quotidian sacrifices, let alone the even greater sacrifices required of statesmen, and that's why our country is regressing so quickly.

US history is full of people who took ten major risks a day before they ate their breakfasts. Now we are a nation full of risk-adverse people. Part of that adventuresome spirit, however, does live on in our DNA, and it needs to be revived. As Renn points out, "in Silicon Valley, people regularly undertake audacious ideas that they aren't sure how they will accomplish or even if it is possible to accomplish them."[23]

Christians know God is with us and works all things together for good. That's not a license to be a fool, but it is an encouragement to stop hiding in a bunker while the world goes to hell. We can afford to experiment and then to try something else if it doesn't work out. We have to act out of hope and faith instead of hiding in apocalyptic despair. We need to occupy space, occupy attention, and start forcing government to get back to securing our rights.

It's easy to look around and complain that we have no Abraham Lincolns to lead our troops in the cold civil war. But it's pretty hard to think: What would I have to do to *become* an Abraham Lincoln? If I couldn't aspire quite so high, could I become the equivalent of an effective Lincoln general? What about one of his captains? One of his infantrymen?

This country can only be as great as its people. We are its people. It is up to all of us who desire national greatness to bring it forth from ourselves and our children. That starts with getting off the smartphone and taking concrete positive action right now.

Notes

Introduction

1   Randy Barnett (@RandyEBarnett), "It's time for establishment Republicans . . .," Twitter, October 23, 2023, 9:55 p.m., https://twitter.com/RandyEBarnett/status/1716634518688322014.

2   Raj Chetty, Nathaniel Hendren, Patrick Kline, and Emmanuel Saez. "Where Is the Land of Opportunity? The Geography of Intergenerational Mobility in the United States." Working Paper. Working Paper Series. National Bureau of Economic Research, January 2014. https://doi.org/10.3386/w19843.

3   Brian Goesling, Hande Inanc, and Angela Rachidi, "Success Sequence: A Synthesis of the Literature," OPRE Report Number 2020–41, Office of Planning, Research, and Evaluation, Administration for Children and Families, U.S. Department of Health and Human Services, December 2020, https://www.acf.hhs.gov/sites/default/files/documents/opre/Success_sequence_review_2020_508_0.pdf.

4   Constitution of Virginia, article 1, section 15, https://law.lis.virginia.gov/constitution/article1/section15/.

5   Thomas G. West, *The Political Theory of the American Founding: Natural Rights, Public Policy, and the Moral Conditions of Freedom* (Cambridge, United Kingdom: Cambridge University Press, 2017), 152.

6   Robert Rector, "How Welfare Undermines Marriage and What to Do about It," The Heritage Foundation, https://www.heritage.org/welfare/report/how-welfare-undermines-marriage-and-what-do-about-it.

7   "Julia's Mother: Why a Single Mom Is Better Off with a $29,000 Job and Welfare than Taking a $69,000 Job," AEIdeas," January 15, 2013, https://web.archive.org/web/20130115115321/http://www.aei-ideas.org/2012/07/julias-mother-why-a-single-mom-is-better-off-on-welfare-than-taking-a-69000-a-year-job; Robert Rector, "Government Supports Would Grow to $76,400 per Poor Family," The Heritage Foundation, November 19, 2021, https://www.heritage.org/welfare/commentary/government-supports-would-grow-76400-poor-family.

8   Jay Belsky, "Universal Preschool: Be Careful What You Wish For?," Institute for Family Studies, October 20, 2015, https://ifstudies.org/blog/universal-preschool-be-careful-what-you-wish-for.

9   Lindsey Burke, "Research Review: Universal Preschool May Do More Harm than Good," The Heritage Foundation, May 11, 2016, https://www.heritage.org/education/report/research-review-universal-preschool-may-do-more-harm-good.

10 Gretchen Livingston, "Fewer than Half of U.S. Kids Today Live in a 'Traditional' Family," Pew Research Center, December 22, 2014, https://www.pewresearch.org/short-reads/2014/12/22/less-than-half-of-u-s-kids-today-live-in-a-traditional-family/.

11 Stephanie Kramer, "U.S. Has World's Highest Rate of Children Living in Single-Parent Households," Pew Research Center, December 12, 2019, https://www.pewresearch.org/short-reads/2019/12/12/u-s-children-more-likely-than-children-in-other-countries-to-live-with-just-one-parent/.

12 Carrie Gress, *The End of Woman: How Smashing the Patriarchy Has Destroyed Us* (Washington, D.C.: Regnery, 2023).

13 Michel Foucault, Frederic Gros (ed.), Robert Hurley (tr.). *Confessions of the Flesh: The History of Sexuality, Volume 4.* (New York, NY: Pantheon, 2021).

14 Massachusetts General Hospital, "Transgender Surgical Program at MGH." August 22, 2021. https://www.massgeneral.org/assets/mgh/pdf/surgery/plastic-surgery/phalloplasty-welcome-packet.pdf.

15 Amandine Baude, et al. "Child Adjustment in Joint Physical Custody Versus Sole Custody: A Meta-Analytic Review." *Journal of Divorce & Remarriage*, vol. 57, no. 5, July 2016, pp. 338–60. DOI.org (Crossref), https://doi.org/10.1080/10502556.2016.1185203.

16 Lathan Watts, "The Biden Administration's Devious Ploy to Get Doctors to Violate Their Oath." National Review Online, December 5, 2023. https://www.nationalreview.com/2023/12/the-biden-administrations-devious-ploy-to-get-doctors-to-violate-their-oath/; Thomas Jipping, "As the Religious Freedom Restoration Act Turns 30, the 'Most Precious of All American Liberties' Is Again at Risk." Heritage Foundation, December 6, 2023. https://www.heritage.org/religious-liberty/report/the-religious-freedom-restoration-act-turns-30-the-most-precious-all.

Chapter 1

1 "Faith Among Black Americans," Pew Research Center, February 16, 2021, https://www.pewresearch.org/religion/2021/02/16/gender-sexuality-and-religion/.

2 Kiana Cox, "Black Americans Firmly Support Gender Equality but Are Split on Transgender and Nonbinary Issues," Pew Research Center, February 16, 2023, https://www.pewresearch.org/race-ethnicity/2023/02/16/black-americans-views-on-transgender-and-nonbinary-issues/.

3 Christopher T. Conner, "How Sexual Racism and Other Discriminatory Behaviors Are Rationalized in Online Dating Apps," *Deviant Behavior*, vol. 44, no. 1, Jan. 2023, 126–42, https://doi.org/10.1080/01639625.2021.2019566.

4 Joyell Arscott, et al., "'That Guy Is Gay and Black. That's a Red Flag.' How HIV Stigma and Racism Affect Perception of Risk Among Young Black Men Who Have Sex with Men," *AIDS and Behavior*, vol. 24, no. 1, Jan. 2020, https://doi.org/10.1007/s10461-019-02607-4.

5 Robert L. Serafino Wani, et al., "Invasive Shigellosis in MSM," *International Journal of STD & AIDS*, vol. 27, no. 10, September 2016, 917–19, https://doi.org/10.1177/0956462415610275.

6 Vera L. Negenborn, et al., "Lethal Necrotizing Cellulitis Caused by ESBL-Producing E. Coli after Laparoscopic Intestinal Vaginoplasty," *Journal of Pediatric and Adolescent Gynecology*, vol. 30, no. 1, Feb. 2017, 19–21, https://doi.org/10.1016/j.jpag.2016.09.005.

7 See, for example: Kimberlé W. Crenshaw, *On Intersectionality: Essential Writings* (New York, NY: The New Press, 2017); and Michel Foucault, Frederic Gros (ed.), Robert Hurley (tr.), *Confessions of the Flesh: The History of Sexuality, Volume 4* (New York, NY: Pantheon, 2021).

8 "LGBT Culture in San Francisco," Wikipedia, https://en.wikipedia.org/w/index.php?title=LGBT_culture_in_San_Francisco&oldid=1207628890.

9 Daniel J. Flynn, *Cult City: Jim Jones, Harvey Milk, and 10 Days That Shook San Francisco* (Wilmington, Delaware: Intercollegiate Studies Institute, 2018).

10 "What Is the Progress Pride Flag?" LGBTQ Nation, June 24, 2022, https://www.lgbtqnation.com/2022/06/progress-pride-flag/.

11 "Gilbert Baker," US National Park Service, https://www.nps.gov/people/gilbert-baker.htm.

12 Joanna Black and Jeremy Prince, "Online Exhibition—Gilbert Baker," GLBT Historical Society, https://archive.is/ntPEl.

13 Sam Landis, "Creating the Change They Wish to See: LGBTQ Artists & Their Activism," *National Center for Civil and Human Rights (blog)*, October 20, 2021, https://www.civilandhumanrights.org/creating-the-change-they-wish-to-see-lgbtq-artists-their-activism/, https://archive.is/Hjmqc.

14 Black and Prince, "Online Exhibition."

15 Blake Stilwell, "How Navy Veteran Monica Helms Created the Transgender Pride Flag," Military.com, March 30, 2022, https://www.military.com/history/how-navy-veteran-monica-helms-created-transgender-pride-flag.html.

16 Jamie Wareham, "Why Many LGBT People Have Started Using a New Pride Flag," *Forbes*, July 12, 2020, https://www.forbes.com/sites/jamiewareham/2020/07/12/why-lgbt-people-have-started-using-a-new-pride-flag-nhs-black-lives-matters/.

17 "The Progress Pride Flag," V&A, https://www.vam.ac.uk/articles/the-progress-pride-flag.

18 "Boston Pride and the City of Boston Today Raise the Pride Flag in a Virtual Ceremony to Kick of Pride Month and Plan to Creating a New Pride Flag for 2021," *Boston Pride (blog)*, https://www.bostonpride.org/2020/06/boston-pride-and-the-city-of-boston-today-raise-the-pride-flag-in-a-virtual-ceremony-to-kick-of-pride-month-and-plan-to-creating-a-new-pride-flag-for-2021/.

19 Wareham, "Why Many . . ."

20 "What Is Intersectionality?," *Encyclopedia Britannica*, https://www.britannica.com/story/what-is-intersectionality.

21 Kerry Byrne, "White House Flew Controversial New Transgender Flag That Troubles Some Critics in the Gay Community," Fox News, June 14, 2023. https://www.foxnews.com/lifestyle/white-house-flew-controversial-transgender-flag-troubles-some-critics-gay-community.

22 Daneil Quasar, "The Work | Design," Danielquasar.com, November 10, 2016. https://danielquasar.com/work/.

23 "LGBTQ+ Progress Pride Flag Flies for First Time over Capitol," TheCityLife.org, June 10, 2022. https://thecitylife.org/2022/06/10/lgbtq-progress-pride-flag-flies-for-first-time-over-capitol/.

24 Shaye Weaver, "New York City's Largest Pride Flag Is Unveiled," *Time Out New York*, June 7, 2022, https://www.timeout.com/newyork/news/new-york-citys-largest-pride-flag-is-unveiled-060722.

25 Gwen Aviles, "New York City's 'largest LGBTQ Pride Flag' Arrives at Four Freedoms Park," NBC News, June 11, 2019, https://www.nbcnews.com/feature/nbc-out/new-york-city-s-largest-lgbtq-pride-flag-arrives-four-n1016601.

26 "Women's March," History.com, https://www.history.com/this-day-in-history/womens-march.

27 See, for example, Duaa Eldab and Marwa Eltagouri, "Thousands Fill Loop After Women's March Rally in Chicago Draws Estimated 250,000," *Chicago Tribune*, January 22, 2017, https://archive.is/rLV5v; Melissa Morris, Los Angeles Women's March Draws Thousands Together in Support of Women's Rights," *Daily Bruin*, July 27, 2023, https://archive.is/wMLJw; California State Library, "Women's March," Google Arts & Culture, https://archive.is/5S1Qn; Elizabeth Rossner, Doree Lewak, and Stephanie Pagones, "Millions of Women in 'Pussyhats' Protest Trump around the World," *New York Post*, July 27, 2023, https://archive.is/CCYAL.

28 Fernando Alfonso III, "How Protest Signs Are Being Used at the Women's March," CNN, January 18, 2020, https://www.cnn.com/2020/01/18/us/best-signs-at-womens-march-2020-trnd/index.html.

29 "Mission and Principles—Women's March," Women's March, February 7, 2019, https://web.archive.org/web/20190207104543/https://womensmarch.com/mission-and-principles.

30 Ryan Mills, "BLM Teaching Students Nationwide to Affirm Transgenderism, Disrupt Nuclear Family," *National Review Online*, February 8, 2022, https://web.archive.org/web/20220208064313/https://www.nationalreview.com/news/blm-week-of-action-teaching-students-nationwide-to-affirm-transgenderism-disrupt-nuclear-family/.

31 Mills, "BLM Teaching Students."

32 Christopher F. Rufo, "Failure Factory," *City Journal*, February 23, 2021, https://www.city-journal.org/article/failure-factory/.

33 Beth Greenfield, "Tamika Mallory of the Women's March Is a Fan of Louis Farrakhan, and People Are Outraged," Yahoo Life, March 7, 2018, https://www.yahoo.com/lifestyle/tamika-mallory-fan-louis-farrakhan-people-outraged-184926181.html.

34 Christopher F. Rufo, *America's Cultural Revolution: How the Radical Left Conquered Everything* (New York: Broadside Books, 2023), 116.

35 Libby Emmons, "Here's Why I'm Not Going Back to the Women's March," *The Federalist*, January 15, 2020, https://thefederalist.com/2020/01/15/heres-why-im-not-going-back-to-the-womens-march/; Georgi Boorman, "Women's March Refusal to Condemn Racism Eviscerates Intersectionalism," *The Federalist*, January 16, 2019, https://thefederalist.com/2019/01/16/womens-march-founder-tamika-mallory-wont-condemn-anti-semitism/.

36 Katelyn Burns, "Why Police Often Single out Trans People for Violence." *Vox*, June 23, 2020, https://www.vox.com/identities/2020/6/23/21295432/police-black-trans-people-violence.

37 Conor Spielmaker and Leah Asmelash, "Statue of Robert E. Lee Gets a Makeover with Pride Flag and 'BLM' Sign," CNN, June 14, 2020, https://www.cnn.com/2020/06/13/us/richmond-robert-e-lee-statue-trnd/index.html.

38 "Queer Nation NY History," *Queer Nation NY*, August 4, 2023, https://web.archive.org/web/20230804101918/https://queernationny.org/history.

39 "Queer Nation NY History," *Queer Nation NY*, August 4, 2023, https://web.archive.org/web/20230804101918/https://queernationny.org/history.

40 Bill Andriette, "Interview with Camille Paglia—Has the Gay Movement Turned down the Wrong Path?," *The Guide*, January 1999, https://brongersma.info/Interview_with_Camille_Paglia_-_Has_the_gay_movement_turned_down_the_wrong_path%3F.

41 Caitlyn Donohue, "When Queer Nation 'Bashed Back' against Homophobia with Street Patrols and Glitter," KQED, June 3, 2019. https://web.archive.org/web/20230307200948/https://www.kqed.org/arts/13858167/queer-nation-lgbtq-activism-90s.

42 "Queer Nation NY History," *Queer Nation NY*, August 4, 2023, https://web.archive.org/web/20230804101918/https://queernationny.org/history.

43 Rufo, *America's Cultural Revolution*, 74.

44 Ibid., 102.

45 Ibid., 115.

46 Denise Cagnon (@4thWaveNow), "Here's the interview w/ Dr. Blair Peters. . . .," Twitter, July 9, 2023, 11:34 a.m., https://twitter.com/4th_WaveNow/Status/1678065148936765440.

47   Jacob P. Warner and John J. Bursch, "Amicus Curiae." *K.C., et al., v. Individual Members of the Medical Licensing Board of Indiana, et al.* US Court of Appeals for the Seventh Circuit, https://adfmedialegalfiles.blob .core.windows.net/files/IndianaMedicalCircuitAmicusBrief.pdf.

48   Robin Respaut and Chad Terhune, "Number of Transgender Children Seeking Treatment Surges in U.S.," Reuters, October 6, 2022, https://www .reuters.com/investigates/special-report/usa-transyouth-data/.

49   Azeen Ghorayshi, "How a Small Gender Clinic Landed in a Political Storm," *New York Times*, August 23, 2023, https://web.archive.org/web /20230823091114/https://www.nytimes.com/2023/08/23/health /transgender-youth-st-louis-jamie-reed.html.

50   Christopher F. Rufo, "Oregon's Castration Machine," *City Journal*, July 5, 2023, https://www.city-journal.org/article/oregon-health-science -universitys-castration-machine/.

51   Ibid.

52   Blair R. Peters, et al., "Challenging the Binary Bias in Gender-Affirming Surgery,'" *Plastic and Reconstructive Surgery*, 151(4): 698e–699e, April 2023, https://web.archive.org/web/20230820200834/https://journals.lww .com/plasreconsurg/fulltext/2023/04000/challenging_the_binary_bias_in _gender_affirming.51.aspx.

53   Eliza Mondegreen, "Gender Surgeon Promotes Bizarre Range of 'Nonbinary Surgeries," *UnHerd*, July 11, 2023, https://unherd.com/newsroom /gender-surgeon-promotes-bizarre-range-of-nonbinary-surgeries/.

54   Christopher F. Rufo, "Barbarism in the Name of Equality," *Christopherrufo .com (blog)*, https://christopherrufo.com/p/barbarism-in-the-name -of-equality.

55   Peters, et al., "Challenging the Binary Bias."

56   Hannah Grossman, "Feminist Medical School Professor Says Trans Kids Identifying as 'Minotaurs' Are Part of 'Gender Revolution,'" Fox News, August 15, 2023, https://web.archive.org/web/20230816163000/https: //www.foxnews.com/media/feminist-medical-school-professor-says-trans -kids-identifying-minotaurs-part-gender-revolution.

57   E. J. Dickson, "Why Are So Many Gen Z Kids Becoming Furries?," *Rolling Stone (blog)*, December 12, 2019, https://web.archive.org/web /20230000000000*/https://www.rollingstone.com/culture/culture-features /furry-fandom-tiktok-gen-z-midwest-furfest-924789/.

58 Ibid.

59 Sarah Stewart, "What It's like to Have Sex as a 'Furry,'" *New York Post*, May 12, 2016, https://web.archive.org/web/20160512142741/https://nypost .com/2016/05/06/inside-the-life-of-a-furry.

60 Ibid.

61 Dylan Matthews, "9 Questions about Furries You Were Too Embarrassed to Ask," *Vox*, December 10, 2014, https://web.archive.org /web/20141226224808/https://www.vox.com/2014/12/10/7362321/9 -questions-about-furries-you-were-too-embarrassed-to-ask.

62 Ibid.

63 Parizaad Khan Sethi, "This Plastic Surgeon Will Happily Split Your Tongue." *Allure*, August 24, 2023, https://web.archive.org/save/https://www.allure .com/story/tongue-splitting-plastic-surgeon.

64 Meirav Devash, "The Risks of Eye Tattoos, according to Body Modification Artist Who Invented Them," *Allure*, January 21, 2021, https://web .archive.org/web/20230531045420/https://www.allure.com/story/eye -tattoo-risk-and-dangers.

65 "The Lizardman (Performer)," Wikipedia, https://en.wikipedia.org/w/index .php?title=The_Lizardman_(performer)&oldid=1188022350.

66 Diana Tourjée, "The Trans Woman Who Became a Dragon," *Vice (blog)*, September 20, 2018, https://web.archive.org/web/20230120084909 /https://www.vice.com/en/article/kz5bxa/eva-tiamat-medusa-dragon -lady-transgender.

67 "Ten Arguments from Social Science against Same-Sex Marriage," *Family Research Council*, https://www.frc.org/issuebrief/ten -arguments-from-social-science-against-same-sex-marriage.

68 Andrew Sullivan, "Here Comes the Groom: A (conservative) case for gay marriage," *The New Republic*, August 28, 1989, https://newrepublic.com /article/79054/here-comes-the-groom.

69 Michael Martin and Mattilda Bernstein Sycamore, "A 'Queer' Argument Against Marriage." "Tell Me More," NPR, June 10, 2010, https://www.npr .org/templates/story/story.php?storyId=127740436.

70 "Against Equality: Queer Critiques of Gay Marriage" Against Equality, February 20, 2012, https://web.archive.org/web/20120220133053 /http://www.againstequality.org/stuff/against-equality-queer-critiques -of-gay-marriage/.

71   Kara Joyner, et al., "Gender and the Stability of Same-Sex and Different-Sex Relationships Among Young Adults." *Demography*, vol. 54, no. 6, Dec. 2017, 2351–74, https://doi.org/10.1007/s13524–017-0633–8..

72   Jeffrey Jones, "In U.S., 10.2% of LGBT Adults Now Married to Same-Sex Spouse," *Gallup*, June 22, 2017, https://news.gallup.com/poll/212702/lgbt-adults-married-sex-spouse.aspx; Jeffrey T. Parsons, et al. "Alternatives to Monogamy Among Gay Male Couples in a Community Survey: Implications for Mental Health and Sexual Risk," *Archives of Sexual Behavior*, vol. 42, no. 2, Feb. 2013, 303–12, https://doi.org/10.1007/s10508–011-9885–3; Kellie L. Barton, "The Lived Experience of Monogamy Among Gay Men in Monogamous Relationships," Walten University, Walden Dissertations and Doctoral Studies Collection, 2020, https://scholarworks.waldenu.edu/cgi/viewcontent.cgi?article=9534&context=dissertations.

73   V. Calef and E. M. Weinshel, "Anxiety and the Restitutional Function of Homosexual Cruising," *The International Journal of Psycho-Analysis*, vol. 65 (Pt 1), 1984, 45–53; Jack Turban, "We Need to Talk about How Grindr Is Affecting Gay Men's Mental Health," *Vox*, April 4, 2018, https://www.vox.com/science-and-health/2018/4/4/17177058/grindr-gay-men-mental-health-psychiatrist.

74   Rufo, "Castration Machine."

75   Stesha Brandon, "Camille Paglia Discusses 'Free Women, Free Men: Sex, Gender, Feminism,'" Seattle public Library and Foundation (podcast), March 17, 2017, https://www.spl.org/Seattle-Public-Library/documents/transcriptions/2017/17–03-20_Camille-Paglia.pdf.

76   Carl Trueman, "Religion, Politics, and American Culture: Carl Trueman Talks with Camille Paglia," Modern Reformation, December 3, 2018, https://modernreformation.org/resource-library/web-exclusive-articles/the-mod-sex-art-and-god-carl-trueman-talks-with-camille-paglia/.

77   Kevin Slack, *War on the American Republic: How Liberalism Became Despotism* (New York: Encounter Books, 2023), 195.

78   Charles Rycroft, "The Case of Wilhelm Reich," *New York Review of Books,* December 4, 1969, https://www.nybooks.com/articles/1969/12/04/the-case-of-wilhelm-reich/.

79   Shulamith Firestone, *The Dialectic of Sex: The Case for Feminist Revolution* (London: Paladin, 1972), 19, qtd. in Carrie Gress, *The End of Woman: How Smashing the Patriarchy Has Destroyed Us* (Washington, D.C.: Regnery Publishing, 2023), 83.

80 Gress, *The End of Woman*, 80.

81 Ibid., 145.

82 Slack, *War on the American Republic*, 216.

83 Mallory Millett, "Marxist Feminism's Ruined Lives," *FrontPage Magazine*, September 1, 2014, https://www.frontpagemag.com/marxist-feminisms -ruined-lives-mallory-millett/, qtd. in Gress, *End of Woman*, 77–78.

84 Gress, 84–85.

85 Ibid, Trueman and Sullivan.

86 Christopher F. Rufo, "The Real Story Behind Drag Queen Story Hour," *City Journal*, Autumn 2022, https://www.city-journal.org/article/the -real-story-behind-drag-queen-story-hour/.

87 J. D. Unwin, *Sex and Culture* (London: Oxford University Press, 1934), 412, qtd. in Gress, 166.

88 Thomas G. West, *The Political Theory of the American Founding: Natural Rights, Public Policy, and the Moral Conditions of Freedom* (Cambridge, United Kingdom: Cambridge University Press, 2017), 223.

89 Ibid.

90 Nathanael Blake, "The Lies of 'Born This Way,'" *World Magazine*, August 8, 2023, https://wng.org/opinions/the-lies-of-born-this-way-1691493975.

91 Jonathan Lambert, "No 'Gay Gene': Massive Study Homes in on Genetic Basis of Human Sexuality," *Nature* 573, no. 7772 (August 29, 2019): 14–15, https://doi.org/10.1038/d41586-019-02585-6.

92 See, for example, Christine E. Kaestle, "Sexual Orientation Trajectories Based on Sexual Attractions, Partners, and Identity: A Longitudinal Investigation From Adolescence Through Young Adulthood Using a U.S. Representative Sample," *The Journal of Sex Research*, vol. 56, no. 7, September 2019, 811–26, https://doi.org/10.1080/00224499.2019.1577351.

93 Becky McCall and Lisa Nainggolan, "Transgender Teens: Is the Tide Starting to Turn?" Medscape, April 26, 2021.https://www.medscape.com /viewarticle/949842?form=fpf#vp_2.

94 As Russell Kirk explains in *The Roots Of American Order* (Wilmington, Del.: ISI Books, 2003) and *America's British Order* (Piscataway, N.J.: Transaction Publishers, 1993), the original source of Western culture is the Christian faith, and that faith is explicit in teaching men are the heads of their households. See, for example, 1 Corinthians 11:3, Ephesians 5:23, 1 Peter 3:7, Ephesians 5:22–24, and Genesis 3:16.

95 Rufo, *America's Cultural Revolution*, 30, 31.

96 Karl Marx and Friedrich Engels, *The Communist Manifesto*, Project Gutenberg, April 1993.

97 Jacques Derrida, *Margins of Philosophy*. (Chicago, IL: University of Chicago Press, 1982.) https://archive.org/details/marginsofphilosoooooderr.

98 Stella Morabito, "Bolshevik Revolution's Six Phases From Freedom To Communist Misery," *The Federalist*, November 6, 2017, https://thefederalist.com/2017/11/06/bolshevik-revolution-reveals-six-phases-freedom-communist-misery/; and Stella Morabito, "The Final 3 Phases In The Slide From Freedom To Communism," *The Federalist*, November 8, 2017, https://thefederalist.com/2017/11/08/final-3-phases-slide-freedom-communism/.

99 Mike Opelka, "Lesbian Activist's Surprisingly Candid Speech: Gay Marriage Fight Is a 'Lie' to Destroy Marriage," *The Blaze*, April 29, 2013, https://web.archive.org/web/20130501084256/https://www.theblaze.com/stories/2013/04/29/lesbian-activists-surprisingly-candid-speech-gay-marriage-fight-is-a-lie-to-destroy-marriage/.

Chapter 2

1 "Appellants' Opening Brief," *Scardina v. Masterpiece Cakeshop*, Colorado Ct. of Appeals, November 18, 2021, https://adflegal-live-drupal-files-delivery.s3.us-east-1.amazonaws.com/public/2021–11/Scardina-v-Masterpiece-Cakeshop-Appellants-Opening-Brief-2021–11-18.pdf.

2 Ibid.

3 Ibid.

4 Jordan Boyd, "Colorado Condemns Jack Phillips for Being a Christian, Again," *The Federalist*, January 26, 2023, https://thefederalist.com/2023/01/26/colorado-condemns-jack-phillips-for-being-a-devout-christian-again/.

5 Andrea Joy Campbell, "Amicus Curiae," *Autumn Scardina v. Masterpiece Cakeshop.* Supreme Court of the State of Colorado, https://ag.ny.gov/sites/default/files/amicus-curiae/scardina-v.-masterpiece-amicus-brief.pdf.

6 Joy Pullmann, "LGBT Activists Have Been Harassing This Christian Baker for Ten Years," *The Federalist*, January 17, 2022, https://thefederalist.com/2022/01/17/lgbt-activists-have-been-using-courts-to-harass-this-christian-baker-for-ten-years/.

7 Philip Hamburger, "Chevron Bias," *George Washington Law Review* 84, no. 1187 (2016), https://papers.ssrn.com/sol3/papers.cfm?abstract_id=2477641.

8   Randy E. Barnett and Evan D. Bernick, "No Arbitrary Power: An Originalist
     Theory of the Due Process of Law," *Social Science Research Network*,
     March 26, 2018, https://doi.org/10.2139/ssrn.3149590.

9   Philip Hamburger, *Is Administrative Law Unlawful?* (Chicago, IL:
     University of Chicago Press, 2015).

10   Peter Cava, "Cisgender and Cissexual," *The Wiley Blackwell Encyclopedia
     of Gender and Sexuality Studies*, edited by Angela Wong et al., 1st ed.,
     Wiley, 2016, 1–4, https://doi.org/10.1002/9781118663219.wbegss131.

11   Hamburger, *Is Administrative Law Unlawful?*

12   Pullmann, "LGBT Activists Have Been Harassing This Christian Baker";
     "We've Got Jack's Back," *GiveSendGo*, May 30, 2022, https://web.archive
     .org/web/20220530052558/https://www.givesendgo.com/G2CUT.

13   Jonathan Lange, "Persecution of Jack Phillips Shows 'Hate Crime' Laws
     End Free Speech," *The Federalist*, July 2, 2021, https://thefederalist
     .com/2021/07/02/the-court-sanctioned-persecution-of-jack-phillips-shows
     -how-hate-crime-laws-end-everyones-freedom-of-speech/.

14   Christopher F. Rufo, "Inside the Transgender Empire." *Imprimis*, October
     5, 2023, https://imprimis.hillsdale.edu/inside-the-transgender-empire/.

15   Libby Palanza, "Massive Turnout for Public Hearing on Last-Minute Bill
     Creating 'Legal Right' to Abortion and 'Gender-Affirming Care' in Maine,"
     The Maine Wire, March 6, 2024, https://www.themainewire.com/2024/03
     /massive-turnout-for-public-hearing-on-last-minute-bill-creating-legal-right
     -to-abortion-and-gender-affirming-care-in-maine/.

16   "TN AG Skrmetti Issues Statement Raising Concerns Over Maine's
     Proposed Legislative Assault on Federalism," Tennessee Office of the
     Attorney General, March 11, 2024, https://www.tn.gov/attorneygeneral
     /news/2024/3/11/pr24–26.html.

17   Jonathan Skrmetti, et al., Letter to Maine's governor, attorney general, Senate
     president, and House speaker, March 11, 2024, https://www.tn.gov/content
     /dam/tn/attorneygeneral/documents/pr/2024/pr24–26MaineLetter.pdf.

18   For example, courts have to allow a lawsuit and outline the parameters of
     permissible discovery.

19   Kevin Stocklin, "Why the Courts Are Failing to Stop Government
     Censorship" *Epoch Times*, November 9, 2023, https://www.theepochtimes.
     com/article/why-the-courts-are-failing-to-stop-government-censorship
     -5526160?src_src=Morningbrief&src_cmp=mb-2023–11-13&est=OwY8g

VTg79ql2%2BeOzAgI5rMTm6ZZ4z6X5pmr%2FTXI3itPDol6lS3sDPrn
bia7fHg%2BJg%3D%3D.

20 "House Bill 4474 (2023)," Michigan Legislature, https://www
.legislature.mi.gov/(S(rdgkrhsuhmuozpfdknzguvwn))/mileg.aspx
?page=BillStatus&objectname=2023-HB-4474.

21 Dave Huber, "Professor: Michigan 'Hate Speech' Bill Could Criminalize
Conservative Opinion," *The College Fix*, July 2, 2023, https://www
.thecollegefix.com/professor-michigan-hate-speech-bill-could-criminalize
-conservative-opinion/.

22 Steven Kovac, "Michigan Supreme Court Becomes First in Nation to
Adopt 'They' Pronoun," *Epoch Times*, September 30, 2023, https://www
.theepochtimes.com/us/michigan-supreme-court-becomes-first-in-nation-to
-adopt-they-pronoun-for-court-proceedings-records-5500939.

23 "HHS Agencies & Roles," US Department of Health and Human Services,
December 10, 2019, https://www.hhs.gov/careers/working-hhs/agencies.

24 Roger Severino (@RogerSeverino_), "HHS today imposed a transgender
pronoun mandate . . . ," Twitter, October 11, 2023, 6:54 p.m., https://twitter
.com/RogerSeverino_/status/1712240245108822323;

25 Roger Severino (@RogerSeverino_), "Although I broke the story on HHS's
unlawful. . . ." Twitter, October 19, 2023, 11:27 a.m., https://twitter.com
/RogerSeverino_/status/1715026894238699529.

26 Raymond Wolfe, "California Court Strikes down Transgender Pronoun
Mandate," *LifeSite News*, July 22, 2021, https://www.lifesitenews.com
/news/california-court-strikes-down-transgender-pronoun-mandate/.

27 Mercedes Schneider, "Roe v. Wade Was Decided by a Republican-
Nominated Supreme Court," *HuffPost*, November 6, 2016. https://web
.archive.org/web/20210520041542/https://www.huffpost.com/entry/trump
-supporters-roe-vs-wade-was-decided-by-a-republican_b_581fbd44e4b04
4f827a78f87.

28 "Attorney General Holder Directs Department to Include Gender Identity
under Sex Discrimination Employment Claims," US Department of Justice
Office of Public Affairs, December 18, 2014, https://www.justice.gov/opa/pr
/attorney-general-holder-directs-department-include-gender-identity-under
-sex-discrimination.

29 Michael Schulman, "The Three People at the Center of the Landmark
Supreme Court Decision," *New Yorker*, June 16, 2020, https://www
.newyorker.com/culture/cultural-comment/the-three-people-at-the
-center-of-the-landmark-supreme-court-decision.

30 Ed Whelan, "Ruling on 'Judge Shopping' in Transgender Cases Finds 11 Lawyers Guilty of Misconduct," National Review Online, March 20, 2024, https://www.nationalreview.com/bench-memos/ruling-on-judge-shopping-in-transgender-cases-finds-11-lawyers-guilty-of-misconduct/.

31 Phillip Picardi, "Meet the Lawyer behind the Biggest LGBTQ+ Legal Victory in History," *GQ*, June 24, 2020, https://web.archive.org/web/20200625115621/https://www.gq.com/story/chase-strangio-aclu-lgbtq-legal-victory.

32 *Bostock v. Clayton County, Georgia,* US Supreme Court, June 15, 2020, https://www.supremecourt.gov/opinions/19pdf/17–1618_hfci.pdf.

33 Chase Strangio, "What President Biden's LGBTQ Executive Order Does and Doesn't Do," *American Civil Liberties Union (blog),* January 21, 2021, https://web.archive.org/web/20210325202733/https://www.aclu.org/news/lgbtq-rights/what-president-bidens-lgbtq-executive-order-does-and-doesnt-do/.

34 *Bostock v. Clayton County, Georgia.* US Supreme Court, June 15, 2020, https://www.supremecourt.gov/opinions/19pdf/17–1618_hfci.pdf.

35 Stacy Manning, "Public School Put Man With Breasts In Our 10-Year-Old's Class," *The Federalist*, September 28, 2023, https://thefederalist.com/2023/09/28/our-public-school-put-a-man-with-fake-breasts-in-our-10-year-olds-classroom/.

36 Picardi, "Meet the Lawyer."

37 Charles Kesler, *Crisis of the Two Constitutions: The Rise, Decline, and Recovery of American Greatness,* (New York, NY: Encounter Books, 2021.)

38 "Executive Order on Preventing and Combating Discrimination on the Basis of Gender Identity or Sexual Orientation," The White House, January 21, 2021, https://www.whitehouse.gov/briefing-room/presidential-actions/2021/01/20/executive-order-preventing-and-combating-discrimination-on-basis-of-gender-identity-or-sexual-orientation/.

39 "Protections Against Employment Discrimination Based on Sexual Orientation or Gender Identity," US Equal Opportunity Employment Commission, June 15, 2021, https://web.archive.org/web/20210629130905/https://www.eeoc.gov/laws/guidance/protections-against-employment-discrimination-based-sexual-orientation-or-gender.

40 *Texas v. EEOC*, US District Court for the Northern District of Texas, October 1, 2022, https://www.eeoc.gov/sites/default/files/2022–10/downloadfile.pdf.

41   Ibid.

42   Ibid; Haywood, "Lyons."

43   "Blueprint for Positive Change 2020," Human Rights Campaign, 2020, https://web.archive.org/web/20201112225917/https://hrc-prod-requests.s3-us-west-2.amazonaws.com/Blueprint-2020.pdf?mtime=2020 1110185320&focal=none.

44   "Human Rights Campaign Announces Eight New Members of Boards of Directors," Human Rights Campaign, October 7, 2021, https://www.hrc.org/press-releases/human-rights-campaign-announces-eight-new-members-of-boards-of-directors.

45   Trudy Ring, "Kelley Robinson, Black Queer Woman, Is New Human Rights Campaign Head," *The Advocate*, September 20, 2022, https://www.advocate.com/news/2022/9/20/kelley-robinson-black-queer-woman-new-human-rights-campaign-head.

46   "JoDee Winterhof," Human Rights Campaign, https://www.hrc.org/about/staff/jodee-winterhof and Human Rights Campaign; "Ryan Matthews," Human Rights Campaign, https://web.archive.org/web/20230501000000*/https://www.hrc.org/about/staff/ryan-matthews.

47   Ibid., Human Rights Campaign, "Blueprint 2020," 3.

48   Ibid., Human Rights Campaign, "Blueprint 2020."

49   Ibid., White House executive order, January 20, 2021.

50   Ibid., Human Rights Campaign, "Blueprint 2020," 9.

51   Greg Baylor, interview with the author on May 5, 2022. Notes in author's possession.

52   Ibid; Pullmann, "K–12 Schools."

53   Paul Light, "The True Size of Government Is Nearing a Record High," *Brookings Institution*, October 7, 2020, https://www.brookings.edu/articles/the-true-size-of-government-is-nearing-a-record-high/.

54   "Five Trends in Government Contracting for FY 2023," *Bloomberg Government*, February 17, 2023, https://about.bgov.com/brief/trends-in-federal-contract-spending/.

55   "Federal Spending: Where Does the Money Go," *National Priorities Project*, https://www.nationalpriorities.org/budget-basics/federal-budget-101/spending.

56   US Office of Management and Budget and Federal Reserve Bank of St. Louis. "Federal Net Outlays as Percent of Gross Domestic Product," FRED, Federal

Reserve Bank of St. Louis, January 1, 1929, https://fred.stlouisfed.org/series
/FYONGDA188S; "Fiscal Data Explains Federal Spending," Treasury.gov,
https://fiscaldata.treasury.gov/americas-finance-guide/federal-spending/.

57 "The Federal Budget in Fiscal Year 2022," Congressional Budget Office,
March 28, 2023, https://www.cbo.gov/publication/58888; US Bureau of
Economic Analysis, "Federal Government Current Transfer Payments:
Government Social Benefits: To Persons." FRED, Federal Reserve
Bank of St. Louis, January 1, 1947, https://fred.stlouisfed.org/series
/B087RC1Q027SBEA.

58 Chris Edwards, "How the Federal Government Spends $6.7 Trillion,"
Briefing Paper No. 174, Cato Institute, March 12, 2024, https://www.cato
.org/briefing-paper/how-federal-government-spends-67-trillion.

59 Thomas Spoehr, "The Rise of Wokeness in the Military," *The Heritage
Foundation*, September 30, 2022, https://www.heritage.org/defense
/commentary/the-rise-wokeness-the-military.

60 Stanley Kurtz, "Biden and Dems Are Set to Abolish the Suburbs," *National
Review Online*, June 30, 2020, https://www.nationalreview.com/corner
/biden-and-dems-are-set-to-abolish-the-suburbs.

61 *Sesame Street* and *Arthur* have both featured queer characters.
See Denise Shick, "'Sesame Street' to Feature Cross-Dressing Gay
Entertainer," *The Federalist*, February 6, 2020, https://thefederalist
.com/2020/02/06/sesame-street-to-feature-cross-dressing-gay
-entertainer-for-impressionable-preschoolers/; and Morning Edition,
"PBS Show 'Arthur' Introduces Children To Same-Sex Marriage,"
NPR, May 15 2019, https://www.npr.org/2019/05/15/723466487
/pbs-show-arthur-introduces-children-to-same-sex-marriage.

62 "Inclusive Curriculum Standards: Representation of LGBTQ+ and
Other Marginalized Communities Promotes Student Achievement and
Wellbeing," *GLSEN*, January 2022, https://www.glsen.org/activity
/inclusive-curricular-standards.

63 Tony Perkins, "Teachers Union Wants Kids to Pursue Gender Transition
Without Parents," *The Daily Signal*, February 24, 2020, https://www
.dailysignal.com/2020/02/24/california-teachers-union-wants-kids-to
-pursue-gender-transition-without-parental-consent/.

64 Joy Pullmann, "How Illinois Schools Teach Preschoolers to Celebrate
Transgenderism," *The Federalist*, October 9, 2019, https://thefederalist

.com/2019/10/09/how-illinois-schools-teach-preschoolers-to-celebrate
-transgenderism/.

65 Howard Blume and Melissa Gomez, "What California Law Requires in
Teaching about LGBTQ People in Public Schools," *Los Angeles Times*,
May 11, 2022. https://www.latimes.com/california/story/2022–05-11
/california-takes-opposite-path-of-florida-texas-on-inclusive-education.

66 Ibid; "Inclusive Curriculum Standards."

67 California State Board of Education, "History Social Science Framework
For California Public Schools Kindergarten Through Grade Twelve,"
California Department of Education, 2017, 532, https://web.archive
.org/web/20171209043321/https://www.cde.ca.gov/ci/hs/cf/documents
/hssfwchapter20.pdf.

68 Pullmann, ibid. "How Illinois Schools..."

69 Ibid; GLSEN, "Inclusive Curriculum Standards."

70 "Religious Freedom Index," The Becket Fund for Religious Liberty, January
2024, https://becketnewsite.s3.amazonaws.com/20240116135226/Religious
-Freedom-Index-2023-Report.pdf.

71 Ibid.

72 Andrea Jones and Emilie Kao, "Sexual Ideology Indoctrination: The
Equality Act's Impact on School Curriculum and Parental Rights," The
Heritage Foundation, May 15, 2019, https://www.heritage.org/civil-society
/report/sexual-ideology-indoctrination-the-equality-acts-impact-school
-curriculum-and.

73 Inez Stepman, "The Equality Act Makes Women Unequal," *The Wall
Street Journal*, February 23, 2021, https://www.wsj.com/articles/the
-equality-act-makes-women-unequal-11614123263.

74 Chad Felix Greene, "How the Equality Act Threatens Speech, Religion,
And Women's Rights," *The Federalist*, April 1, 2019, https://thefederalist
.com/2019/04/01/called-equality-act-threatens-freedom-speech-religion
-womens-rights/.

75 Joy Pullmann, "K–12 Schools Must Put Boys In Girls' Privvies To Get
Federal Lunch Money," *The Federalist*, May 25, 2022, https://thefederalist
.com/2022/05/25/biden-admin-k-12-schools-must-put-boys-in-girls
-bathrooms-to-get-federal-lunch-money/.

76 "USDA Promotes Program Access, Combats Discrimination Against
LGBTQI+ Community," Food and Nutrition Service, US Department

of Agriculture, May 5, 2022, https://www.fns.usda.gov/news-item
/usda-0100.22.

77 Ibid.

78 Jordan Boyd, "Biden Admin's Title IX Rewrite Obliterates Female Spaces,
Free Speech, And Due Process," *The Federalist*, April 19, 2024, https:
//thefederalist.com/2024/04/19/biden-admins-title-ix-rewrite-obliterates
-female-spaces-free-speech-and-due-process.

79 "First amended complaint," *Compassion v. Johnson, et al.* US
District Court for the Southern District Court of California, June 2,
2023, https://adfmedialegalfiles.blob.core.windows.net/files/Church
OfCompassionAmendedComplaint.pdf.

80 "CA Church, Preschool Again Free to Serve Children as Part of Food
Program," Alliance Defending Freedom, January 16, 2024, https://adfmedia
.org/case/church-compassion-v-johnson.

81 "Days after ADF Lawsuit, Biden, Fried to Approve Tampa Christian School's
Lunch Money Application." Alliance Defending Freedom, August 8, 2022,
https://adflegal.org/press-release/days-after-adf-lawsuit-biden-fried-approve
-tampa-christian-schools-lunch-money.

82 "USDA Holds Low-Income Children Hostage on Controversial Transgender
Policy," SaveServices.org (press release), August 14, 2023, https://web
.archive.org/web/20230812102825/https://www.saveservices.org/2023/08
/usda-holds-low-income-children-hostage-on-controversial-transgender
-policy/.

83 Charles Haywood, "Lyons on the Managerial Regime," *American
Conservative*, September 11, 2023, https://www.theamericanconservative
.com/haywood-lyons-managerial-regime/.

84 Scott Yenor (@scottyenor), "Texas A&M Administrators were caught
on camera," Twitter, February 16, 2023, 10:10 a.m., https://web.archive
.org/web/20230305040125/https://twitter.com/scottyenor/status
/1626237539999977489.

85 Louis K. Bonham, "DEI Laws Are Meaningless without Enforcement,"
The James G. Martin Center for Academic Renewal, July 19, 2023,
https://www.jamesgmartin.center/2023/07/dei-laws-are-meaningless
-without-enforcement/.

86 Mark Walsh, "Biden Administration Outlines How Colleges Can Pursue
Racial Diversity after Court Ruling," *Education Week*, August 14, 2023, sec.

Policy & Politics, Law & Courts, https://www.edweek.org/policy-politics
/biden-administration-outlines-how-colleges-can-pursue-racial-diversity
-after-court-ruling/2023/08.

Chapter 3

1   Kevin Slack, *War on the American Republic*, 363.

2   Fred Lucas, "House GOP Questions Biden for Targeting Chris Rufo's Use of Pronouns," *The Daily Signal*, September 13, 2023, https://www.dailysignal
.com/2023/09/13/house-gop-questions-biden-admin-probe-of-christopher
-rufos-use-of-pronouns/.

3   Cat Zakrzewski, "Musk May Have Violated FTC Privacy Order, New Court Filing Shows," *Washington Post*, September 13, 2023, https://www
.washingtonpost.com/technology/2023/09/12/elon-musk-consent-order-ftc/.

4   "US Sues Elon Musk's SpaceX over Hiring Policy," BBC, August 25, 2023, https://www.bbc.com/news/business-66610725.

5   Clyde Wayne Crews, "Tens of Thousands of Pages and Rules in the Federal Register," Competitive Enterprise Institute, June 30, 2021. https://cei.org
/publication/tens-of-thousands-of-pages-and-rules-in-the-federal-register-2/.

6   Philip Hamburger, *Is Administrative Law Unlawful?* (Chicago, London: University of Chicago Press, 2015); Charles Murray, *By the People: Rebuilding Liberty Without Permission* (New York: Forum Books, 2016).

7   Joy Pullmann, "SCOTUS Cowardice Lets Colorado Keep Persecuting Christians," *The Federalist*, January 30, 2023, https://thefederalist
.com/2023/01/30/supreme-courts-cowardice-allows-colorado-to-keep
-persecuting-christians/.

8   Gordon L. Crovitz, "You Commit Three Felonies a Day," *Wall Street Journal*, September 27, 2009, https://www.wsj.com/articles/SB100014240
52748704471504574438900830760842.

9   Mariam Jaffery. Email on behalf of the US Department of Housing and Urban Development on Sept. 27, 2023. In author's possession.

10 With a nod to theologian Dr. Greg Schulz for these insights, expressed in different words in a pre-publication paper he sent to me privately in 2023.

11 "'The Idiot Class': David Schweikert Absolutely Hammers Congressional Colleagues Over Spending," Forbes Breaking News YouTube Channel, September 29, 2023. https://www.youtube.com/watch?v=sRi9rEpc4JI

12 Romina Boccia and Dominik Lett, "National Security Implications of Unsustainable Spending and Debt," *Cato Institute (blog)*, July 27, 2023,

https://www.cato.org/blog/national-security-implications-unsustainable
-spending-debt.

13   Thomas West, *The Political Theory of the American Founding: Natural
     Rights, Public Policy, and the Moral Conditions of Freedom*, Cambridge
     (U.K.: Cambridge University Press, 2017), 82.

14   Thomas G. West, *Vindicating the Founders: Race, Sex, Class, and Justice
     in the Origins of America* (Oxford: Rowman and Littlefield, 1997), 64.

15   Ibid., 59.

16   Ibid., 271, 272.

17   Ibid., 25.

18   Ibid., 60.

19   Ibid., 221.

20   Ibid., 219.

21   See, for example: David Hackett Fischer. *Albion's Seed: Four British
     Folkways in America.* (Oxford, U.K.: Oxford University Press, 1989.); and
     Charles Murray. *Coming Apart: The State of White America, 1960–2010.*
     (New York, NY: Crown Forum, 2012).

22   Ibid., 233.

23   Ibid., 229.

24   Ibid., 222.

25   Ibid., 225.

26   Katy Faust and Stacy Manning, *Them Before Us: Why We Need a Global
     Children's Rights Movement* (New York: Post Hill Press, 2021).

27   Center for Opportunity Now. "Fact Sheet: Fatherhood and Crime," America
     First Policy Institute, May 30, 2023, https://americafirstpolicy.com/issues
     /fact-sheet-fatherhood-and-crime.

28   Jack Brewer, "Issue Brief: Fatherlessness and Its Effects on American Society,"
     America First Policy Institute, May 15, 2023, https://americafirstpolicy.com
     /latest/issue-brief-fatherlessness-and-its-effects-on-american-society.

29   Robert Detlefsen, *Civil Rights Under Reagan* (San Francisco: ICS Press,
     1991), 17, https://archive.org/details/civilrightsunderooo0detl/page/16
     /mode/2up?view=theater.

30   West, *The Political Theory*, 149.

31   Ibid., 81.

32   Often, has been demagogued into wanting.

33 James Madison, *Federalist No. 10*, *The Federalist Papers*, Library of Congress. https://guides.loc.gov/federalist-papers/text-1–10#s-lg-box -wrapper-25493273.

34 West, *Vindicating*, 125.

35 Kevin Slack, *War on the American Republic: How Liberalism Became Despotism* (New York: Encounter Books, 2023), 72.

36 Herbert Croly, *The Promise of American Life* (Boston: Northeastern University Press), 1989, 400, cited in Slack, *War on the American Republic*, 72.

37 See, for example, Deuteronomy 15:11, Mark 14:7, John 16:33, John 15:18–27.

38 Slack, *War on the American Republic*, 65.

39 Murray, *By the People*, 13.

40 Woodrow Wilson, "What Is Progress?" *The New Freedom: A Call for the Emancipation of the Generous Energies of a People* (New York and Garden City: Doubleday, Page & Company, 1913), 56, 57, https://www.gutenberg .org/files/14811/14811-h/14811-h.htm.

41 "Die Lösung," Wikipedia, https://en.wikipedia.org/w/index .php?title=Die_L%C3%B6sung&oldid=1181857777.

42 Slack, *War on the Republic*, 90–91.

43 Charles Kesler, *Crisis of the Two Constitutions* (New York: Encounter Books, 2021), 152.

44 Ibid., 150.

45 Ibid., 151.

46 Slack, *War on the Republic*,118.

47 West, *Vindicating*, 59.

48 Ibid., 60.

49 "President Franklin Roosevelt's Annual Message (Four Freedoms) to Congress (1941)," National Archives, September 21, 2021. https://www .archives.gov/milestone-documents/president-franklin-roosevelts -annual-message-to-congress.

50 James Quinn (@James_t_Quinn), "New: State Department issues press release. . . .," Twitter, October 26, 2023, 8:16 a.m., https://twitter.com /james_t_quinn/status/1717515599717560824.

51 Greg Price (@greg_price11) "Left: the White House's statement on Laken Riley. . ." Twitter, March 14, 2024, 5:07 p.m. https://twitter.com /greg_price11/status/1768383470407995559.

52   West, *The Political Theory*, 286.

53   Diana West, *American Betrayal: The Secret Assault on Our Nation's Character* (New York: St. Martin's Press, 2013). See also Stanton M. Evans and Herbert Romerstein, *Stalin's Secret Agents: The Subversion of Roosevelt's Government* (Threshold, 2012).

54   Slack, *War on the Republic*, 131.

55   Murray, *By the People*, 17–20.

56   Ibid., 20.

57   "Policy Basics: Where Do Our Federal Tax Dollars Go?" Center on Budget and Policy Priorities, September 28, 2023, https://www.cbpp.org/research /federal-budget/where-do-our-federal-tax-dollars-go.

58   Murray, *By the People*, 28.

59   Philip Hamburger, *Purchasing Submission* (Cambridge, Massachusetts: Harvard University Press, 2021), 16.

60   Slack, *War on the American Republic*, 139.

61   Ibid., 162.

62   Charles Murray, *Facing Reality: Two Truths About Race in America* (New York: Encounter Books), 2021), 88.

63   Robert R. Detlefsen, "Affirmative Action and Business Deregulation: On the Reagan Administration's Failure to Revise Executive Order No. 11246" *Policy Studies Journal* 21, no. 3 (September 1993): 556–64. https://doi .org/10.1111/j.1541–0072.1993.tb01810.x.

64   Slack, *War on the Republic*, 162.

65   Hamburger, *Is Administrative Law Unlawful?*

66   Slack, *War on the Republic*, 141.

67   Ibid., 208.

68   Ibid.

69   Ibid., 206.

70   Detlefsen, *Civil Rights Under Reagan*, 32.

71   Christopher Caldwell, *Age of Entitlement* (New York: Simon & Schuster, 2020), 146.

72   Detlefsen, *Civil Rights Under Reagan*, 27.

73   Ibid., 27.

74   Detlefsen, "Affirmative Action."

75 Christopher F. Rufo, *America's Cultural Revolution: How the Radical Left Conquered Everything* (New York: Broadside Books, 2023), 265.

76 Ibid., 9.

77 Ibid., 33.

78 Ibid., 215.

79 Ibid., 229.

80 Brendan Cole, "Obama Tweets Rainbow White House Image and Wishes Happy Pride Month," *Newsweek*, June 16, 2020. https://www.newsweek.com/barack-obama-lgbtq-supreme-court-civil-rights-act-1511077.

81 Ilya Somin, "A Great Decision on Same-Sex Marriage—but Based on Dubious Reasoning" *Washington Post*, October 23, 2021, https://www.washingtonpost.com/news/volokh-conspiracy/wp/2015/06/26/a-great-decision-on-same-sex-marriage-but-based-on-dubious-reasoning/.

82 Ibid.

83 West, *Vindicating the Founders*, 73.

84 As wives traditionally agree to when they consent to their choice of husband.

Chapter 4

1 Freddie DeBoer, "How Elites Ate the Social Justice Movement," *The Free Press*, October 2, 2023, https://www.thefp.com/p/how-elites-ate-the-social-justice.

2 Becky Bowers, "President Barack Obama's Shifting Stance on Gay Marriage," PolitiFact.com, May 11, 2012, https://www.politifact.com/factchecks/2012/may/11/barack-obama/president-barack-obamas-shift-gay-marriage.

3 Norimitsu Onishi, "U.S. Support of Gay Rights in Africa May Have Done More Harm Than Good," *New York Times*, December 20, 2015, https://www.nytimes.com/2015/12/21/world/africa/us-support-of-gay-rights-in-africa-may-have-done-more-harm-than-good.html.

4 Max Bearak, "There's a Rising Global Tide of Crackdowns on LGBT Communities," *Washington Post*, December 1, 2021, https://www.washingtonpost.com/news/worldviews/wp/2017/10/20/theres-a-rising-global-tide-of-crackdowns-on-lgbt-communities.

5 Stefano Gennarini, "Their Refusal to Tolerate Is Creating Global Backlash on LGBT People," *The Federalist*, January 11, 2018, https://thefederalist.com/2018/01/11/refusal-tolerate-dissent-creating-global-backlash-lgbt-people/.

6   Mohamad El Chamaa, "Anti-LGBTQ Backlash Grows across Middle East, Echoing U.S. Culture Wars," *Washington Post*, August 4, 2023. https://www.washingtonpost.com/world/2023/08/03/middle-east-lgbtq-gay-transgender.

7   Jackson Elliott, "How the US Spent $4.1 Billion on Global LGBT Initiatives," *Epoch Times*, November 6, 2023, https://www.theepochtimes.com/article/how-the-us-spent-4–1-billion-on-global-lgbtq-initiatives-5524073.

8   Daniel A. Cox, et al., "Generation Z and the Transformation of American Adolescence: How Gen Z's Formative Experiences Shape Its Politics, Priorities, and Future," The Survey Center on American Life, November 9, 2023, https://www.americansurveycenter.org/research/generation-z-and-the-transformation-of-american-adolescence-how-gen-zs-formative-experiences-shape-its-politics-priorities-and-future/.

9   Ben Johnson, "'Enough': Fewer Republicans and Democrats Believe Homosexuality Is Moral, Poll Finds," *The Washington Stand*, June 20, 2023. https://washingtonstand.com/news/enough-fewer-republicans-and-democrats-believe-homosexuality-is-moral-poll-finds.

10 Jeffrey M. Jones, "More Say Birth Gender Should Dictate Sports Participation," *Gallup*, June 12, 2023, https://news.gallup.com/poll/507023/say-birth-gender-dictate-sports-participation.aspx.

11 "The Politics of Gender, Pronouns, and Public Education," PRRI, June 8, 2023. https://www.prri.org/research/the-politics-of-gender-pronouns-and-public-education/.

12 McLaughlin and Associates, "Poll: Over 70 Percent Strongly Object to Transgender Industry's Targeting of Kids and Teens," *Summit Ministries*, March 13, 2023. https://www.summit.org/about/press/poll-over-70-percent-strongly-object-to-transgender-industrys-targeting-of-kids-and-teens/.

13 Ibid.

14 Samuel Boehlke, "Bud Light's Brand Is So Trashed It Can't Even Give Beer Away," *The Federalist*, May 25, 2023, https://thefederalist.com/2023/05/25/bud-lights-brand-is-so-trashed-it-cant-even-give-beer-away-for-free/.

15 Reyes, Ronny, "Target Loses $10B Following Boycott Calls over LGBTQ-Friendly Clothing," *New York Post*, May 28, 2023, https://nypost.com/2023/05/28/target-loses-10b-following-boycott-calls-over-lgbtq-friendly-clothing/.

16 Nathaniel Meyersohn, "Pride Month Backlash Hurt Target's Sales. They Fell for the First Time in Six Years," CNN, August 16, 2023. https://www.cnn.com/2023/08/16/investing/target-stock-earnings/index.html.

17 "LGBTQ+ Americans Fight Back: A Guidebook for Action," *Human Rights Campaign*, June 6, 2023, https://web.archive.org/web/20230606130919 /https://hrc-prod-requests.s3-us-west-2.amazonaws.com/LGBTQ -Guidebook-for-Action.pdf.

18 "Support for Gay Marriage Has 'Declined' in the Last Year," *Sky News*, https://www.youtube.com/shorts/WMn30aAJJrs.

19 Not hyperbole. Those interested in investigating this merger in process should read N. S. Lyons, "The China Convergence," *The Upheaval (blog)*, August 3, 2023, https://theupheaval.substack.com/p/the-china-convergence.

20 Colum Murphy, "How Life in China Has Gotten Tougher for LGBTQ People: QuickTake," *Bloomberg News*, April 27, 2022, https://web .archive.org/web/20220428000707/https://www.bloomberg .com/news/articles/2022–04-27/how-lgbtq-life-in-china-has-gotten-tougher -under-xi-quicktake.

21 Colum Murphy, "Being Gay in China Has Gotten Harder Under Xi Jinping," *Bloomberg News*, February 17, 2022, https://www.bloomberg .com/news/newsletters/2022–02-17/being-gay-in-china-has-gotten -harder-under-xi-jinping.

22 Chad Felix Greene, "Lesbians Targeted for Objecting to Transgenderism at London Pride," *The Federalist*, July 10, 2018, https://thefederalist .com/2018/07/10/lesbians-accused-hate-crimes-objecting-transgenderism -london-pride-festival/.

23 "Caitlyn Jenner," Wikipedia, https://en.wikipedia.org/wiki/Caitlyn _Jenner#Gender_transition and Lauren Turner, "Even More Gorgeous Pictures of Caitlyn Jenner!," *Popsugar*, June 1, 2015, https://www.popsugar .com/celebrity/caitlyn-jenner-vanity-fair-pictures-37611764.

24 David Rozado, "The Great Awokening as a Global Phenomenon," *Rozado's Visual Analytics (blog)*, April 6, 2023. https://davidrozado.substack.com/p /gag.

25 Brandon Griggs, "America's Transgender Moment," CNN, April 23, 2015, https://web.archive.org/web/20150801000000*/https://www.cnn .com/2015/04/23/living/transgender-moment-jenner-feat/index.html. Thanks to Abigail Shrier referencing this article in Abigail Shrier, *Irreversible Damage: The Transgender Craze Seducing Our Daughters* (Washington, D.C.: Regnery Publishing, 2020), 144.

26 "Interview with Jann Wenner of 'Rolling Stone,'" The American Presidency Project, https://www.presidency.ucsb.edu/documents /interview-with-jann-wenner-rolling-stone.

27 Christopher Caldwell, *Age of Entitlement* (New York: Simon & Schuster, 2020), 230.

28 Carrie Gress, *The End of Woman: How Smashing the Patriarchy Has Destroyed Us* (Washington, D.C.: Regnery Publishing, 2023), 138.

29 Trudy Ring, "This Year's Michigan Womyn's Music Festival Will Be the Last," The Advocate, April 21, 2015, https://www.advocate.com /michfest/2015/04/21/years-michigan-womyns-music-festival-will-be-last.

30 Annalise Frank, "Why Finding a Lesbian Bar near You is Almost Impossible," Axios, June 30, 2023, https://web.archive.org/web/20230630100737/https: //www.axios.com/2023/06/30/lesbian-bars-america-2023.

31 Greggor Mattson, "The Changing Mix of Gay Bar Subtypes after COVID-19 Restrictions in the United States, 2017–2023" (preprint), SocArXiv, June 16, 2021, https://doi.org/10.31235/osf.io/4uw6j.

32 "The Future Is Female: Feminism as (Wearable) Cultural Capital," *Feminist Legal Theory (blog)*, January 20, 2016, https://femlegaltheory.blogspot .com/2016/01/the-future-is-female-feminism-as.html.

33 Abigail Shrier, *Irreversible Damage: The Transgender Craze Seducing Our Daughters* (Washington, D.C.: Regnery, 2021), 202.

34 Tucker Carlson (@TuckerCarlson), "Ep. 28 Trans, Inc: genital mutilation is not just," Twitter, October 4, 2023, 6:00 p.m., https://twitter.com /TuckerCarlson/status/1709689853661913465.

35 Shannon Keating, "Can Lesbian Identity Survive the Gender Revolution?" *BuzzFeed News*, February 11, 2017, https://www.buzzfeednews.com/article /shannonkeating/can-lesbian-identity-survive-the-gender-revolution.

36 Freddie DeBoer, "How Elites."

37 Brynn Tannehill, "Is Refusing to Date Trans People Transphobic?" *The Advocate*, December 14, 2019. https://www.advocate.com/commentary /2019/12/14/refusing-date-trans-people-transphobic.

38 Shannon Keating, "Can Lesbian Identity Survive the Gender Revolution?" *BuzzFeed News*, February 11, 2017, https://www.buzzfeednews.com/article /shannonkeating/can-lesbian-identity-survive-the-gender-revolution.

39 Tannehill, "Is Refusing?"

40 "Video Unavailable: This Video Is Private," Youtube, https://www.youtube. com/watch?v=2X-PgHSZh6U.

41 Taylor Fogarty, "Why Trans Activists Will Destroy Homosexual Rights," *The Federalist*, May 2, 2017, https://thefederalist.com/2017/05/02 /trans-activists-will-destroy-homosexual-rights/.

42 "RE: 'Are genital preferences transphobic?' Give it up, Riley!" Magdalen Berns, YouTube, March 30, 2017, https://www.youtube.com /watch?v=F_5FFGrGzJw&t=44s.

43 Caroline Lowbridge, "The Lesbians Who Feel Pressured to Have Sex and Relationships with Trans Women," *BBC News*, October 26, 2021. https://web.archive.org/web/20211102085923/https://www.bbc.com/news /uk-england-57853385.

44 "We're Being Pressured into Sex by Some Trans Women, bbc.co.uk Finding by the Head of the Executive Complaints Unit (ECU)," *BBC News*, May 31, 2022, https://web.archive.org/web/20230319211555/https://www.bbc .co.uk/contact/ecu/newsonlineoctober2021.

45 "We're Being Pressured into Sex by Some Trans Women," Wikipedia, https://en.wikipedia.org/w/index.php?title=%22We%27re_being _pressured_into_sex_by_some_trans_women%22&oldid=1207656286; Alexandra Topping, "BBC Changes Online Article at Centre of Transphobia Row," *The Guardian*, November 4, 2021, https://web.archive.org /web/20230316130725/https://www.theguardian.com/society/2021/nov/04 /bbc-changes-online-article-at-centre-of-transphobia-row.

46 Mary Margaret Olohan, "Half of Jailed Men Identifying as Transgender Convicted of Sex Crimes," *The Daily Signal*, August 24, 2023, https: //www.dailysignal.com/2023/08/24/exclusive-half-imprisoned-men-identify -transgender-women-convicted-least-one-sexual-assault/.

47 Nathanael Blake, "OK, Groomer: Why Some in the LGBT Movement Are Focusing on Kids," *Public Discourse*, March 28, 2022, https://www .thepublicdiscourse.com/2022/03/81314/.

48 Pam Belluck, "Many Genes Influence Same-Sex Sexuality, Not a Single 'Gay Gene,'" *New York Times*, August 29, 2019, https://www.nytimes .com/2019/08/29/science/gay-gene-sex.html.

49 "Understanding Sexual Orientation and Homosexuality," *American Psychological Association*, 2008, https://www.apa.org/topics/lgbtq /orientation.

50 "Romantic Opportunities Appear to Influence Women's Sexual Identities, But Not Men's," *American Sociological Association*, August 25, 2015. https://web.archive.org/web/20230205222214/https://www.asanet.org /wp-content/uploads/savvy/documents/press/pdfs/AM_2015_McClintock _News_Release_FINAL.pdf.

51 Ibid.

52 Lisa Littman, "Correction: Parent Reports of Adolescents and Young Adults Perceived to Show Signs of a Rapid Onset of Gender Dysphoria." *PLOS ONE* 14, no. 3 (March 19, 2019): e0214157, https://doi.org/10.1371/journal.pone.0214157.

53 Joy Pullmann, "Study Repressed for Finding Trans Kids May Be Social Contagion," *The Federalist*, August 31, 2018, https://thefederalist.com/2018/08/31/explosive-ivy-league-study-repressed-for-finding-transgender-kids-may-be-a-social-contagion/.

54 Ibid.

55 Littman, "Correction: Parent Reports."

56 Pullmann, "Study Repressed."

57 Colin Wright, "Anatomy of a Scientific Scandal," *City Journal*, June 12, 2023. https://www.city-journal.org/article/anatomy-of-a-scientific-scandal/.

58 Lisa Littman (@LisaLittman1), "I am thrilled to announce. . . .," Twitter, August 31, 2020, 7:59 p.m., https://twitter.com/LisaLittman1/status/1300583913283354628.

59 Michael Bailey, "My Research on Gender Dysphoria Was Censored. But I Won't Be," *The Free Press*, July 10, 2023. https://archive.is/afcuG#selection-1251.437–1259.24.

60 Suzanna Diaz and J. Michael Bailey, "RETRACTED ARTICLE: Rapid Onset Gender Dysphoria: Parent Reports on 1655 Possible Cases," *Archives of Sexual Behavior* 52, no. 3 (April 1, 2023): 1031–43, https://doi.org/10.1007/s10508-023-02576-9.

61 Jamie Reed, "I Thought I Was Saving Trans Kids. Now I'm Blowing the Whistle," *The Free Press*, February 9, 2023, https://www.thefp.com/p/i-thought-i-was-saving-trans-kids.

62 Belluck, "Many Genes."

63 "Medicine and Gender Transidentity in Children and Adolescents," *Académie Nationale de Médecine*, February 25, 2022. https://www.academie-medecine.fr/la-medecine-face-a-la-transidentite-de-genre-chez-les-enfants-et-les-adolescents/?lang=en.

64 Jonathan Lambert, "No 'Gay Gene': Massive Study Homes in on Genetic Basis of Human Sexuality," *Nature* 573, no. 7772 (August 29, 2019): 14–15. https://doi.org/10.1038/d41586-019-02585-6.

65 Ibid; "Medicine and Gender Transidentity."

66   Albert R. Mohler Jr., "Polymorphous Perversity in the Heartland," *World*, November 15, 2023, https://wng.org/opinions/polymorphous -perversity-in-the-heartland-1700050198.

67   Jennifer A. Marshall and Jason Richwine, "The Regnerus Study: Social Science on New Family Structures Met with Intolerance," *The Heritage Foundation*, October 2, 2012. https://www.heritage.org/marriage-and-family/report /the-regnerus-study-social-science-new-family-structures-met-intolerance.

68   "LGBT+ Pride 2021 Global Survey Points to a Generation Gap around Gender Identity and Sexual Attraction," Ipsos, June 9, 2021, https://www .ipsos.com/en-us/news-polls/ipsos-lgbt-pride-2021-global-survey.

69   Margaret Peppiatt, "Almost 40 Percent of Students Identify as LGBTQ at Liberal Arts Colleges: Survey," *The College Fix*, December 16, 2022. https: //www.thecollegefix.com/almost-40-percent-of-students-identify-as-lgbtq -at-liberal-arts-colleges-survey/.

70   Mark Regnerus, "What the Surge in LGBTQ Self-Identity Means," *Public Discourse*, June 25, 2023. https://www.thepublicdiscourse.com /2023/06/89539/.

71   "Letter from the Attorney General to Congress on Litigation Involving the Defense of Marriage Act," Office of Public Affairs, US Department of Justice, February 23, 2011. https://www.justice.gov/opa/pr /letter-attorney-general-congress-litigation-involving-defense-marriage-act.

72   Glenn T. Stanton, "Why Are Lesbian Teens Having More Babies Than Heterosexual Peers?" *The Federalist*, August 7, 2017. https://thefederalist .com/2017/08/07/lesbian-teens-two-seven-times-many-babies-heterosexual -peers/.

73   Kinnon R. MacKinnon, et al., "Health Care Experiences of Patients Discontinuing or Reversing Prior Gender-Affirming Treatments." *JAMA Network Open* 5, no. 7 (July 25, 2022): e2224717. https://doi.org/10.1001 /jamanetworkopen.2022.24717; Kelsey Bolar, "'Detransitioners' Are Being Abandoned By Medical Professionals," *The Federalist*, February 10, 2023; "Growing Focus on Detransition," Society for Evidence-Based Gender Medicine, October 18, 2021, https://segm.org/new_detransition _study_2021; and Lisa Selin Davis, "The Urgency of Detransition Care," BROADview, April 17, 2023, https://www.broadview.news/p /the-urgency-of-detransition-care.

74   Denise Cagnon (@4thWaveNow), "Here's the interview w/ Dr. Blair Peters. . . .," Twitter, July 9, 2023, 11:34 a.m., https://twitter.com/4th_WaveNow /Status/1678065148936765440. Video minute 19:10.

75   Ibid, video minute 11:11.

76   Ibid, video minute 23:35.

77   Ibid, minute 30:19.

78   Ibid, minute 34:45.

79   Ibid; "Medicine and Gender Transidentity."

80   Ibid.

81   Rachel E. Gross, "Half the World Has a Clitoris. Why Don't Doctors Study It?" *New York Times*, October 17, 2022, https://web.archive.org/web/20221101024511/https://www.nytimes.com/2022/10/17/health/clitoris-sex-doctors-surgery.html.

82   Noah Herring, "Nike to Invite Child Sex Change Surgeon to Panel Discussion for Pride Month," *One America News Network*, June 6, 2023, https://web.archive.org/web/20230606203717/https://www.oann.com/newsroom/nike-to-invite-child-sex-change-surgeon-to-panel-discussion-for-pride-month/.

83   Ibid; McLaughlin and Associates, "Poll: Over 70 Percent Strongly Object."

84   Annelise Hanshaw, "Missouri AG Alleges Federal Involvement in Washington University Investigation," *Missouri Independent*, December 7, 2023, https://missouriindependent.com/2023/12/07/missouri-ag-alleges-federal-involvement-in-washington-university-investigation; Melissa Brown and Kelly Puente, "Vanderbilt Turns over Transgender Patient Records to State in Attorney General Probe," *The Tennessean*, June 20, 2023, https://www.tennessean.com/story/news/health/2023/06/20/vanderbilt-university-m-turns-over-transgender-patient-medical-records-to-tennessee-attorney-general/70338356007/.

85   Christopher Wiggins, "Google Bans Anti-Trans Hate Group Gays Against Groomers," *The Advocate*, September 21, 2022, https://www.advocate.com/news/2022/9/21/google-bans-anti-trans-hate-group-gays-against-groomers-venmo-paypal.

86   "About," GaysAgainstGroomers.com, https://www.gaysagainstgroomers.com/about.

87   Bari Weiss, "We're Number One—Thanks to You," *The Free Press*, April 10, 2024, https://www.thefp.com/p/were-number-one-thanks-to-you.

88   Bari Weiss, "Subscribe to The Free Press," *The Free Press*, https://www.thefp.com/subscribe?simple=true&next=https%3A%2F%2Fwww.thefp.com%2Fp%2Fwelcome-to-the-free-press.

89 Bari Weiss, "I'm Glad the Dyke March Banned Jewish Stars" (opinion), *New York Times*, June 27, 2017, https://web.archive.org/web/20200715124322 /https://www.nytimes.com/2017/06/27/opinion/im-glad-the-dyke-march -banned-jewish-stars.html.

90 Bari Weiss, "End DEI," *The Free Press*, November 9, 2023, https://www .thefp.com/p/end-dei-woke-capture.

91 Bari Weiss, "You Are the Last Line of Defense," *The Free Press*, November 13, 2023, https://www.thefp.com/p/you-are-the-last-line-of-defense.

92 Ibid.

93 Ibid.

94 Ibid.

95 "Bari Weiss," Wikipedia, January 29, 2024, https://en.wikipedia.org/w /index.php?title=Bari_Weiss&oldid=1200271122.

96 Weiss, "You Are the Last."

97 Annie Goldsmith, "Bari Weiss Brings the Culture Wars Home," *The Information*, January 27, 2023. https://www.theinformation.com/articles /bari-weiss-brings-the-culture-wars-home.

98 Katy Faust and Stacy Manning, *Them Before Us: Why We Need a Global Children's Rights Movement* (New York: Post Hill Press, 2021).

99 Suzy Weiss, "Motherloading: Inside the Surrogacy Boom," *The Free Press*, April 11, 2023, https://www.thefp.com/p/motherloading-inside -the-surrogacy.

100 Bari Weiss (@bariweiss), "'I'm not a handmaid'," Twitter, April 11, 2023, 8:41 a.m., https://twitter.com/bariweiss/status/1645768979833667594.

101 Peppiatt, "Almost 40 Percent."

102 Tom Kertscher, "Fact-Check: U.S. Billionaire Wealth Could Run the U.S. Government for about 8 Months," *Austin American-Statesman*, November 5, 2021, https://www.statesman.com/story/news/politics/politifact/2021/11/05 /billionaire-wealth-could-run-u-s-government-8-months/6281374001/.

103 Chris Edwards, "Federal Debt and Unfunded Entitlement Promises," *Cato Institute* (blog), January 21, 2022, https://www.cato.org/blog /federal-debt-unfunded-entitlement-promises.

104 Camille Paglia and Carl R. Trueman, "Religion, Politics, and American Culture: Carl Trueman Talks with Camille Paglia," *Modern Reformation*, December 3, 2018. https://modernreformation.org/resource-library/web-exclusive-articles /the-mod-sex-art-and-god-carl-trueman-talks-with-camille-paglia/.

Chapter 5

1   Thomas G. West, *The Political Theory of the American Founding: Natural Rights, Public Policy, and The Moral Conditions of Freedom* (Cambridge, UK: Cambridge University Press, 2017), 141.

2   "The US Military Oath of Enlistment." Military.com, May 12, 2021, https://www.military.com/join-armed-forces/swearing-in-for-military-service.html.

3   "Department of Defense Diversity, Equity, and Inclusion Statement," Office for Diversity, Equity, and Inclusion, US Department of Defense. https://archive.is/jgCDK.

4   Sarah Jacobs, Letter to the Chairmen and Ranking Members of the House and Senate Committees on Armed Services, September 21, 2023, https://web.archive.org/web/20230925185707/https://sarajacobs.house.gov/uploadedfiles/fy24_ndaa_conference_letter_on_anti-equality_provisions.final.pdf.

5   Shawn Fleetwood, "18 GOPers Help Dems Kill Measure Axing Pentagon 'Pride' Parties," *The Federalist*, September 28, 2023, https://thefederalist.com/2023/09/28/18-house-republicans-help-democrats-kill-amendment-defunding-pentagon-pride-month-parties/; Bradley Jaye (@bradleyajaye), 'Amendment from @chiproytx to prohibit. . . .," Twitter, September 27, 2023, 7:03 p.m., https://twitter.com/bradleyajaye/status/1707169184159768985; "Final Vote Results for Roll Call 441 on H. R. 4365," Clerk of the US House of Representatives, September 27, 2023, https://clerk.house.gov/evs/2023/roll441.xml.

6   Rebecca Kheel, "Pentagon Abortion, Transgender Policies Safe, But Diversity Programs Take a Hit in Compromise Defense Bill," Military.com, December 7, 2023, https://www.military.com/daily-news/2023/12/07/pentagon-abortion-transgender-policies-safe-diversity-programs-take-hit-compromise-defense-bill.html.

7   John Haughey, "In-Depth: Pentagon Paying the Price for Going 'Woke,'" *Epoch Times*, June 19, 2023, https://www.theepochtimes.com/us/in-depth-pentagon-paying-the-price-for-going-woke-5340824.

8   "Executive Order on Advancing Racial Equity and Support for Underserved Communities through the Federal Government," The White House, January 21, 2021, https://www.whitehouse.gov/briefing-room/presidential-actions/2021/01/20/executive-order-advancing-racial-equity-and-support-for-underserved-communities-through-the-federal-government/.

9   Eric Pahon, "Readout of Deputy Secretary of Defense Dr. Kathleen Hicks' Meeting With LGBTQ+ Advocacy Groups," US Department of Defense, August 9, 2022, https://web.archive.org/web/20220810145624/https://www.defense.gov/News/Releases/Release/Article/3122189/readout-of-deputy-secretary-of-defense-dr-kathleen-hicks-meeting-with-lgbtq-adv/.

10   Haughey, "In Depth."

11   See, for example, Helen Pluckrose and James A. Lindsay, *Cynical Theories: How Activist Scholarship Made Everything about Race, Gender, and Identity—and Why This Harms Everybody* (Durham, North Carolina: Pitchstone Publishing, 2020); Christopher F. Rufo. *America's Cultural Revolution: How the Radical Left Conquered Everything* (Broadside Books, 2023).

12   Steven Ertelt, "Senator Tom Cotton: 'Military Should Not Be Paying for Abortion Tourism,'" LifeNews.com, July 17, 2023, https://www.lifenews.com/2023/07/17/senator-tom-cotton-military-should-not-be-paying-for-abortion-tourism/.

13   Jordan Boyd, "Senate GOP Can Back Tuberville or Fail Americans on Abortion," *The Federalist*, July 17, 2023, https://thefederalist.com/2023/07/17/senate-republicans-have-a-choice-back-tuberville-or-fail-a-majority-of-americans-on-abortion-again/.

14   Penny Nance, "In Defense of Tommy Tuberville's Hold over Pentagon Abortion Policy," *The Hill*, July 15, 2023, https://thehill.com/opinion/congress-blog/4098741-in-defense-of-tommy-tubervilles-hold-over-pentagon-abortion-policy/.

15   10 US Code § 1093. https://www.law.cornell.edu/uscode/text/10/1093; Ertelt, "Senator Tom Cotton."

16   Kimberley Strassel, "The Biden-Schumer Military-Promotion Blockade," *Wall Street Journal*, September 21, 2023. https://www.wsj.com/articles/the-biden-schumer-war-games-abortion-policy-military-politics-pentagon-9b4fd1a3.

17   "In an Exclusive Interview, Secretaries of the US Navy, US Army and US Air Force Join *The Lead* to Condemn Sen. Tommy Tuberville's Hold on Military Nominations," *The Lead*, CNN, September 5, 2023, https://www.cnn.com/videos/tv/2023/09/05/the-lead-army-navy-air-force-secretaries.cnn.

18   Carlos Del Toro, Frank Kendall, and Christine Wormuth, "Three Service Secretaries to Tuberville: Stop This Dangerous Hold on Senior Officers," *Washington Post*, September 5, 2023, https://www.washington

post.com/opinions/2023/09/04/army-navy-air-force-secretaries-tuberville -military-hold.

19   Laura Seligman, Paul McLeary, and Connor O'Brien, "Pentagon Goes on the Attack amid Tuberville Blockade," *Politico*, September 6, 2023, https://www .politico.com/news/2023/09/06/pentagon-media-blitz-tuberville-00114284.

20   That's exactly what's happened. See documentation in J. Michael Waller, *Big Intel: How the CIA and FBI Went from Cold War Heroes to Deep State Villains,* (Washington, DC: Regnery Publishing, 2024).

21   Jordan Boyd, "GOPers Dogpile on Tuberville for Fighting DOD Abortion Racket," *The Federalist*, July 12, 2023, https://thefederalist.com/2023/07/12 /mcconnell-thune-join-bad-faith-dogpile-on-tuberville-for-fighting-militarys -taxpayer-funded-abortion-racket/.

22   Doug G. Ware, "Marine commandant nominee says blocking military promotions compromises national security," *Stars and Stripes*, June 13, 2023, https://www.stripes.com/branches/marine_corps/2023–06-13/marine -commandant-senate-tuberville-promotions-abortion-10426722.html.

23   William Perry, William S. Cohen, Robert M. Gates, Leon E. Panetta, Chuck Hagel, James Mattis, and Mark T. Esper, *Letter from Seven Former United States Secretaries of Defense to Chuck Schumer and Mitch McConnell*, May 4, 2023, https://web.archive.org/web/20230505041210/https://www .democrats.senate.gov/imo/media/doc/letter_from_seven_former_united _states_secretaries_of_defense.pdf.

24   Jeremy Hunt, "Hearing On Ensuring Force Readiness: Examining Progressivism's Impact on an All-Volunteer Military," Statement before the House Committee on Oversight and Accountability Subcommittee on National Security, the Border, and Foreign Affairs, March 28, 2023, https://oversight.house.gov/wp-content/uploads/2023/03/Hunt _CongressionalTestimony_28MAR23.pdf.

25   Brent Scher, "Pentagon Officials Worked To Finalize Climate Plan During Botched Afghanistan Withdrawal, Emails Show," *Daily Wire*, August 30, 2023, https://www.dailywire.com/news/pentagon-frantically-worked-to -finalize-climate-plan-during-botched-afghanistan-withdrawal-emails-show.

26   Lolita C. Baldor, "Biden Picks Female Admiral to lead Navy. She'd Be First woman on Joint Chiefs of Staff," Associated Press, July 21, 2023, https: //apnews.com/article/navy-chief-first-woman-franchetti-3508e41a3e9ff0e1 7782de81299acf13.

27 Sara Eschleman, "Commander, Naval Air Forces Hosts 2nd Annual DEI Summit," US Navy Press Office, November 9, 2022, https://archive.is/RE68r#selection-347.1–395.0

28 Mary Margaret Olohan, "Drag Shows on USS Ronald Reagan Occurred under This Navy Captain," *The Daily Signal*, May 19, 2023, https://www.dailysignal.com/2023/05/19/tuberville-blocking-promotion-navy-captain-who-allowed-drag-shows-uss-ronald-reagan/.

29 American Accountability Foundation (@ExposingBiden), "He also praised a movie about LGBT activist. . . .," Twitter, August 24, 2023, 11:57 a.m., https://twitter.com/ExposingBiden/status/1694740630189052099.

30 American Accountability Foundation (@ExposingBiden), "He says that 'A system of de facto. . . .," Twitter, August 24, 2023, 11:57 a.m., https://twitter.com/ExposingBiden/status/1694740616519762415.

31 "Navy Observes LGBT Pride Month," Navy Office of Information, June 4, 2019, https://www.militarynews.com/news/navy-observes-lgbt-pride-month/article_3715b2b5-10d8-5c34-8aef-0c76ab7c47ce.html.

32 American Accountability Foundation (@ExposingBiden), "BREAKING: This is Vice Adm. Craig A. Clapperton. . . .," Twitter, August 22, 2023, 5:41 p.m., https://twitter.com/ExposingBiden/status/1694102556631298527.

33 American Accountability Foundation (@ExposingBiden), "Brig. Gen. Scott A. Cain (Air Force), nominated. . . .," Twitter, August 22, 2023, 5:41 p.m., https://twitter.com/ExposingBiden/status/1694102569184903581.

34 American Accountability Foundation (@ExposingBiden), "This is Lt. Gen. Kevin B. Schneider (Air Force). . . .," Twitter, August 21, 2023, 5:13 p.m., https://twitter.com/ExposingBiden/status/1693733073353851160.

35 Fred Lucas, "Biden Taps Woke Generals for Top Air Force Promotions," *The Daily Signal*, June 6, 2023, https://www.dailysignal.com/2023/06/06/1-biden-nominee-wants-wokeness-in-air-forces-dna-another-decries-whiteness/.

36 Shawn Fleetwood, "Space Force Nominee Fired Service Member Over DEI Opposition," *The Federalist*, July 25, 2023, https://thefederalist.com/2023/07/25/bidens-space-force-nominee-previously-canned-service-member-for-speaking-out-against-marxism-in-the-military/.

37 "LGBT Pride Month Inaugural Speaker—'Honoring Diversity Solves Problems and Creates Innovative Products' (press release) " US Navy, July 27, 2015, https://archive.is/sxHiD.

38 Haughey, "In Depth."

39 "Amanda Simpson," Wikipedia, February 18, 2024, https://en.wikipedia.org/wiki/Amanda_Simpson.

40 "Amanda Simpson, Formerly Test Pilot Mitchell Simpson, Gets Senior Post in Commerce Department," *New York Daily News*, January 4, 2010, https://www.nydailynews.com/2010/01/04/amanda-simpson-formerly-test-pilot-mitchell-simpson-gets-senior-post-in-commerce-department/.

41 Elaine Donnelly, "Legislative History of the Law Regarding Homosexuals in the Military," Testimony before the House Armed Services Personnel Subcommittee, July 23, 2008, https://www.cmrlink.org/issues/full/legislative-history-of-the-law-regarding-homosexuals-in-the-military-1.

42 Fiona Dawson. "In a First, Openly Transgender Service Member Promoted," NBC News, Sept. 15, 2016, https://archive.is/LIj4t.

43 Meghann Myers, "She's One of the Army's First Transitioned Transgender Soldiers—and an Infantryman—but Now Her Future Is Uncertain," *Army Times*, August 1, 2017, https://www.armytimes.com/news/your-army/2017/08/01/shes-one-of-the-armys-first-transitioned-trangender-soldiers-and-an-infantryman-but-now-her-future-is-uncertain/.

44 Caroline Downey, "Army's First Trans Officer Indicted for Spying for Russia," *Yahoo News*, September 29, 2022. https://news.yahoo.com/army-first-trans-officer-indicted-183103671.html.

45 Chris Geidner, "The First Out Transgender Active-Duty US Army Officer: 'My Story Is Not Unique,'" *BuzzFeed News,* June 9, 2015. https://www.buzzfeednews.com/article/chrisgeidner/the-first-out-transgender-active-duty-us-army-officer-my-sto.

46 Dawson, "In a First."

47 Tim Teeman, "Top Trans Officer Bree Fram on the Military, Marriage, and Joining Space Force," *The Daily Beast*, August 21, 2021. www.thedailybeast.com, https://www.thedailybeast.com/top-trans-officer-bree-fram-on-the-military-marriage-and-joining-space-force.

48 Brandan O'Connor, "Forty Years Have Passed Since the First Women Graduated from West Point in the Class of 1980," US Army, May 27, 2020, https://archive.is/4Wte2

49 "Navy Ignores Warnings of Health Issues for Women on Submarines," Center for Military Readiness, May 13, 2010, https://www.cmrlink.org/issues/full/navy-ignores-warnings-of-health-issues-for-women-on-submarines.

50 Laura Sessions Stepp, "Rates of Unintended Pregnancies in the Navy Are Surprisingly High," *Washington Post*, July 1, 2013, https://www .washingtonpost.com/national/health-science/rates-of-unintended -pregnancies-in-the-navy-are-surprisingly-high/2013/07/01/b8f86630-b0dc -11e2-baf7–5bc2a9dc6f44_story.html.

51 Will Heilpern, "Meet the First Openly Transgender Infantryman in the US Army," *Business Insider*, June 27, 2016, https://www.businessinsider.com /tricia-king-the-first-transgender-infantryman-in-the-us-army-2016–6.

52 Fiona Dawson, "'Transgender, at War and in Love'" (opinion) *New York Times*, June 4, 2015, https://www.nytimes.com/2015/06/04/opinion /transgender-at-war-and-in-love.html.

53 Myers, "She's One of the Army's First Transitioned Transgender Soldiers."

54 *Transmilitary* (documentary), SideXSide Studios, Free Lion Productions, Archer Gray, 2018, https://www.imdb.com/title/tt7297156/

55 See, for example, the documentation of abortion activists inflating figures for illegal abortions in Carrie Gress, *The End of Woman: How Smashing the Patriarchy Has Destroyed Us* (Washington, DC: Regnery Publishing, 2023), 83.

56 SPARTA, "Commitment to Serve," June 7, 2018, https://web.archive.org /web/20190803145542/https://spartapride.org/commitment-to-serve/.

57 Gerhard Peters and John T. Woolley, "Press Release - President Biden Announces Key Administration Nominations in National Security Online," The American Presidency Project, April 23, 2021, https://www.presidency .ucsb.edu/node/349630.

58 Leo Shane III, "Controversial Pentagon Nominee Will Be Put into VA Leadership Instead," *Military Times*, June 8, 2022, https://www .militarytimes.com/veterans/2022/06/08/controversial-pentagon-nominee -will-be-put-into-va-leadership-instead/, https://archive.is/zNjNW.

59 Jonathan S. Tobin, "Rachel Levine's Only Qualification Was Punching the Diversity Ticket," *The Federalist*, March 31, 2021, https://thefederalist .com/2021/03/31/rachel-levines-only-qualification-was-punching-the -diversity-ticket/.

60 Libby Emmons, "What Everyone Knows About Rachel Levine but Isn't Allowed to Say on Social Media," *The Federalist*, March 23, 2022, https://thefederalist.com/2022/03/23/everybody-knows-rachel -levine-is-truly-a-man-including-rachel-levine/.

61 "Rachel Levine," Wikipedia, https://en.wikipedia.org/w/index .php?title=Rachel_Levine&oldid=1210950532.

62 John A. Lucas, "How The 'Four-Star Admiral' Photo-Op Will Damage US Security," *The Federalist*, October 25, 2021, https://thefederalist .com/2021/10/25/how-the-rachel-levine-four-star-admiral-photo-op-will -damage-u-s-security/.

63 Tristan Justice, "Senate Confirms Transgender Nominee Rachel Levine to Science Position," *The Federalist*, March 25, 2021, https://thefederalist .com/2021/03/25/democrats-war-on-science-ramps-up-with-confirmation -of-bidens-trans-nominee-rachel-levine-to-health-position/.

64 Social Media Chronicles, "Russian Propaganda Ad Mocking US Wokeness," 2023, https://www.youtube.com/watch?v=UVy7yjPyO98.

65 Eddie Scarry, "TikTok Is a Ground Zero For Kids Learning About Transgenderism," *The Federalist*, June 2, 2022, https://thefederalist .com/2022/06/02/cbs-mini-doc-shows-tik-tok-is-a-ground-zero-for-kids- learning-about-transgenderism; and Clare Morell, "If Parents Don't Get a Grip on Their Kids' Social Media, Trans Activists Will," *The Federalist*, August 1, 2022, https://thefederalist.com/2022/08/01/parents-if-you-dont -get-a-grip-on-your-kids-social-media-trans-activists-will/.

66 Helen Raleigh, "3 Key Takeaways From The US-China Summit In Alaska," *The Federalist*, March 23, 2021, https://thefederalist.com/2021/03/23/3-key -takeaways-from-the-u-s-china-summit-in-alaska/. .

67 Jordan Boyd, "Biden's Department of Defense Denies Drag Shows on Bases Even When Confronted with Undeniable Evidence," *The Federalist*, March 31, 2023, https://thefederalist.com/2023/03/31/bidens-department -of-defense-denies-drag-shows-on-bases-even-when-confronted-with -undeniable-evidence/.

68 Caitlin Doornbos, "US Navy Denied Recruitment Program That Featured Drag Queen 'Digital Ambassador': Rep. Jim Banks," *New York Post*, May 9, 2023, https://archive.is/1IBOR.

69 Chaya Raichik (@LibsofTikTok), "The US Navy hired this non-binary drag queen. . . .," Twitter, May 2, 2023, 3:27 p.m., https://twitter.com /libsoftiktok/status/1653481253650288652.

70 Shawn Fleetwood, "Navy Puts The Kibosh On Digital Recruiting Program After Discovering Enlistees Aren't Into Drag Queens," *The Federalist*, September 15, 2023, https://thefederalist.com/2023/09/15/navy-puts-the

-kibosh-on-digital-recruiting-program-after-discovering-enlistees-arent
-into-drag-queens/.

71   Boyd, "Department of Defense."

72   "Rep. Gaetz Demands Answers from Secretary Austin, General Milley
      on Military Drag Show Events" (press release), May 23, 2023, http://gaetz
      .house.gov/media/press-releases/rep-gaetz-demands-answers-secretary
      -austin-general-milley-military-drag-show.

73   Hank Berrien, "Sec Def Austin Smirks, Denies Drag Events Held At Military
      Bases Were Supported By Defense Department," *The Daily Wire*, March 29,
      2023, https://www.dailywire.com/news/sec-def-austin-smirks-denies-drag
      -events-held-at-military-bases-were-supported-by-defense-department.

74   Jon Simkins, "Sailor by Day, Performer by Night—Meet the Navy's Drag
      Queen, 'Harpy Daniels,'" *Military Times*, August 30, 2018, https://archive
      .is/klco8.

75   Kirstin Cole and Charline Charles, "Navy Expands Recruitment Efforts
      with One of Their Own; Drag Queen 'Harpy Daniels,'" PIX11, June 16,
      2023, https://pix11.com/news/morning/navy-expands-recruitment-efforts
      -with-one-of-their-own-drag-queen-harpy-daniels/.

76   Carl Herzog, "Drag in the Navy: An Interview with Harpy Daniels," *USS
      Constitution Museum (blog,)* August 19, 2022: https://archive.is/a5ctv, https:
      //ussconstitutionmuseum.org/wp-content/uploads/dlm_uploads/2018/09
      /USS-Constitution-Museum-03–31-2022-Financial-Statements.pdf.

77   Simkins, "Sailor by Day."

78   John Paul Brammer, "Navy drag queen 'Harpy Daniels' is serving looks—and
      the country," NBC News, August 30, 2018, https://www.nbcnews.com/feature
      /nbc-out/navy-drag-queen-harpy-daniels-serving-looks-country-n905056.

79   TRMLX (@realtrmlx), "Rear Admiral Lex Walker (he/him), commander
      of Navy. . . .," Twitter, May 4, 2023, 8:36 p.m., https://web.archive.org
      /web/20230718194013/https://twitter.com/realtrmlx/status/16542838
      74774441985.

80   Rebecca Kheel, "Top Military Officials Questioned over Drag Shows on
      Military Bases," Military.com, March 29, 2023, https://archive.is/T3GZD.

81   Berrien, "Sec Def Austin Smirks."

82   Ian Whitaker, "The secret world of Nellis: Inside the military marvel
      mere miles from the Las Vegas Strip," *Las Vegas Sun*, September 4,
      2016, https://lasvegassun.com/news/2016/sep/04/the-secret-world-of
      -nellis-inside-the-military-mar/.

83 Zoe Kalen Hill, "US Military Defends Drag Show at Largest Training Center as 'Essential to Morale,'" *Newsweek*, June 24, 2021, https://archive.is/KM255.

84 Heather Mongilio, "VCNO: Navy Set to Miss FY 2023 Recruiting Goals for Enlisted Sailors by Nearly 16%," *USNI News*, April 20, 2023, https://news.usni.org/2023/04/20/vcno-navy-set-to-miss-fy-2023-recruiting-goals-for-enlisted-sailors-by-nearly-16.

85 Courtney Kube and Molly Boigon, "Every Branch of the Military Is Struggling to Make Its 2022 Recruiting Goals, Officials Say." *NBC News*, June 27, 2022, https://www.nbcnews.com/news/military/every-branch-us-military-struggling-meet-2022-recruiting-goals-officia-rcna35078.

86 Cody Anderson, "Navy Recruiting Command Announces Mission Results for Fiscal Year 2022 and Goals for 2023," *United States Navy*, October 3, 2022. https://www.navy.mil/Press-Office/News-Stories/Article/3177917/navy-recruiting-command-announces-mission-results-for-fiscal-year-2022-and-goal/.

87 Mongilio, "VCNO."

88 Stephen Sorace, "US Army Cutting Force by 24K amid Recruiting Shortfalls," *Fox News*, February 27, 2024, https://www.msn.com/en-us/news/us/us-army-cutting-force-by-24k-amid-recruiting-shortfalls/ar-BB1iYRQd.

89 Ben Kesling, "The Military Recruiting Crisis: Even Veterans Don't Want Their Families to Join," *Wall Street Journal*, June 23, 2023, https://www.wsj.com/articles/military-recruiting-crisis-veterans-dont-want-their-children-to-join-510e1a25.

90 Shawn Fleetwood, "Poll: Faith in US Military Hits Lowest Level In More Than 20 Years," *The Federalist*, August 1, 2023, https://thefederalist.com/2023/08/01/poll-faith-in-americas-military-plummets-to-lowest-level-in-more-than-20-years/.

91 Ed Thomas, "86% of Air Force Pilots Are White Men. Here's Why This Needs to Change," *Yahoo! News*, October 20, 2020, https://archive.is/Cr2OA.

92 Rachel S. Cohen, "Air Force Leaders Set New Goals to Diversify officer corps," *Air Force Times*, August 30, 2022, https://archive.is/Q2EtO

93 Elaine Donnelly, "As DOD Queers the Military, It's No Wonder Recruiting Tanked," *The Federalist*, October 21, 2022, https://thefederalist.com/2022/10/21/with-drag-shows-and-genderfluid-internships-its-no-wonder-military-recruiting-is-down/.

94 Shawn Fleetwood, "Biden's Joint Chiefs Pick Prioritized in Air Force Personnel Choices," *The Federalist*, May 8, 2023, https://thefederalist .com/2023/05/08/bidens-pick-for-joint-chiefs-chair-made-diversity-and -inclusion-focal-points-in-air-force-personnel-decisions/.

95 Ben Kesling, "The Military Recruiting Crisis: Even Veterans Don't Want Their Families to Join," *Wall Street Journal*, June 30, 2023, https://www .wsj.com/articles/military-recruiting-crisis-veterans-dont-want-their -children-to-join-510e1a25.

96 Elizabeth Fender, "Poll: Nearly Seven in 10 Active Service Members Have Witnessed Politicization in US Military," The Heritage Foundation, January 30, 2023, https://www.heritage.org/defense/report/poll-nearly-seven-10 -active-service-members-have-witnessed-politicization-us.

97 Jeff Schogol, "Army Secretary Concerned 'Woke Military' Criticism Could Hurt the Service," *Task and Purpose*, June 14, 2023, https://taskandpurpose .com/news/army-secretary-woke-military/.

98 Aaron Renn, "Military Recruitment Challenges Show American Leadership Failures," *AaronRenn.com (blog)*, July 5, 2023, https://www.aaronrenn .com/p/military-recruitment-challenges-show

99 "The 'Military Personnel Eligibility Act of 1993': Gays in the Military: Give the Law a Name," *CMR Notes 85*, July 2007, https://www.cmrlink.org /data/Sites/85/CMRDocuments/CMR%20Notes%20Issue85–0707.pdf.

100 Paul Holston, "'Don't Ask Don't Tell' repeal training in progress," *US Army*, May 23, 2011, https://www.army.mil/article/56925/dont_ask_dont_tell _repeal_training_in_progress; Kent Klein, "Obama: 'Don't Ask, Don't Tell' Repeal 'A Historic Milestone,'" Voice of America News, December 21, 2010, https://www.voanews.com/a/obama-dont-ask-dont-tell-repeal-a-historic -milestone-112327614/132648.html; Valerie Jarrett, "The End of Don't Ask, Don't Tell," White House (blog), July 22, 2011, https://obamawhitehouse .archives.gov/blog/2011/07/22/end-dont-ask-dont-tell.

101 "LGBTQ Activism," Library of Congress US History Primary Source Timeline, https://www.loc.gov/classroom-materials/united-states -history-primary-source-timeline/post-war-united-states-1945–1968 /lgbtq-activism/.

102 "DOD LGBTQ+ Timeline" (notes to Diversity, Equity, and Inclusion webinar "Pride Panel: A Historical Perspective + The Way Ahead"), *Naval History and Heritage Command*, October 13, 2016, https://www.history .navy.mil/content/dam/nhhc/news-and-events/events/DoD%20LGBTQ%20 Timeline.pdf.

103 Thomas Brading, "Serving with Pride: LGBTQ Soldiers Celebrate Diversity, Speak Their Truth," *Army News Service*, June 29, 2021, https://www.army.mil/article/247931/serving_with_pride_lgbtq_soldiers _celebrate_diversity_speak_their_truth.

104 Sean Kimmons, "Transgender Soldier Finds Inclusion, Support in Army," *US Army Garrison Japan Public Affairs*, June 1, 2022, https://archive.is /Y5YQ3.

105 Brading, "Serving with Pride."

106 Sarah Patterson, "Living Authentically Saves Soldier's Life," *Army Sustainment Command Public Affairs*, June 22, 2023, https://archive.is /haX4B.

107 Jon Micheal Connor, "Army Sustainment Command employee chosen as DA-Level Civilian Videographer of Year; ASC Also Rocks in AMC Public Affairs Competition," *Army Sustainment Command Public Affairs*, April 21, 2023, https://www.army.mil/article/265992/army_sustainment _command_employee_chosen_as_da_level_civilian_videographer_of_year _asc_also_rocks_in_amc_public_affairs_competition.

108 Sarah Patterson, image of Major Rachel Jones, *Army Sustainment Command Public Affairs*, June 22, 2023, https://archive.is/lqRk9.

109 Daniel J. Flynn, *Cult City: Jim Jones, Harvey Milk, and 10 Days That Shook San Francisco* (ISI Books, 2018); "Harvey Milk," Wikipedia. https: //en.wikipedia.org/w/index.php?title=Harvey_Milk&oldid=1210921451.

110 Ibid.

111 Deepa Shivaram, "The US Navy Has Christened a Ship Named after Slain Gay Rights Leader Harvey Milk," *NPR*, November 7, 2021, sec. National. https://www.npr.org/2021/11/07/1053330774/navy-ship-harvey-milk.

112 TRMLX (@realtrmlx), "Fort Novosel, formerly Fort Rucker, has a gay pride. . . .," Twitter, June 23, 2023, 12:20 p.m., https://web .archive.org/web/20230718191307/https://twitter.com/realtrmlx/status /1672278429213896714.

113 TRMLX (@realtrmlx), "Children's section of the Laughlin Air Force Base library. . . .," Twitter, June 16, 2023, 2:00 p.m., https://web .archive.org/web/20230718191815/https://twitter.com/realtrmlx /status/1669766937881051168.

114 See note 6 in this chapter.

115 Jordan Schachtel (@JordanSchachtel), "National Guard recruiting video: 'gender doesn't matter.'. . .," Twitter, July 18, 2023, 9:40 a.m., https://web .archive.org/web/20230718193711/https://twitter.com/JordanSchachtel /status/1681297933994541059.

116 Sarah Sicard, "Comment Section Removed from Army Recruiting Ad Featuring Soldier with Two Moms," *Army Times*, May 20, 2021, https: //archive.is/QcwbH.

117 Shawn Fleetwood, "This Book Exposes The DEI Rot Plaguing US Military Academies." *The Federalist*, April 8, 2024, https://thefederalist .com/2024/04/08/30-year-naval-academy-teacher-details-depth-of-dei-rot -in-americas-military-institutions/.

118 Evan Smith, "Inside the 'Woke' Takeover of the US Air Force Academy," *Washington Examiner*, June 20, 2023, https://www .washingtonexaminer.com/opinion/beltway-confidential/2788090 /inside-the-woke-takeover-of-the-us-air-force-academy-2/.

119 "The DEI Threat to Our Military Academies" (editorial), *Washington Examiner*, August 6, 2023, https://www.washingtonexaminer.com/opinion /editorials/2748442/the-dei-threat-to-our-military-academies/.

120 "Diversity and Inclusion Resource List," *US Air Force*, August 2021, https: //web.archive.org/web/20211116144843/https://www.af.mil/Portals/1 /images/diversity/D-I_Resource_Handout_Aug2021_v2.pdf.

121 President Joe Biden, "LGBTQ+ Leaders Share Advice on Coming Out," Facebook, June 29, 2021, https://www.facebook.com/POTUS /videos/274194004474730/.

122 "Waltz: Banks Seek Answers from US Military Academies on Remarks Made at DEI Conference" (press release), *Mike Waltz*, September 21, 2023, https://web.archive.org/web/20230924203534/https://waltz.house.gov/news /documentsingle.aspx?DocumentID=76.

123 "Dr. Joseph Currin" (faculty profile), *United States Airforce Academy*, https://web.archive.org/web/20210228191540/https://www.usafa.edu /facultyprofile/?smid=31180.

124 Matthew J. Sharkey, Joseph M. Currin, Kassidy Cox, Brittney L. Golden, Amelia E. Evans, and Sheila Garos, "'Horny and Wanting to Watch Something': An Exploratory Qualitative Analysis of Heterosexual Men's Pornography Viewing Preferences," *Psychology & Sexuality* 13, no. 2 (April 3, 2022): 415–28, https://doi.org/10.1080/19419899.2020.1824937.

125 Kassidy Cox, Joseph M. Currin, Sheila Garos, Amelia E. Evans, Kimberly Rubio, and Alyssa Stokes, "'That Was Fun, I Gotta Run': Comparing Exit Strategies of a One-Time Sexual Encounter to Buyer–Seller Relationship Dissolution," *Sexuality & Culture* 25, no. 5 (October 1, 2021): 1771–88, https://doi.org/10.1007/s12119-021-09849-2.

126 Joseph M. Currin, Randolph D. Hubach, and Julie M. Croff, "Sex-Ed without the Stigma: What Gay and Bisexual Men Would Like Offered in School Based Sex Education," *Journal of Homosexuality* 67, no. 13 (November 9, 2020): 1779–97, https://doi.org/10.1080/00918369.2019.161 6429.

127 "Dr. Joseph Currin."

128 Karin De Angelis, Michelle Sandhoff, Kimberly Bonner, and David R. Segal, "Sexuality in the Military," in *International Handbook on the Demography of Sexuality*, ed. Amanda K. Baumle, International Handbooks of Population (Dordrecht, the Netherlands: Springer Netherlands, 2013) 363–81, https://doi.org/10.1007/978-94-007-5512-3_18.

129 David G. Smith and Karin De Angelis, "Lesbian and Gay Service Members and Their Families," in *Inclusion in the American Military: A Force for Diversity*, ed. David E. Rohall, Morten G. Ender, and Michael D. Matthews (New York: Lexington Books, 2017), 129–48.

130 Ryan Kelty, Karin K. De Angelis, Morten G. Ender, and Michael D. Matthews, "American Attitudes toward Military Service of Transgender People," in *Attitudes Aren't Free: A Call to Action, Volume II*, ed. James E. Parco, David A. Levy, Daphne DePorres, and Alfredo Sandoval (Palmer Lake, Colorado: Enso Books, 2023), 305–17.

131 Chaya Raichik (@LibsofTikTok), "The military is using your tax dollars to pay queer doctors....," Twitter, August 16, 2023, 12:01 p.m., https://twitter.com/libsoftiktok/status/1691842592890335561.

132 Raichik, "The military is using"; Chaya Raichik (@LibsofTikTok), "Apparently the Military has a base in Texas which houses....," Twitter, August 4, 2023, 8:13 p.m., https://twitter.com/libsoftiktok/status/1687617762842263554.

133 emmettheyo, TikTok, https://www.tiktok.com/@emmettheyo.

134 "Procedural Instruction," Defense Health Agency, US Department of Defense, No. 6025.21, May 12, 2023, 28–29, https://www.health.mil/Reference-Center/DHA-Publications/2023/05/12/DHA-PI-6015-21.

135 Ibid, 29.

136 Raichik, "Apparently the Military."

137 Tom Vanden Brook, "Exclusive: Pentagon Spent Nearly $8 Million to Treat 1,500 Transgender Troops since 2016," *USA Today*, February 27, 2019, https://www.usatoday.com/story/news/politics/2019/02/27/exclusive-report -shows-8-million-spent-more-than-1–500-transgender-troops-pentagon -dysphoria/2991706002/.

138 James Hasson, "New Army Training Tells Female Soldiers To 'Accept' Naked Men in Their Showers," *The Federalist*, July 5, 2017, https://thefederalist.com/2017/07/05/new-army-training-tells-female -soldiers-put-naked-men-showers/.

139 "Biden Pentagon Quietly Expands Woke Transgender Policies in the Military" (policy analysis), Center for Military Readiness Policy Analysis, February 2023. https://cmrlink.org/data/sites/85/CMRDocuments/CMR _PolicyAnalysis_February2023.pdf.

140 Greg Norman, "Biden Joint Chiefs Chairman Nominee Pressed on Transgenderism in Military amid Recruiting Challenges," FoxNews. com, July 11, 2023, https://www.foxnews.com/politics/biden-joint-chiefs -chairman-nominee-military-shouldnt-make-recruits-uncomfortable-push -inclusivity.

141 Hannah Grossman, "Military Recruit Considers Resignation after Being Forced to Shower with Trans Women with Full Male Genitalia: Report," *Fox News*, July 18, 2023, https://www.foxnews.com/media /female-recruit-considered-resigning-being-forced-shower-trans-women -full-male-genitalia.

142 Shawn Fleetwood, "Senate Republicans Grill Biden's Pick for Joint Chiefs Chair over DEI, Transgenderism in the Military," *The Federalist*, July 12, 2023, https://thefederalist.com/2023/07/12/senate-republicans-grill-bidens -pick-for-joint-chiefs-chair-over-dei-transgenderism-in-the-military/? _thumbnail_id=296157.

143 Micaela Burrow, "The Military Is Quietly Using a Little-Known Program to Enable Child Sex Changes," *The Daily Caller*, August 1, 2023, https://dailycaller.com/2023/08/01/military-sex-change-gender-transition -minors-special-needs/.

144 Ibid.

145 "Navy Ignores."

146 "Biden Pentagon Quietly Expands Woke Transgender Policies in the Military" (analysis), *Center for Military Readiness*, February 2023, 4, https://cmrlink.org/data/sites/85/CMRDocuments/CMR_PolicyAnalysis_February2023.pdf.

147 Walt Heyer, *Paper Genders: Pulling the Mask Off the Transgender Phenomenon* (Singapore: Make Waves Publishing, 2011).

148 Jordan Schachtel, "Confidential DOD Memo Reveals 'Transgender' Service Members Can Skip Deployments and Receive Indefinite Physical Fitness/Standards Waivers," *The Dossier*, July 18, 2023. https://www.dossier.today/p/confidential-biden-dod-memo-reveals.

149 Jordan Schachtel, "New DOD Docs Show 'Transgender' Service Members Receive Fitness Exemptions, Drug Testing Waivers, & Paid Vacations," *The Dossier*, July 10, 2023. https://www.dossier.today/p/new-dod-docs-show-transgender-service?publication_id=69009&post_id=135308985&isFreemail=true.

150 Ted Macie (@ted_macie), "Just pulled the count," Twitter, July 21, 2023, 1:55 p.m., https://web.archive.org/web/20230827201207/https://twitter.com/ted_macie/status/1682449319469764611.

151 "Petition for Writ of Mandamus to the Department of Veterans Affairs," *In re: Transgender American Veterans Association (24–108)*, Court of Appeals for the Federal Circuit, January 25, 2024, 3, https://law.yale.edu/sites/default/files/documents/area/clinic/1-petition-with-appendix.pdf.

152 Schactel, "Confidential DOD Memo" and "New DOD Docs Show."

153 "Medical Conditions That Can Keep You from Joining the Military," Military.com, May 8, 2012, https://www.military.com/join-armed-forces/disqualifiers-medical-conditions.html.

154 Schactel, "Confidential DOD Memo."

155 Fender, "Poll."

156 Kesling, "The Military Recruiting Crisis."

157 Conor Finnegan, "US Embassies Authorized to Hang Black Lives Matter Flags, Banners on Anniversary of Floyd's Murder," *ABC News*, May 26, 2021. https://archive.is/qD1om.

158 Nathan Place, "Biden Administration Allows LGBTQ Pride Flag to Fly over US Embassies After Trump Banned It," *The Independent*, April 23, 2021, https://archive.is/BpwM4.

159 Josh Lederman, "Trump Admin Tells US Embassies They Can't Fly Pride Flag on Flagpoles," *NBC News*, June 9, 2019, https://archive.is/snWUQ.

160 Adam Ashton, "California National Guard to Transgender Troops: 'Nobody's Going to Kick You Out,'" *Sacramento Bee*, February 6, 2019, https://www.sacbee.com/news/politics-government/the-state-worker/article225587070.html.

161 David Choi, "'This Is Our Answer to the White House': California Is Bucking Trump's Controversial Policies in an Unprecedented Way," *Business Insider*, February 12, 2019, https://www.businessinsider.com/california-national-guard-defies-trump-transgender-southern-border-policy-2019–2.

162 "National Guard Fact Sheet," *Army National Guard*, May 3, 2006, https://www.nationalguard.mil/About-the-Guard/Army-National-Guard/Resources/News/ARNG-Media/FileId/137011/

163 US Embassy to the Holy See (@USinHolySee), "Today is the start of #Pride Month. The United. . . .," Twitter, June 2, 2022, 6:33 a.m., https://twitter.com/USinHolySee/status/1531947017450176515.

164 "Pride Flags Have Been Flown by US Embassies in Muslim Majority Countries during Biden Presidency" (fact check) Reuters, June 13, 2022, https://www.reuters.com/article/idUSL1N2Y01EU/.

165 Thom Senzee, "9 Unexpected Places Where Pride Flags Flew During Pride Month" *The Advocate*, June 30, 2014, https://www.advocate.com/pride/2014/06/30/9-unexpected-places-where-pride-flags-flew-during-pride-month.

166 Vanessa Gera, "US Ambassador Marches in Warsaw Pride Parade, Sending Message to NATO Ally," *Associated Press*, June 17, 2023, https://apnews.com/article/poland-pride-parade-lgbtq-ece6478ccd23353ff4613e50f84283df.

167 Polina Ivanova and Tom Balmforth, "US Ambassador Marches in Warsaw Pride Parade, Sending Message to NATO Ally," *Associated Press*, June 17, 2023, https://archive.is/ocQgq.

Chapter 6

1 Bill Andriette, "The Guide Interviews Camille Paglia," *The Guide*, January 1999, https://www.ipce.info/library_2/files/paglia_guide.htm.

2 "Weather History for Appomattox, VA," Almanac.com, August 25, 2021, https://www.almanac.com/weather/history/zipcode/24522/2021–08–25.

3 "2021–2022 ACPS Instructional Calendar," Appomattox County Public Schools, https://drive.google.com/file/d/1OEhJs-_UMNZoljBrI22drkM9D160YMSe/view; "2022–2023 ACPS Instructional Calendar," Appomattox County Public Schools, https://web.archive.org/web

/20220813082217/https://drive.google.com/file/d/1OEhJs-_UMNZoljBrI22drkM9D16oYMSe/view

4   "Appomattox County High" (2022–2023 school year), National Center for Education Statistics, https://nces.ed.gov/ccd/schoolsearch/school_detail.asp?Search=1&InstName=appomattox+high&State=51&SchoolType=1&SchoolType=2&SchoolType=3&SchoolType=4&SpecificSchlTypes=all&IncGrade=-1&LoGrade=-1&HiGrade=-1&ID=510024000076.

5   The Family Foundation, "Sage's Law Press Conference," YouTube, January 19, 2023, https://www.youtube.com/watch?v=_tocH6U_G2w.

6   Sarah Wilder (@SarahHopeWilder), "Sage was repeatedly trafficked after her school. . . . .," Twitter, September 11, 2023, 5:38 p.m., https://twitter.com/SarahHopeWeaver/status/1701349470649139408.

7   "Appomattox County Public Schools" (home page), Appomattox County Public Schools, July 26, 2021, https://web.archive.org/web/20210726011521/https://www.acpsweb.net/.

8   "Appomattox County Public Schools Return and Recovery Planning Guide," Appomattox County Public Schools Return and Recovery Task Force, August 31, 2020. https://drive.google.com/file/d/1LCOzByAyrzOxpInJhNLmA_HWINAslI55/view.

9   Ibid.

10   "Appomattox County High" (2022–2023 school year).

11   *Blair v. Appomattox County School Board*, et al., US Dist. Ct. for Western District of Va., August 22, 2023, 10. https://drive.google.com/file/d/1otUr8dXTM—w_fvNddjPQh7IFx9Vbppp/view?pli=1.

12   Ibid., 8.

13   "Dena Olsen's Brief in Support of Motion to Dismiss." *Blair v. Appomattox County School Board*, et al., US Dist. Ct. for Western District of Va., September 20, 2023, 12. https://storage.courtlistener.com/recap/gov.uscourts.vawd.129352/gov.uscourts.vawd.129352.13.0.pdf.

14   "Plaintiff's Brief In Opposition To Defendant Appomattox County School Board's Motion To Dismiss," *Blair v. Appomattox County School Board*, et al., US Dist. Ct. for the Western District of Va., October 16, 2023, 9, https://storage.courtlistener.com/recap/gov.uscourts.vawd.129352/gov.uscourts.vawd.129352.50.0.pdf.

15   Ibid., 9, 10.

16   Ibid., 13.

17 Wilder, "Sage."

18 Wilder, "Sage."

19 *Blair v. Appomattox*, 40.

20 Wilder, "Sage."

21 *Blair v. Appomattox*, 50.

22 *Blair v. Appomattox*, 21.

23 *Blair v. Appomattox*, 16 and 40.

24 *Blair v. Appomattox*, 22.

25 Wilder, "Sage."

26 "About the Interstate Compact for Juveniles," Interstate Commission for Juveniles, https://JuvenileCompact.com/about.

27 Zeke Miller and Colleen Long, "Biden: Families of Separated Children Deserve Compensation," Associated Press, November 6, 2021, https://apnews.com/article/immigration-joe-biden-lifestyle-mexico-2bdb31fdb7e2f661db482e8c081a0d69.

28 "Blueprint for Positive Change 2020," Human Rights Campaign, 2020, https://web.archive.org/web/20201112225917/https://hrc-prod-requests.s3-us-west-2.amazonaws.com/Blueprint-2020.pdf?mtime=20201110185320&focal=none.

29 Asaf Orr, Joel Baum, Jay Brown, Elizabeth Gill, Ellen Kahn, and Anna Salem, "Schools in Transition," ACLU, National Center for Lesbian Rights, Gender Spectrum, the National Education Association, and the Human Rights Campaign, June 3, 2016, https://www.aclu.org/publications/schools-transition.

30 Ibid.

31 Helen M. Alvare, "Families, Schools, and Religious Freedom," *Loyola University Chicago Law Journal* 54, no. 2, March 31, 2022, https://doi.org/10.2139/ssrn.4119844.

32 Lara Korte, "California Is Suing to Stop Schools from Outing Trans Kids to Their Parents," *Politico*, August 28, 2023, https://www.politico.com/news/2023/08/28/california-suing-stop-schools-outing-trans-kids-00113143.

33 Jordan Boyd, "School Board Fights AG Trying To Make Them Secretly Trans Kids," *The Federalist*, September 12, 2023, https://thefederalist.com/2023/09/12/school-district-gears-up-to-fight-california-ag-trying-to-make-them-secretly-trans-kids/.

34 Chris Bray, "The Culture War Is 100% Misdirection," *Tell Me How This Ends (blog)*, August 30, 2023, https://chrisbray.substack.com/p /the-culture-war-is-100-misdirection.

35 Ryan Mills, "BLM 'Week of Action' Teaching Students Nationwide to Affirm Transgenderism, Disrupt Nuclear Family," *National Review*, February 1, 2022, https://web.archive.org/web/20220208064313/https: //www.nationalreview.com/news/blm-week-of-action-teaching-students -nationwide-to-affirm-transgenderism-disrupt-nuclear-family/.

36 Jon Miltimore, "5 Things Marx Wanted to Abolish (besides Private Property)," *Foundation for Economic Education (blog)*, October 31, 2017, https://fee .org/articles/5-things-marx-wanted-to-abolish-besides-private-property/.

37 Dustin Gardner, Lara Korte, Melanie Mason, and Jeremy B. White, "The Trans Bill That Wasn't," *Politico*, September 21, 2023, https: //www.politico.com/newsletters/california-playbook/2023/09/21/the-trans -bill-that-wasnt-00117281.

38 Denise Lite, "The Irony of 'Stay Safe, California,'" *Santa Clarita Valley Signal*, August 26, 2023, https://signalscv.com/2023/08 /denise-lite-the-irony-of-stay-safe-california/.

39 "AB-665 Minors: Consent to Mental Health Services," California Legislative Information, 2023–24, https://leginfo.legislature.ca.gov/faces /billStatusClient.xhtml?bill_id=202320240AB665.

40 Brandon Poulter, "'What the Hell Is Going On?': California Parents, School Board Members Slam Dems' Targeting Of Parental Rights," *The Daily Caller*, September 17, 2023, https://dailycaller.com/2023/09/17/what-the-hell -is-going-on-california-parents-school-board-members-slam-dems -targeting-of-parental-rights/.

41 "AB-957 Family Law: Gender Identity," California Legislative Information, 2023–24, https://leginfo.legislature.ca.gov/faces/billHistoryClient .xhtml?bill_id=202320240AB957.

42 "Broad Support for Oregon Mother Blocked by State from Adopting Children," Alliance Defending Freedom, January 22, 2024, https://adfmedia .org/case/bates-v-pakseresht.

43 "Burke v. Walsh," The Becket Fund for Religious Liberty, August 8, 2023, https://www.becketlaw.org/case/burke-v-walsh/.

44 "Family Services Policy 76," *Family Services Policy Manual*, Vermont Department for Children and Families, October 13, 2017, https://outside .vermont.gov/dept/DCF/Shared%20Documents/FSD/Policies/Policy76.pdf.

45 Nathanael Blake, "The Biden Administration Is Scheming to Take Your Kids Away," *The Federalist*, November 27, 2023, https://thefederalist.com/2023/11/27/the-biden-administration-is-scheming-to-take-your-kids-away/.

46 The Administration for Children and Families, "Safe and Appropriate Foster Care Placement Requirements for Titles IV-E and IV-B," Federal Register, 88 FR 66752, September 28, 2023, https://www.federalregister.gov/documents/2023/09/28/2023–21274/safe-and-appropriate-foster-care-placement-requirements-for-titles-iv-e-and-iv-b.

47 Rachel N. Morrison, "Non-Affirmation of Child's 'LGBTQI+' Identity Is Abuse Under Proposed Foster Care Rule," *The Federalist Society (blog)*, November 19, 2023, https://fedsoc.org/commentary/fedsoc-blog/non-affirmation-of-child-s-lgbtqi-identity-is-abuse-under-proposed-foster-care-rule.

48 Jordan Boyd, "Treating a Foster Child's Dysphoria Would Be 'Abuse' under HHS Rule." *The Federalist*, November 21, 2023, https://thefederalist.com/2023/11/21/not-encouraging-a-foster-childs-rainbow-identity-would-be-abuse-under-proposed-hhs-rule/.

49 "AB-957 Family Law: Gender Identity."

50 Abigail Shrier, "Child Custody's Gender Gauntlet," *City Journal*, February 7, 2022, https://www.city-journal.org/article/child-custodys-gender-gauntlet.

51 Walt Heyer, "Six-Year-Old Texas Boy on Track for Repressed Puberty Due to Dysphoria Diagnosis," *The Federalist*, January 29, 2019. https://thefederalist.com/2019/01/29/6-year-old-texas-boy-track-repressed-puberty-due-gender-dysphoria-diagnosis/.

52 Gabe Kaminsky, "Judge Awards Full Custody of James Younger to Mother Who Wants to Transition Him," *The Federalist*, August 9, 2021, https://thefederalist.com/2021/08/09/judge-awards-custody-of-nine-year-old-james-younger-to-trans-activist-mother-who-wants-to-transition-him/.

53 "List of School District Transgender–Gender Nonconforming Student Policies," Parents Defending Education, March 7, 2023, updated February 29, 2024, https://defendinged.org/investigations/list-of-school-district-transgender-gender-nonconforming-student-policies/.

54 Christopher F. Rufo, "Concealing Radicalism," *City Journal*, September 14, 2022, https://archive.is/OqooW.

55 Rufo, *America's Cultural Revolution*, 167. Citing Jay P. Greene and James Paul, 2021.

56 Bethany Mandel, "The Revolt of Religious Parents in Montgomery County," *The Free Press*, August 29, 2023, https://www.thefp.com/p /revolt-religious-parents-montgomery-county?publication_id=260347 &post_id=136419583&isFreemail=true.

57 Alvare, "Families, Schools."

58 Sarah Parshall Perry, "Stuff of Parents' Nightmares: Washington State Bill Hides Runaway Kids from Transgender-'Unsupportive' Parents," *The Daily Signal*, April 17, 2023, https://www.dailysignal.com/2023/04/17 /washington-state-bill-hides-runaway-kids-parents-unsupportive-their -gender-transition-abortion/.

59 "AB-665 Minors: Consent to Mental Health Services."

60 Wesley J. Smith, "California Bill to Exclude Parents from Children's Mental-Health Care," National Review Online, April 14, 2023, https: //www.nationalreview.com/corner/california-bill-to-exclude-parents -from-childrens-mental-health-care/.

61 Kiara Alfonseca, "At Least 19 States to Offer Refuge to Trans Youth and Families amid Anti-LGBTQ Legislation Wave," ABC News, May 3, 2022, https: //abcnews.go.com/US/19-states-offer-refuge-trans-youth-families-amid /story?id=84472645.

62 Scott Wiener, "LGBTQ Lawmakers in 19 States Have or Will Introduce Laws to Protect Trans Kids from Civil and Criminal Penalties When Seeking Gender-Affirming Care," May 3, 2022, https://sd11.senate.ca.gov /news/20220503-lgbtq-lawmakers-19-states-have-or-will-introduce-laws -protect-trans-kids-civil-and.

63 Jerry Cornfield, "Gay Lawmaker's Persistence Led to Conversion Therapy Ban," HeraldNet.com, March 29, 2018, https://www.heraldnet.com/news /new-law-bans-conversion-therapy-practice-in-state/.

64 Robert Price, "DA: Sex Traffickers Pick up Runaways Almost Immediately After They Hit the Streets," KGET, October 30, 2023, https://www .kget.com/news/local-news/da-sex-traffickers-pick-up-runaways-almost -immediately-after-they-hit-the-streets/.

65 Perry, "Stuff of Parents' Nightmares."

66 Mary Eberstadt, *Primal Screams: How the Sexual Revolution Created Sexual Politics* (West Conshohocken, Pennsylvania: Templeton Press, 2019), 138.

67 Ibid, 135.

68 Raj Chetty, Nathaniel Hendren, and Lawrence Katz, "The Effects of Exposure to Better Neighborhoods on Children: New Evidence from the Moving to Opportunity Project," *American Economic Review* 106, no. 4 (2016).

69 Eberstadt, *Primal Screams*, 9.

70 Ibid., 11.

71 Allyn Walker, *A Long, Dark Shadow: Minor-Attracted People and Their Pursuit of Dignity* (Oakland, California: University of California Press, 2021).

72 W. Bradford Wilcox, "The Evolution of Divorce," *National Affairs*, fall 2009. https://www.nationalaffairs.com/publications/detail /the-evolution-of-divorce.

73 Eberstadt, *Primal Screams*, 91.

74 Gwen Farrell, "Over 50% Of Liberal, White Women under 30 Have a Mental Health Issue. Are We Worried Yet?," *Evie Magazine*, April 13, 2021, https: //www.eviemagazine.com/post/over-50-percent-white-liberal-women-under -30-mental-health-condition; Greg Lukianoff and Jonathan Haidt, "'Coddling' the Afterword Part 1: Gen Z's Mental Health Continues to Deteriorate," The Foundation for Individual Rights and Expression (FIRE), September 16, 2021, https://www.thefire.org/news/blogs/eternally-radical-idea /coddling-afterword-part-1-gen-zs-mental-health-continues.

75 See, for example, Abigail Shrier, *Bad Therapy: Why the Kids Aren't Growing Up* (New York, NY: Sentinel, 2024).

76 Joel Kotkin and Samuel J Abrams, "The Rise of the Single Woke (and Young, Democratic) Female," RealClearInvestigations, January 17, 2023, https://www.realclearinvestigations.com/articles/2023/01/17/the_rise_of _the_single_woke_and_young_democratic_female_875047.html.

77 Frank Newport, Marriage Remains Key Predictor of Party Identification," Gallup, July 13 2009, https://news.gallup.com/poll/121571/Marriage -Remains-Key-Predictor-Party-Identification.aspx.

78 W. Brad Wilcox, "Who Is Happiest? Married Mothers and Fathers, per the Latest General Social Survey," Institute for Family Studies, September 12, 2023, https://ifstudies.org/blog/who-is-happiest-married-mothers-and -fathers-per-the-latest-general-social-survey.

79 Stella Morabito, "Why Women Are So Susceptible to Political Correctness," *The Federalist*, November 2, 2022, https://thefederalist.com/2022/11/02 /why-women-are-so-susceptible-to-political-correctness/.

80   Daniel A. Cox, Kelsey Eyre Hammond, and Kyle Gray, "Generation Z and the Transformation of American Adolescence: How Gen Z's Formative Experiences Shape Its Politics, Priorities, and Future," American Enterprise Institute, November 9, 2023, https://www.americansurveycenter.org/research/generation-z-and-the-transformation-of-american-adolescence-how-gen-zs-formative-experiences-shape-its-politics-priorities-and-future/.

81   Robert Karen, *Becoming Attached: First Relationships and How They Shape Our Capacity to Love,* (Oxford: Oxford University Press, 2024).

82   Jonathan Rothwell, "Parenting Is the Key to Adolescent Mental Health," Institute for Family Studies, November 3, 2023, https://ifstudies.org/blog/parenting-is-the-key-to-adolescent-mental-health.

83   Nicolás de Cárdenas, "Priest Says 'Trans' People He Has Ministered to Have Deep Wounds," *National Catholic Register,* April 4, 2024, https://www.ncregister.com/cna/priest-says-trans-people-he-has-ministered-to-have-deep-wounds.

84   Rob Henderson, "The Paradox of Liberation," *RobKHenderson.com (blog),* September 17 ,2023, https://www.robkhenderson.com/p/the-paradox-of-liberation.

85   Phillip M. Hughes et al., "Adverse Childhood Experiences across Birth Generation and LGBTQ+ Identity, Behavioral Risk Factor Surveillance System, 2019," *American Journal of Public Health* 112, no. 4, April 2022, 662–70, PubMed, https://doi.org/10.2105/AJPH.2021.306642.

86   Amy Wright Glenn, "Child Abuse Is 40 Times More Likely When Single Parents Find New Partners," Philly Voice, March 25, 2019, https://www.phillyvoice.com/child-abuse-single-parenting-divorce-marriage-new-partners-advice/; Bettina Arndt, "Mum's Boyfriend—the Worst Sexual Risk to Children," *Sydney Morning Herald,* February 13, 2014, https://www.smh.com.au/opinion/mums-boyfriend—the-worst-sexual-risk-to-children-20140213-32n3s.html.

87   Scott Yenor, "Conservatives and Our Queer Constitution," *American Greatness,* June 18 2023, https://amgreatness.com/2023/06/17/conservatives-and-our-queer-constitution/.

88   Wilcox, "The Evolution of Divorce."

89   Benjamin Scafidi, "The Taxpayer Costs of Divorce and Unwed Childbearing: FirstEver Estimates for the Nation and All Fifty States," Institute for American Values and Georgia Family Council, 2008, https://www.healthymarriageinfo.org/wp-content/uploads/2017/12/costofdivorce.pdf.

90   Wilcox, "The Evolution of Divorce."

91   Katy Faust and Stacy Manning, *Them Before Us: Why We Need a Global Children's Rights Movement* (Post Hill Press, 2021).

92   Joy Pullmann, "Study Repressed for Finding Trans Kids May Be Social Contagion," *The Federalist*, August 31, 2018, https://thefederalist.com/2018/08/31/explosive-ivy-league-study-repressed-for-finding-transgender-kids-may-be-a-social-contagion/.

93   James Poulos, "Welcome to the Pink Police State: Regime Change In America," *The Federalist*, 17 July 2014, https://thefederalist.com/2014/07/17/welcome-to-the-pink-police-state-regime-change-in-america/.

94   Henderson, "The Paradox."

95   Amy Dockser Marcus, "A Sperm Donor Chases a Role in the Lives of the 96 Children He Fathered," *Wall Street Journal*, August 27, 2023, https://www.wsj.com/lifestyle/relationships/sperm-donor-family-children-146617c8.

96   Choire Sicha, "Keeping Up With the Laverys: The Brooklyn literary power throuple all working and baby-raising from home," *New York Magazine*, April 10, 2024, https://www.thecut.com/article/daniel-lavery-grace-lavery-lily-woodruff-brooklyn-interview.html.

97   Daniel Bergner, "Lessons From a 20-Person Polycule," *The New York Times Magazine*, April 15, 2024, https://www.nytimes.com/interactive/2024/04/15/magazine/polycule-polyamory-boston.html.

98   Thanks to Stella Morabito for her work clarifying some of the language and connections here. See Stella Morabito, "How the Trans-Agenda Seeks to Redefine Everyone," *The Federalist*, June 23, 2014, https://thefederalist.com/2014/06/23/how-the-trans-agenda-seeks-to-redefine-everyone/; Stella Morabito, "Bait and Switch: How Same Sex Marriage Ends Family Autonomy," *The Federalist*, April 9, 2014, https://thefederalist.com/2014/04/09/bait-and-switch-how-same-sex-marriage-ends-marriage-and-family-autonomy/.

99   Katy Faust (@Advo_Katy), "Would Shane Dawson have passed an adoption screening? . . .," Twitter, December 10, 2023, 11:41 p.m., https://twitter.com/Advo_Katy/status/1734070815203983772.

100 Katy Faust, "Disaster Surrogacy Cases Sanctioned by Washington State's SB 6037," *Them Before Us*, February 12, 2018, https://thembeforeus.com/disaster-surrogacy-cases-sanctioned-washington-states-sb-6037/.

101 "Hugh LaFollette," Hughlafollette.com, https://web.archive.org/web/20231207203214/https://www.hughlafollette.com/.

102 Stella Morabito, "How Leftists Are Building the Framework For 'Parenting Licenses,'" *The Federalist*, November 10, 2021, https://thefederalist .com/2021/11/10/if-the-left-ends-parent-rights-you-might-need-a-license-to -raise-your-own-child/.

103 Stella Morabito, "Licensing Parents: A Statist Idea in Libertarian Drag," *The Federalist*, September 10, 2014, https://thefederalist.com/2014/09/10 /licensing-parents-a-statist-idea-in-libertarian-drag/.

104 Morabito, "Bait and Switch"; Stella Morabito, "5 Questions for Libertarians Who Support Privatizing Marriage," *The Federalist*, July 28, 2015, https: //thefederalist.com/2015/07/28/5-questions-for-libertarians-who-support -privatizing-marriage/.

105 Roger Kimball, "The Perversions of M. Foucault," *New Criterion* 11 no. 7 (March 1993), 10, https://web.archive.org/web/20181225091105/https: //www.newcriterion.com/issues/1993/3/the-perversions-of-m-foucault.

106 Ibid.

107 Dupont Lajoie, "Queer Theory and the Destruction of Normality," *WrongSpeak*, August 10, 2023, https://www.wrongspeakpublishing.com/p /queer-theory-and-the-destruction.

108 Ibid.

109 Albert R. Mohler Jr., "Polymorphous Perversity in the Heartland," *World*, November 15, 2023, https://wng.org/opinions/polymorphous -perversity-in-the-heartland-1700050198.

110 Lajoie, "Queer Theory."

111 Nick Sheppard, "It's Time for the Left to Stop Idolizing Oscar Wilde. He's a Pervert," *The Federalist*, September 18, 2018, https://thefederalist .com/2018/09/18/time-left-stop-idolizing-oscar-wilde-hes-pervert/.

112 Jeremy Lynbarger, "Walt Whitman's Boys," *Boston Review*, May 30, 2019, https://www.bostonreview.net/articles/jeremy-lybarger-walt -whitmans-boys/.

113 Chad Felix Greene, "What Happens When Men Have Sex with Teenage Boys," *HuffPost*, February 20, 2017, https://www.huffpost.com/entry/what -happens-when-men-have-sex-with-teenage-boys_b_58ab8c69e4b029c1d 1f88e02.

114 Danielle Berjikian, "11-Year-Old Becomes Youngest Grand Marshal at Orlando Pride Parade," *Louder With Crowder*, October 24, 2023, https: //www.louderwithcrowder.com/orlando-pride-marshal.

115 TheLadyWithTheHammer (@FreyaManslayer), "Brief about @Roblox. . . .," Twitter, January 2, 2023, 6:02 p.m., https://web .archive.org/web/20230121055206/https://twitter.com/FreyaManslayer /status/1609973328160198657.

116 Clifton French, "Reporter Covering Library Policy Is a Convicted Child Molester," *REAL News Central Indiana*, August 22, 2023, https: //realnewscentralindiana.com/2023/08/22/reporter-covering-library -policy-is-a-convicted-child-molester/.

117 Chad Felix Greene, "No, It's Not Bigoted for Lawmakers to Ban Child Drag Queens," *The Federalist*, April 29, 2019, https://thefederalist .com/2019/04/29/no-not-bigoted-lawmakers-ban-child-drag-queens/.

118 See, for example: Jordan Liles, "Did Videos Show Naked Men at 2023 Seattle Pride Parade, with Families and Children Present?" Snopes.com, June 29, 2023, https://www.snopes.com/fact-check/seattle-pride-parade -naked/; Ariel Zilber, "Megyn Kelly blasts 'open penis showing' at Pride parades in front of children," *New York Post*, June 27, 2023, https://nypost .com/2023/06/27/megyn-kelly-blasts-open-penis-showing-at-pride-parades -with-kids/; Shaye Weaver, "Go Topless Parade 2022 guide," TimeOut, July 19, 2022, https://www.timeout.com/newyork/things-to-do/go-topless-day.

119 Phil Willon, "Newsom Signs Bill Intended to End Discrimination against LGBTQ People in Sex Crime Convictions," *Los Angeles Times*, September 11, 2020, https://www.latimes.com/california/story/2020–09-11 /sb145-sex-crimes-law-gavin-newsom-lgbtq-rights.

120 "Senator Wiener's Work on LGBTQ Issues," Senator Scott Wiener, November 19, 2018, https://sd11.senate.ca.gov/senator-wiener %E2%80%99s-work-lgbtq-issues.

121 Greg Owen, "Gay Lawmaker Scott Wiener Speaks Out After Right's 'Groomer' Slur Led to Threat against Him," LGBTQ Nation, December 2, 2022, https://www.lgbtqnation.com/2022/12 /gay-lawmaker-scott-wiener-speaks-rights-groomer-slur-led-threat/.

122 Hannah Nightingale, "'We're Coming for Your Children': San Francisco Gay Men's Chorus Pushes Woke Agenda," *The Post Millennial*, July 7, 2021, https: //thepostmillennial.com/were-coming-for-your-children-san-francisco-choir.

123 Tyler Kingkade, "'We're Coming For Your Children' Chant at NYC Drag March Elicits Outrage, but Activists Say It's Taken out of Context," NBC News, June 27, 2023, https://archive.is/cPe4X.

124 Scott Lynch, "Photos: Drag March Kicks Off Pride Weekend 2022 with Rage and Defiance," *Gothamist*, June 25, 2022, https://gothamist.com/news/photos-drag-march-kicks-off-pride-weekend-2022-with-rage-and-defiance.

125 Wylie C. Hembree et al, "Endocrine Treatment of Gender-Dysphoric/Gender-Incongruent Persons: An Endocrine Society Clinical Practice Guideline," *Journal of Clinical Endocrinology and Metabolism* 102, no. 11 (November 2017), https://doi.org/10.1210/jc.2017–01658; James M. Cantor, "Transgender and Gender Diverse Children and Adolescents: Fact-Checking of AAP Policy," *Journal of Sex & Marital Therapy* 46, no. 4, 2020, https://doi.org/10.1080/0092623X.2019.1698481; "Independent Review of Gender Identity Services for Children and Young People," *The Cass Review*, April 2024, https://cass.independent-review.uk/wp-content/uploads/2024/04/CassReview_Final.pdf.

126 Thomas D. Steensma et al., "Factors Associated with Desistence and Persistence of Childhood Gender Dysphoria: A Quantitative Follow-up Study," *Journal of the American Academy of Child and Adolescent Psychiatry* 52, no. 6 (June 2013), https://doi.org/10.1016/j.jaac.2013.03.016.

127 Libby Emmons, "NBC News DEFENDS 'We're Coming for Your Children' Chant at NYC Drag March, Arguing It's 'Been Used for Years at Pride Events,'" *The Post Millennial*, June 28, 2023. https://thepostmillennial.com/nbc-news-defends-were-coming-for-your-children-chant-at-nyc-drag-march-arguing-its-been-used-for-years-at-pride-events.

128 Harper Keenan and Lil Miss Hot Mess, "Drag Pedagogy: The Playful Practice of Queer Imagination in Early Childhood," *Curriculum Inquiry* 50, no. 5 (October 2020), https://doi.org/10.1080/03626784.2020.1864621.

129 "Harper Keenan," Stanford Graduate School of Education, September 6, 2018, https://ed.stanford.edu/community/harper-keenan.

130 "Dr. Harper Keenan," University of British Columbia, https://educ.ubc.ca/dr-harper-keenan/.

131 Chrissy Clark, "Texas Teacher Claims 20 Fourth Graders Out Of 32 Students Identify As LGBTQ," *Daily Caller*, March 29, 2022, https://dailycaller.com/2022/03/29/texas-teacher-fourth-grade-students-lgbt-pride-week/.

132 Breccan F. Thies, "Pornhub Pushes Gay, Transgender Videos to 'Convert' Straight Men, Secret Recordings Suggest," *Washington Examiner*, December 7, 2023, https://www.washingtonexaminer.com/news/pornhub-pushes-gay-transgender-videos-convert-straight-men.

133 Amanda L. Giordano, "What to Know About Adolescent Pornography Exposure," *Psychology Today*, February 27, 2022, https://www.psychologytoday.com/us/blog/understanding-addiction/202202/what-know-about-adolescent-pornography-exposure.

134 Marc Novicoff, "A Simple Law Is Doing the Impossible. It's Making the Online Porn Industry Retreat," *Politico*, August 8, 2023, https://www.politico.com/news/magazine/2023/08/08/age-law-online-porn-00110148.

135 Giordano, "What to Know."

136 "Poll: Majority of Voters Say Introducing LGBTQ Issues to Children Hurts Their Development," Summit Ministries, June 26, 2023, https://web.archive.org/web/20230627224755/https://www.summit.org/about/press/introducing-lgbtq-issues-to-children-hurts-their-development/.

137 Pascal-Emmanuel Gobry, "A Science-Based Case for Ending the Porn Epidemic," *American Greatness*, December 15, 2019, https://amgreatness.com/2019/12/15/a-science-based-case-for-ending-the-porn-epidemic/.

138 Myles Bonnar, "I Thought He Was Going to Tear Chunks out of My Skin," BBC, March 23, 2020, https://www.bbc.com/news/uk-scotland-51967295.

139 Debby Herbenick et al., "Diverse Sexual Behaviors and Pornography Use: Findings from a Nationally Representative Probability Survey of Americans Aged 18 to 60 Years," *Journal of Sexual Medicine* 17, no. 4, (April 2020), https://doi.org/10.1016/j.jsxm.2020.01.013.

140 "What Violent Porn Taught Me at 13," Fight the New Drug, https://fightthenewdrug.org/what-violent-porn-taught-me-at-13/.

141 Martin J. Downing et al., "Sexually Explicit Media Use by Sexual Identity: A Comparative Analysis of Gay, Bisexual, and Heterosexual Men in the United States," *Archives of Sexual Behavior* 46, no. 6 (August 2017), https://doi.org/10.1007/s10508-016-0837-9./

142 Andrea Long Chu, *Females*, (Brooklyn, NY: Verso, 2019); Helen Lewis, "The Worst Argument for Youth Transition," *The Atlantic*, March 19, 2024, https://www.theatlantic.com/ideas/archive/2024/03/trans-youth-transition-andrea-long-chu/677796/.

143 Andrea Long Chu, "Did Sissy Porn Make Me Trans?" *Queer Disruptions* 2, Columbia University, New York, NY, March 1–2, 2018, https://static1.squarespace.com/static/5a9b1c0812b13f48e686fdc4/t/5a9c17e1f9619a449856c4fe/1520179170246/Chu-Did+Sissy+Porn+Make+Me+Trans%20percent3F+%20percent28QD2%20percent29.pdf.

144 Andrea Long Chu, "Freedom of Sex: The moral case for letting trans kids change their bodies," New York magazine, March 11, 2024, https://nymag .com/intelligencer/article/trans-rights-biological-sex-gender-judith-butler .html.

145 Gobry, "A Science-Based Case."

146 Lianne Kolirin, "Billie Eilish Says Watching Porn from Age 11 'Really Destroyed My Brain,'" CNN, December 15, 2021, https://www.cnn .com/2021/12/15/entertainment/billie-eilish-porn-scli-intl/index.html.

147 Christopher F. Rufo, "The Real Story behind Drag Queen Story Hour," *City Journal*, autumn 2022, https://www.city-journal.org/article /the-real-story-behind-drag-queen-story-hour.

148 Ibid.

149 Ibid.

150 Ibid.

151 Matt Walsh, *What Is a Woman?: One Man's Journey to Answer the Question of a Generation* (Nashville, Tennessee: DW Books, 2022).

152 Kaylee Greenlee, "Proposed House Rules Eliminate Gendered Terms like 'Father' And 'Daughter,'" January 1, 2021, https://dailycaller.com /2021/01/01/proposed-house-rules-gender-terms/.

153 Elle Purnell, "If Ketanji Brown Jackson Doesn't Know What A 'Woman' Is, Why Does She Use the Word So Much?" *The Federalist*, March 23, 2022, https://thefederalist.com/2022/03/23/if-ketanji-brown-jackson-doesnt-know -what-a-woman-is-why-does-she-use-the-word-so-much/.

154 Pat Califia, "Feminism, Pedophilia, and Children's Rights," in *The Culture of Radical Sex* (San Francisco, California: Cleis Press, 1994), https://www .ipce.info/ipceweb/Library/califa_feminism.htm.

155 Jennifer Oliver O'Connell, "Agent Who Inspired Box Office Smash 'Sound of Freedom' Warns: 'Trans Voice' Agenda Is Straight out of the Pedophile Playbook," Redstate.com, July 9, 2023, https://redstate.com /jenniferoo/2023/07/09/agent-who-inspired-box-office-smash-sound -of-freedom-warns-trans-voice-agenda-is-straight-out-of-the-pedophile -playbook-n773994.

156 Meghan J. Goff, "Naked Ambitions," *Harper's Magazine*, November 2006, 14. https://archive.is/y5K7d/image.

157 Mike Pearl, "Whatever Happened to NAMBLA?" *Vice*, March 24, 2016, https://www.vice.com/en/article/7bd37e/whatever-happened-to-nambla.

158 Justin Lee, "The Pedophile Apologist," *Arc Digital*, December 4, 2018, https://web.archive.org/web/20190111220517/https://arcdigital.media/the-pedophile-apologist-40ee80bf5d58?gi=87700d930d4d.

159 "Editors" *Sexuality and Culture: An Interdisciplinary Journal*, SpringerLink, https://link.springer.com/journal/12119/editors.

160 Lee, "The Pedophile".

161 Mark Regnerus, "No Long-Term Harm? The New Scientific Silence on Child-Adult Sex and the Age of Consent," Public Discourse, September 18, 2017, https://www.thepublicdiscourse.com/2017/09/20057/.

162 "NAMBLA," NewgonWiki, https://www.newgon.net/wiki/NAMBLA.

163 "Boylove," NewgonWiki. https://www.newgon.net/wiki/Boylove.

164 Ibid.

165 "MAP visibility on Twitter," NewgonWiki, https://www.newgon.net/wiki/MAP_visibility_on_Twitter.

166 Bly Rede, "Reviews: Safe from Harm and Let's Talk: Child Sexual Abuse," *MAP for Life (blog)*, September 9, 2021, https://web.archive.org/web/20230204102006/https://mapforlife.substack.com/p/reviews-1.

167 "Association for Sexual Abuse Prevention" (homepage), ASAPinternational.org, https://asapinternational.org/.

168 "Our Supporters," VirPed.org. https://archive.is/3QvuX.

169 Emma Mayer, "Abuse Center Explains Allyn Walker Hiring after Pedophilia Comments Fallout," *Newsweek*, May 13, 2022, https://www.newsweek.com/abuse-center-explains-allyn-walker-hiring-after-pedophilia-comments-fallout-1706533.

170 Walker, *A Long, Dark Shadow*, 1.

171 Bly Rede, "A Short Bright Elucidation," *MAP for Life (blog)*, October 18, 2021, https://web.archive.org/web/20230204102006/https://mapforlife.substack.com/p/long-dark-shadow.

172 Walker, *A Long, Dark Shadow*, 7.

173 Ibid.

174 Ibid., 8.

175 Ibid.

176 Ibid., 20.

177 Ibid., 172–75.

178 Ibid., 57.

179 Ibid., 25.

180 Ibid., 25, 26.

181 Ibid., 123.

182 Ibid., 125, 128.

183 Benedict Carey, "Preying on Children: The Emerging Psychology of Pedophiles." *New York Times*, September 29, 2019, https://www.nytimes .com/2019/09/29/us/pedophiles-online-sex-abuse.html.

184 Ibid.

185 Walker, *A Long, Dark Shadow*, 123.

Chapter 7

1 Whittaker Chambers, "A Witness," in *Conservatism In America Since 1920: A Reader*. Ed. Gregory L. Schneider. (New York, NY: New York University Press, 2023), 147.

2 Susan Stryker, "My Words to Victor Frankenstein above the Village of Chamounix: Performing Transgender Rage," *GLQ: A Journal of Lesbian and Gay Studies* 1, no. 3, 1994, 237–54. DOI.org (Crossref), https://doi .org/10.1215/10642684-1-3-237.

3 Peter Burfeind, "Why the Word 'Woke' Encapsulates an Evil, Self-Defeating Ideology," *The Federalist*, September 18, 2017, https://thefederalist .com/2017/09/18/word-woke-encapsulates-evil-self-defeating-ideology/.

4 Peter Burfeind, "Gnostic Mysticism Grounds Modern Progressive Ideology," *The Federalist*, June 29, 2015, https://thefederalist.com/2015/06/29 /gnostic-mysticism-grounds-modern-progressive-ideology/.

5 Following the illogical form of "the fallacy of the undistributed middle": Socrates is a man. Socrates is wise. Therefore all men are wise. Another flaw in McWhorter's argument is that it assumes all religion is irrational rather than proving that to be the case. Just because he can't understand something doesn't mean it's irrational. Perhaps it is McWhorter who is so irrational that he cannot understand the rational.

6 John McWhorter, *Woke Racism: How a New Religion Has Betrayed Black America* (New York: Portfolio, 2021), 27.

7 Jonathan Capehart, "'Hands up, Don't Shoot' Was Built on a Lie," *Washington Post*, December 2, 2021, https://www.washingtonpost

.com/blogs/post-partisan/wp/2015/03/16/lesson-learned-from-the
-shooting-of-michael-brown/.

8   Michael Shellenberger and Peter Boghossian, "Why Wokeism Is a Religion," *Public* (Substack), November 11, 2021, https://public.substack.com/p
/why-wokeism-is-a-religion.

9   James Lindsay, "The Cult Dynamics of Wokeness," *New Discourses*, June 6, 2020, https://newdiscourses.com/2020/06/cult-dynamics-wokeness/.

10   See the Supreme Court case *Missouri v. Biden*, later renamed *Missouri v. Murthy*.

11   "Instances of Viewpoint-Based De-Banking," Viewpoint Diversity Score, February 28, 2024, https://storage.googleapis.com/vds_storage/document
/resources/Debanking%20Incidences.pdf.

12   Sarah Coffey, "What Is Debanking? Political and Religious Discrimination by Financial Institutions," The Foundation for Government Accountability, August 21, 2023, https://thefga.org/blog
/what-is-debanking-political-and-religious-discrimination/.

13   Justin Hart, "Diabolical 'Debanking': A Distressing Trend in the Great White North," Rational Ground, October 6, 2023, https://covidreason.substack
.com/p/diabolical-debanking-a-distressing.

14   Szu Ping Chan, "Debanking Complaints Surge in Wake of Nigel Farage's NatWest Scandal," *The Telegraph*, November 8, 2023, www
.telegraph.co.uk, https://www.telegraph.co.uk/business/2023/11/08
/debanking-complaint-surge-wake-nigel-farage-natwest-scandal/.

15   James Cook and Paul Hastie, "JK Rowling in 'arrest me' challenge over hate crime law," BBC, April 2, 2024, https://www.bbc.com/news/articles
/c51j64lk2l8o.

16   Emily Burns and Aaron Kheriaty, "The Politics of Disdain," *City Journal*, October 20, 2023. https://www.city-journal.org/article/the-politics-of
-disdain/.

17   Michael Shellenberger and Peter Boghossian, "Why This One Simple Chart Will End Wokeism," *Public* (Substack), October 4, 2023, https://public
.substack.com/p/why-this-one-simple-chart-will-end.

18   "Marxist–Leninist Atheism," Wikipedia, https://en.wikipedia.org/wiki/
Marxist%E2%80%93Leninist_atheism; Jean-Louis Panné, et al., *The Black Book of Communism* (Cambridge, Mass: Oxford University Press, 1999).

19 Bill Dunn, "John McWhorter," Freedom from Religion Foundation, October 6, 2021, https://ffrf.org/ftod-cr/item/40813-john-mcwhorter.

20 Leah MarieAnn Klet, "Michael Shellenberger Tells Joe Rogan He Returned to Christianity in Response to Societal 'Hatred, Anger,'" *Christian Post*, April 10, 2023, https://www.christianpost.com/news/michael-shellenberger -tells-joe-rogan-why-hes-a-christian.html.

21 Chad Felix Greene, "Data Says The Violence 'Epidemic' Against Transgender People Is A Myth," *The Federalist*, November 4, 2019, https://thefederalist .com/2019/11/04/the-left-is-lying-about-a-hatred-and-violence-epidemic -against-transgender-people/.

22 And I'm not defending either.

23 Paul Coleman, *Censored: How European 'Hate Speech' Laws are Threatening Freedom of Speech* (Wien, Austria: Kairos Publications, 2016), 22; "Drew University Mourns the Passing of Longtime Professor Hans Morsink," Drew University, https://drew.edu/stories /drew-university-mourns-the-passing-of-longtime-professor-hans-morsink/.

24 Coleman, *Censored*, 22, 23.

25 Interview with author Dec. 15, 2023. Notes in author's possession.

26 Christopher F. Rufo, *America's Cultural Revolution: How the Radical Left Conquered Everything* (Broadside Books, 2023).

27 Ibid, 22, 23.

28 Aaron Kheriaty, "Rebellion, Not Retreat," *American Mind*, June 27, 2023, https://americanmind.org/salvo/rebellion-not-retreat.

29 Ibid.

30 Ibid.

31 "Brief of Alliance Defending Freedom as Amicus Curiae in Support of Appellant and for Reversal," *Parents Defending Education v. Olentangy School District*, US District Court for the Southern District of Ohio, Case No. 2:23-cv-01595-ALM-KAJ, October 20, 2023, https://adfmedialegalfiles.blob .core.windows.net/files/ParentsDefendingEducation6thCircuitAmicusBrieft .pdf.

32 Kirsty Bosley, "Everything That Happened at the Commonwealth Games Opening Ceremony," Birmingham Live, 28 July 2022, https: //www.birminghammail.co.uk/whats-on/whats-on-news/everything -happened-commonwealth-games-opening-24616390.

33 Sarah Carson, "The Commonwealth Games Opening Ceremony Was a Bostin' Celebration of Birmingham," Inews.Co.Uk, July 28, 2022, https://inews.co.uk/culture/television/commonwealth-games-2022-opening-ceremony-review-malala-birmingham-bull-duran-duran-steven-knight-1767757.

34 John Nathan. "How Iqbal Khan Enlisted Malala to Challenge the Commonwealth Games' Colonial Past," *Metro*, November 4, 2022, https://web.archive.org/web/20221104064724/https://metro.co.uk/2022/11/04/iqbal-khan-on-terrifying-birmingham-commonwealth-games-ceremony-17693454/.

35 "2022-07-29 Commonwealth Games Baal Worship." *Online Dreams*, YouTube, August 13, 2022. https://www.youtube.com/watch?v=WZl16pXoD2A.

36 Barry Glendenning, "Commonwealth Games 2022 Opening Ceremony—as It Happened," *The Guardian*, July 28 2022, https://web.archive.org/web/20220802101642/https://www.theguardian.com/sport/live/2022/jul/28/commonwealth-games-2022-opening-ceremony-live-latest-birmingham?page=with:block-62e2c7ab8f08c00147326646.

37 Ibid; Nathan, "How Iqbal Khan Enlisted Malala."

38 "The Making of Raging Bull," Commonwealth Games Birmingham 2022, July 29, 2022, https://www.birmingham2022.com/video/2696096/the-making-of-raging-bull.

39 Amrita Dhar, "Iqbal Khan: Postcolonial Shakespearean Voices in Pakistan, India, and the UK," Ohio State University, September 26, 2023, https://web.archive.org/web/20231117192313/https://u.osu.edu/shakespearepostcolonies/interviews-and-transcripts/iqbal-khan/.

40 Ibid; "2022–07-29 Commonwealth Games Baal Worship."

41 Matthew 12:27.

42 Ronny Reyes, "'Satanic' RGB Tribute Statue Slammed for Horns and Tentacles," *The Daily Mail Online*, January 26, 2023, https://web.archive.org/web/20230126210631/https://www.dailymail.co.uk/news/article-11680847/Gold-statue-horns-tentacles-paying-homage-Ruth-Bader-Ginsburg-gets-trolled-online.html.

43 Dan Bilefsky. "Move Over Moses and Zoroaster: Manhattan Has a New Female Lawgiver," *New York Times*, January 25 2023, https://web.archive.org/web/20230126210816/https://www.nytimes.com/2023/01/25/arts/design/discrimination-sculpture-madison-park-sikander-women.html.

44 Luke Gentile, "Target's Newest Pride Strategist Bringing a Whole New LGBT Spirit to Christmas," *Washington Examiner*, November 16, 2023, https://www.washingtonexaminer.com/news/target-pride-strategist-christmas.

45 Sam Smith and Kim Petras, "Unholy," *Gloria*, Westlake Studios (Los Angeles), January 27, 2023. https://genius.com/Sam-smith-and-kim-petras-unholy-lyrics.

46 Thaddeus Williams, "Satanism on Display at the Grammy Awards," *World Magazine*, February 10, 2023. https://wng.org/opinions/satanism-on-display-at-the-grammy-awards-1676031920.

47 Joy Pullmann, "TikTok's Hottest Trend Is as Old as Demonic Possession," *The Federalist*, July 26, 2021, https://thefdrlst.wpengine.com/2021/07/26/tiktoks-hottest-trend-is-as-old-as-demonic-possession/.

48 Acts 16.

49 Joy Pullmann, "*Washington Post* Reports on Demonic Energy Behind Left's Culture War," *The Federalist*, November 1, 2021, https://thefederalist.com/2021/11/01/washington-post-reports-on-demonic-energy-behind-the-lefts-culture-war/.

50 "Lilith," Wikipedia, https://en.wikipedia.org/wiki/Lilith.

51 Jacob Adams, "Satan Comes to Georgetown," *First Things*, November 3, 2023, https://www.firstthings.com/web-exclusives/2023/11/satan-comes-to-georgetown.

52 "About Us," The Satanic Temple, TheSatanicTemple.com, https://thesatanictemple.com/pages/about-us.

53 Serena Sonoma, "Satanic Temple Says It Will "Fight to the Death" for LGBTQ+ Rights," *Out*, August 24, 2019, https://www.out.com/activism/2019/8/24/satanic-temple-says-it-will-fight-death-lbgtq-rights.

54 Kate Ryan, "How the Satanic Temple Became a Queer Haven," *Vice*, July 24, 2017. https://www.vice.com/en/article/zmv7my/how-the-satanic-temple-became-a-queer-haven.

55 These four paragraphs are modified portions of an essay I published in *The Federalist* in 2021 Pullmann, "*Washington Post* Reports on Demonic Energy."

56 Mark 12:17.

57 Freddie Sayers, "Ayaan Hirsi Ali Answers Her Critics," *UnHerd*, November 16, 2023, https://unherd.com/2023/11/ayaan-hirsi-ali-answers-her-critics/.

Chapter 8

1 Christopher F. Rufo, *America's Cultural Revolution: How the Radical Left Conquered Everything* (New York: Broadside Books, 2023), 273.

2 Carter Sherman, "US abortion rates rise post-Roe amid deep divide in state-by-state access," *The Guardian*, October 24, 2023, https://www.theguardian.com/world/2023/oct/24/us-abortion-rates-post-roe-v-wade.

3 "The New Conservative Voter," *American Compass*, September 2023, https://americancompass.org/wp-content/uploads/2023/09/GOP-Voter-Survey_Sept-2023_Final.pdf.

4 Christopher F. Rufo, "Bring on the Counterrevolution," ChristopherRufo.com, August 9, 2023, https://christopherrufo.com/p/bring-on-the-counterrevolution.

5 Ibid.

6 Ibid.

7 Regulation 9.016, "Prohibited Expenditures," Florida Board of Education, January 24, 2021, https://www.flbog.edu/wp-content/uploads/2024/01/Regulation-9.016.pdf.

8 Tristan Justice, "Florida Devises New Rules for Rooting DEI Out of Higher Ed," *The Federalist*, October 17, 2023. https://thefederalist.com/2023/10/17/florida-devises-new-rules-for-rooting-dei-out-of-higher-ed/.

9 Shawn Fleetwood, "Other Red States Should Follow Florida's Legislative Blueprint," *The Federalist*, May 23, 2023. https://thefederalist.com/2023/05/23/florida-republicans-are-crafting-a-legislative-blueprint-other-red-states-should-follow/.

10 Michael Hartney, "Revitalizing Local Democracy: The Case for On-Cycle Local Elections," *Issue Brief*, Manhattan Institute, October 14, 2021, https://manhattan.institute/article/revitalizing-local-democracy-the-case-for-on-cycle-local-elections.

11 See Philip Hamburger, *Is Administrative Law Unlawful?* (Chicago, London: University of Chicago Press, 2015).

12 W. Bradford Wilcox, "The Evolution of Divorce," *National Affairs*, Fall 2009, https://www.nationalaffairs.com/publications/detail/the-evolution-of-divorce.

13 Beverly Willett, "There Is No Republican Plot to End No-Fault Divorce—but There Should Be," *Washington Examiner*, August 18, 2023, https:

//www.washingtonexaminer.com/opinion/beltway-confidential/2771905/there-is-no-republican-plot-to-end-no-fault-divorce-but-there-should-be/.

14 Ibid; Wilcox, "The Evolution of Divorce."

15 Scott Yenor, "Challenging the No-Fault Divorce Regime," *Institute for Family Studies (blog)*, July 31, 2023. https://ifstudies.org/blog/challenging-the-no-fault-divorce-regime.

16 Joy Pullmann, "Christopher Rufo's New Book Shows DEI Is Communism," *The Federalist*, September 5, 2023, https://thefederalist.com/2023/09/05/christopher-rufos-new-book-shows-diversity-equity-and-inclusion-are-the-new-face-of-communism/.

17 Richard Hanania, "Woke Institutions Is Just Civil Rights Law," *RichardHanania.com (blog)*, June 1, 2021, https://www.richardhanania.com/p/woke-institutions-is-just-civil-rights.

18 Aaron M. Renn, "Where Is the Right Wing Virtue?," *AaronRenn.com (blog)*, Oct. 27, 2023. https://www.aaronrenn.com/p/weekly-digest-where-is-the-right.

19 "Civic Values and Virtues," School Choice Bibliography, EdChoice, June 28, 2023, https://www.edchoice.org/school-choice-bibliography/.

20 Jack Brewer, "Issue Brief: Fatherlessness and Its Effects on American Society," America First Policy Institute, May 15, 2023, https://americafirstpolicy.com/latest/issue-brief-fatherlessness-and-its-effects-on-american-society.

21 Arguably, both the Covid response and the last fifty years of lost wars are not a matter of capability, but of a lack of will to combat lies driven by media hyenas, but the outcome is the same.

22 Rod Dreher, *The Benedict Option: A Strategy for Christians in a Post-Christian Nation,* (New York, NY: Sentinel), 2017.

23 Aaron M. Renn, "The Case Against Pragmatism," *AaronRenn.com (blog)*, December 18, 2023, https://www.aaronrenn.com/p/newsletter-83-the-case-against-pragmatism.